# Ethnologia Europaea

Journal of European Ethnology

Volume 34:2 2004

MUSEUM TUSCULANUM PRESS ❦ UNIVERSITY OF COPENHAGEN

Copyright © 2004 Ethnologia Europaea, Copenhagen
Printed in Sweden by Grahns Tryckeri AB, Lund 2005
Illustrations (pp. 18, 30, 40, 70, 112, 158) Gösta Arvastson
ISBN 87-635-0371-9
ISSN 0425-4597

*Editors*  Orvar Löfgren (main editor) & Peter Niedermüller

*Editorial assistant*  Margareta Tellenbach

*Editorial Board*  Albert Baiburin (Russia), Jeremy Boissevain (Netherlands), Wolfgang Brückner (Germany), Reginald Byron (Wales UK), Palle O. Christiansen (Denmark), John W. Cole (USA), Claudio Esteva Fabregat (Spain), Alexander Fenton (Scotland), Jonas Frykman (Sweden), Ueli Gyr (Switzerland), Tamás Hofer (Hungary), Konrad Köstlin (Austria), Orvar Löfgren (Sweden), Ruth-E. Mohrmann (Germany), Peter Niedermüller (Germany), Ján Podolák (Slovakia), Klaus Roth (Germany), Bjarne Rogan (Norway), Thomas Schippers (France), Martine Segalen (France), Zofia Sokolewicz (Poland), Bjarne Stoklund (Denmark).

This journal is published with the support of the Nordic board for periodicals in the humanities and social sciences.

Museum Tusculanum Press
University of Copenhagen
Njalsgade 94
DK-2300 Copenhagen S
www.mtp.dk

# Multicultures
# and Cities

Edited by
Gösta Arvastson
and Tim Butler

MUSEUM TUSCULANUM PRESS • UNIVERSITY OF COPENHAGEN

# Contents

Gösta Arvastson and Tim Butler: Metamorphoses, Transformation and European Cities .................................................................................. 5

Àngel Cebollada-Frontera and Carme Miralles-Guasch: Mobility and Urban Transport in Metropolitan Barcelona. Accessibility versus Exclusion ............................................................................................... 19

Margaret Byron: Labour Market Trajectories of Caribbean People in Britain and France. Multi-ethnic Societies, Multiculturalism, or Assimilation ........................................................................................... 31

Stephen Shaw and Joanna Karmowska: The Multicultural Heritage of European Cities and its Re-presentation through Regeneration Programmes .......................................................................................... 41

John Eade: Class and Ethnicity in a Globalising City. Bangladeshis and Contested Urban Space in London's 'East End' ........................................ 57

Graeme Evans and Jo Foord: Rich Mix Cities. From Multicultural Experience to Cosmopolitan Engagement ........................................... 71

Elisabeth Högdahl: Urban Strategies and Loophole Tactics. Claiming Space in Cape Town and Malmö ........................................................ 85

Urban Ericsson: Haunting Experiences of Images. Blind Spots and Fantasy-Frames in the Mass Mediated Suburb ..................................... 97

Per-Markku Ristilammi: Afterthoughts on Modernist Necropoles ................ 107

Alexa Färber and Cordula Gdaniec: Shopping Malls and Shishas. Urban Space and Material Culture as Approaches to Transformation in Berlin and Moscow ............................................................................. 113

Beate Binder: National Narratives and Cosmopolitan Dreams. Becoming a Capital in Late Modernity ................................................. 129

Nora Räthzel: Creating Spaces of Fear and Spaces of Safety. Young Natives and Migrants in Metropolitan Neighbourhoods .................. 141

# Metamorphoses, Transformation and European Cities

*Gösta Arvastson*
*Tim Butler*

The first thing that meets the observer who takes the airport coach towards a city centre somewhere in Europe is the sight of monotonous suburbs, run-down factory areas, slum housing and the ruined remains of small companies that the market created. It is still possible to decipher posters on fire- and brick walls that illustrated a time of special emphasis on the few texts displayed in the public space. The city erodes and is exposed to stresses and strains that can't be repaired, neighbourhood social safety disappears, cars take over the streets and the district crumbles. Symbols and monuments are not replaced. The city expands into the suburbs and beyond and the suburbs devour the city centre.

Scholars looking for perspectives have often chosen to investigate the city as an expression for the processes of civilisation. The city was seen as a homogenising force and transformed incomers from the countryside into modern citizens. The power of the city crumbles and homogeneity amongst its inhabitants is no longer preserved. It cannot control all the cultures, interest groups and organisations that spring up, and it can't manipulate its inhabitants and sustain the myth of an immediate disintegration. The city crises of the 1990s were mainly enacted at institutional and government levels.

In the new heterogeneity, inhabitants established their districts and recreated ways of life that should really have vanished somewhere along modernisation's straight line of development. Even during the 1990s, the city was on the frontline in this continuous revolution; a centre of tourism and information and communication technologies. The city continued to be the physical coating of desire. Nothing of the playful and unpredictable disappeared just because homogeneity and the concept of the city proved to be impossible. The city has always held a fascination both as a landscape and for its unplanned encounters between people. New innovations in our time include the architecture and the idioms of global culture that are developed in conflict with those national and local cultural hegemonies that also make claims on the city. The global economy's centres of glass and concrete convey sweeping changes in the city's appearance. The modern city has changed and industrial premises stand empty. The dwindling labour market makes its mark on the city. Life is condensed in new forms, places are given new meaning and the old is dismantled. The European city is born and dies at the same time.

This anthology focuses on European cities. It's about how new worlds of life have been developed and how people's experiences of the city have been dictated by change and mobility. While it is mainly the last half century that has captured the authors' interest, a longer time perspective is often essential to an understanding of today's debate on the city.

## Urban Movements

Already by the 1820s London could boast a population of just over a million, and Paris was developing in similar vein. Large numbers of people moving to the city led to overcrowding and poverty. Their colonisation was beyond the control of the authorities. Travellers who found their way to Europe's metropolises in the 1880s moved like spectators through the crowds and were often affected by a pensive melancholy. A society was in process of disappearing and, at the same time, they could imagine that dramatic changes were taking place.

The stream of people from countryside to city is common to European urban history. One great concern was the overpopulation caused by the previous industrialisation wave during the latter part of the 1800s. Cities grew at a much faster rate than the authorities had resources. Many lacked passports and official papers and this caused huge problems for the authorities. The need to take stock of the cities led to a renewed interest in identities. Originally, the need to establish identity with physical evidence had a policing purpose. At the end of the 1800s, fingerprinting was introduced by the police in London. City dwellers gradually became subject to increasing cataloguing and registering.

When Eugène Haussmann's columns spread during the 1800s and the city gained in aesthetics, powerful visual markers of "cityness" appeared. The idea of Parisian bourgeois dwellings along open boulevards spread to many other European cities. The first floor of a block of flats was the best. Facades were adorned with pilasters and personified mouldings. Wide and straight fashionable streets of Parisian and English mould described the city dweller's enthusiasm for overstepping cultures. Grecian symbols and a neutralised aesthetics in terms of lines, ellipses, rhomboids and mathematical forms, restored the city dweller to a community-creating classical inheritance.

## Circulation, Pulse and Flow

The European city also became an international prototype. Europe's capital cities, especially Paris and Vienna, also became prototypes for city cultures in other parts of the world. They were especially significant to the American city culture – North and South; Buenos Aires was known as "the Paris of the South". In the colonies of Africa and Asia, experimental cities were built that had no European counterpart and that cultivated an aesthetic and European feature in a more complete way than had been possible in Europe.

The planning of the European city at the end of the 1800s dealt with a complete machinery of life. To a great extent, the city was the result of an engineering that sought parallels in nature. The access paths of the ant-hills and the well-organised beehive represented a model for the cities that elevated the status of engineer and stationed the architect as lord of creation. Production and service sectors were amalgamated with public entertainment and were given their own space. The planned flow of city people was indicated by transport tracks between home and work. Already at the beginning of the previous century engineers had developed mobile pavements so that people would be well catered for. Cities were built for mobility.

At the same time, the city was a symbol of life and circulation and the pulsing flow of goods, capital and people – the functional whole. Historians used headings like *the urban revolution* or *the capitalist city* whenever they described these sweeping transformations of the city. The emphasis on revolution led thoughts towards the idea of a stagnating peasant society. Of course that was not the case. The big European cities had been founded on urban culture since medieval times, and had been places of public ceremonies as well as ritual contacts with other citizens outside the family circle long before the dawn of industrialisation. The difference during the industrialisation phase was the speed of the transformation.

Modern society was characterised by standardisation; an abolition of cultural differences. Prior to the First World War, the cities of Europe had become symbols of development and modernity (Sennett 1978:133). Here were institutions and authorities that exercised control, but despite the constant presence of police, individuals discovered that they had plenty of opportunities in which to investigate sections of society other than the officially recognised. Anti-modern movements opposed international exhibitions and new cultural chasms appeared. The cultural boundaries of the city were transformed. From this perspective, the city could be read as a conflict zone between antagonistic interests.

## Opinion Creation and Mass Culture

Film was a fitting medium for those who wanted to portray people in the city. As an instrument of reflection and cultural critique it was unbeatable and united city dweller with modern times, development and the ideas of the permanent revolution. Sequences and movements were there on the streets. Every visual impression could be captured in a continuous present. The made-up beds and the beggar's park bench were contemporaries. So too were a street washed down with a hose and a girl that washed in her room. One situation slid into the other. Encounters between people were swift and profiled social competence.

The photographers of the 1920s and 1930s absorbed themselves in architecture, people's movements and light variations between dawn and dusk. One of the pioneers of international documentary film was Dziga Vertov. In *The Man with the Camera* (1928–29), he simply allowed the city to march past in front of the lens. He fixed his camera to the front of motorcycles and railway engines. He was obsessed with capturing the busyness of the traffic, engineering workshops and factories, and he allowed the lens to wander its way over chimneys, radio masts, facades of houses and right into the rooms of both rich and poor. It was his idea that the eye of the camera should mediate an intense feeling of the present (Weiss 1956:89).

During the interwar period, architects, doctors, journalists and psychologists had focused on the city as an organism, an "inner expediency". They had turned the city into a laboratory for a rational modernity. Any useless branches had to be cut off, just as in the plant kingdom, so that what was healthy could grow and strengthen.

After the Second World War, such conclusions were not negotiable. The European cities had shown another face; an arena for secret police in search of critics of the regime. Seen from the perspective of power, and mindful of the totalitarian regimes of the Nazi period and the later post-war period in Eastern Europe, the difference between a city and a labour camp was insignificant. Short distances contributed to that, as did the possibilities for the enclosure of the population, and with that continuous surveillance, the lack of escape routes, the media, propaganda and a system of street addresses. In general, the humanistic idea was easier to implement in the home and more difficult in the workplace. Later during the post-war period, dormitory town planning gathered the experiences of the darker years in Europe to put an emphasis on smaller "neighbourhood units". New housing areas that were built as small urban communities on the outskirts of the cities – with shops, schools and public institutions, dominated during the 1960s and 1970s.

## Changes in Working Conditions

Consumption was given a different slant when supermarkets started to spring up around towns and cities at the beginning of the 1960s. Journeys to work came into being. Many people lived a long way away from their workplaces and travel on a daily basis became time consuming.

The economic intensity that had been uncompromising during the 1950s and 1960s gave rise to the protest movements of the 1970s. Harsh criticism was directed against motoring and air pollution, town centre commercialisation and "gentrification", i.e. that housing for the lower social classes was pulled down or converted to provide more room for the well-to-do middle class. Cities gained their protest singers and superstores their commercial music. Bicycles were painted by hand. The password of the 1970s was *tools for transformation* and alluded to user-friendliness and a politics of activity and social fellowship.

At the beginning of the 1970s, criticism against the ideas of mass production became almost total; one of the linchpins of the industrial city. Disturbances at the end of the 1960s and employees' demands for reforms in 1968 had brought about a different view of people's work. At the same time it was a revolt that could not be enacted anywhere other than in the city. Class theories taken from the ideas of the history of civilisation gave European ethnology new perspectives. Culture was a stabilising order that the individual attached him/herself to through socialisation processes controlled by outside powers; a way of living that was conditioned by his/her role as a creature of class.

It is sometimes said that the social visions of the 1980s seemed to be sealed in black cabin bags. That is an exaggeration, but a lot had changed since the 1970s. The grassroots were in jeopardy and the fight against social segregation was no longer on the agenda. The architecture of the 1980s aimed at showing work in progress; those who passed the big glass windows of the city centre areas could look straight into shiny polished work environments with their white desks. Insurance companies became just as transparent as ladies' hairdressers. People moved around like spectators in the galleries – and could see themselves reflected in the glass panes.

Conservative welfare models and the establishment of the European free market in the 1980s introduced strict economic measures for the development of cities. Society's disorders were seen as a result of a costly public sector. Vulnerable minorities and marginal ethnic groups no longer attracted society's concern; the labour market itself started to have cultural overtones. Ethnic groups in the workplace started to be graded according to an imagined scale of loyalty; national characteristics and countenances again started to be of interest.

## The New Monumentality

The recession at the beginning of the 1990s showed that market forces would deepen the crisis in Europe. Professional finance analysts' interest in deregulation affected the cities and confronted the politicians with difficult decisions. As the market "as such is amoral", political intervention was called upon to manage such debatable market-oriented phenomena as drug-dealing and prostitution. The New Age Movement emerged to address a wide range of issues. Cuts in public spending imposed a moralising view on citizens. Industriousness and stable family relations were important factors, and in the background an image of "the Others" was outlined as parasites of the welfare state. The homogeneous class structure was decomposing, and the new solidarity – with the home as starting point – contributed to the commercialisation of the public milieu. The result seemed to be a predictable "death of the classes". Robert Venturi gained great success among cultural scholars when he emphasised the industrial parenthesis (Venturi, Scott Brown & Izenour 1977). Han talked about architecture and "the new monumentality", which meant that the city wasn't only built to be big and impressive, but long and low. The discussion can continue for an eternity for a flexible adaptation of capitalism's ideas as the basis of planning the city. Instead of point-by-point positioning, people were expected to look for freedom by being on the move, and the city was dominated by a demand for space and above all temporary solutions that make it possible to leave every single place without any worry. What is interesting is that it is not the places but transport systems that become fundamentally important for people on the move. The speed theoretician, Paul Virilio, also had something to say about that when he described monumental impact in the city as invisible. Having an overview of the city no longer calls for the presence of towers, but a functional and efficient electronic network (Morris 1992:4).

## City Person

From some points of view, living in a city is a truly modern phenomenon. European history provides us with many examples of "cityness" that translate into materialised objects and the consumption of goods. Many attempts to understand the city have been made in terms of their general appearance and their *raison d'être*. The concentration of technology and economic opportunities in world cities comprised the general features of an accelerating growth of transnational economies at the end of 20th century. Hence, the concept of *city* implies the notion of an urban community by virtue of "some legal or conventional distinction" (*Encyclopædia Britannica* 2005).

The permanent revolution was perceived as a high speed journey towards a higher civilisation, similar to the Fordist vision of the early production environments of the 20th century. The outlines of modern progress and the journey are still in place. The grand narrative of modernity is still at work and landscapes of power and repression continue to be created.

Every minute the city produces an enormous amount of facts about health, social welfare, unemployment, medical care, schools, the flow of transport, and the financial affairs of companies and the public sector. Information is dependent on computer technology and is so extensive that many avoid it. The city's official information is also often stamped with the hallmark of monotony. It is a city person's nature to evade information they find uninteresting. Both consciously and unconsciously, they take a stand against information and shun advertising texts in the tube, shop windows and frontages. They economise with impressions because they gain no pleasure from what they see and read in their own significance, and find that they can get along with the help of cultural simplifications. It's the city person's prerogative to choose information that matches their interests. The city person prepares for events and goes into social situations that they have no control over in terms of a clear escape route. The majority of people that move around in unfamiliar neighbourhoods are aware of the emergency procedures. The forms of contemporaneousness, convergence and encounter force the need for cultural checklists for quick meetings at the supermarket checkout, on the bus or at a restaurant. Ritual reality happens on a plane other than the planned city. This is the complex of problems that several cultural scholars have found interesting. "Cityness" is something that is happening now, in the present, that develops without people noticing it and is changed as a social reality. Many cultural scholars are inspired by Henri Lefebvre and start out from the double process of industrialisation and urbanisation, or with reference to the city's social life, explosion and implosion. "Cityness" can be the implosion, a compress of feelings that can unfurl and be pulled in again, depending on the social situation.

Most cultural scholars would agree that culture means the knowledge that people use when facing the realities of daily life. Its meaning is affected by a cultural understanding of humanity, sometimes affected by a more philosophical view on humanity's uniqueness as a creator of a human world in order to use it for her own benefit. There is also an emotional side to culture, which has to do with the fabric of perceptions, fantasies, desires and fears that have become very noticeable in recent theoretical discourses. When recognizing the city from this perspective – in terms of multiculturalism – there might be a need for detailed descriptions and further analyses of the routines of the city, concentrating on social meetings, faces and the daily exhibition of codes and styles in the street. Street ethnography is a very promising methodology, as it depicts the symbolic landscape of transforming the city into rituals and social actions. In effect it says that "games are not always played in order to win", but the processes of categorization are continuing and the world is changing – like an urban version of *schismogenesis* that Gregory Bateson explains in terms of cultural change from within (Bateson 1972).

At a distance, the city looks like a functioning whole. The perspective gained from great altitudes, maps and the interest for observation towers indicates how the city is often treated as an anatomical illustration in the world of notions – a homogenous creation that lends itself to the drawing-table. The perspective based on a closer view of the crowded street offers a challenge. A long accustomed habit of cultural scholars has been to position perspectives in opposition – high versus low, the elite versus the commonplace and seeing versus doing. But the notion of the planned city's impact on consciousness should not be over emphasised. De Certeau's return to the street after having visited the observation tower's symbolic planning position also represents the new conditions of research. The concept-city was on its way out during the 1980s and with it an urban sociology that subsequently reached its climax in Europe shortly after World War II.

The emphasis on reading faces, movements and bodies, and with directions as to an important "facialisation" in the encounters between people, creates new possibilities of assembling a new ethnography of the city (de Certeau 1984; Deleuze & Gauttari 2003:63). It can create new possibilities for a cultural research that has partly turned its back on the material, clothing and consumer habits in preference to studying people and the city as a mixed "semiotic of meaning and subjectivism, paranoia and monomania, interpretation and passion". The modern person is pushed into their existential reproductions, goes backwards towards the future and keeps a check on the make of car they used to like and formulates the dialects of the consumer landscape. But at the same time, they are interested in reading faces as something more than just their shapes; an expression of people, categories, those in power and frames of mind.

## Right to the City

The question of the right to the city was made topical by Henri Lefebvre (Lefebvre 1968). The critics appear again today; it is often sociologists and cultural scholars who say that the traditional urbanity has been neglected. Artistically designed consumption streets dominated the metropolises of Eastern Europe following the Velvet Revolution of 1989. Memories of Stalinistic architecture and Soviet times were not at a premium, although interested parties are to be found even in these fields. That is not to say that anything was changed. Cities have always been in process of dissolution and genesis, but the ardour of transformation in Eastern Europe increased after the Velvet Revolution. The production of goods gradually disappeared from the city when factories were dismantled and replaced by information companies. The city appeared as a more refined place of desires; an ecstatic circulation of goods. It was a phase in modern society where capitalism's aesthetics were united with the patterns of consumption. The consumption landscape led to new routines, interests, meeting places and forms of integration. The theme can be recognised in the writings of Jean Baudrillard (Baudrillard 1988a:125; Baudrillard 1988b:23).

The image of the information industry's success has dominated the theory of cities in recent decades. There is reason to investigate which research perspectives disappear and which representations fade into oblivion. *Mixing* is one such representation; the city that has always been a place of encounter between strangers. Other representations include *smoothing*; the city with its lifestyle improvisations, black economies and survival strategies. An interpretation may suggest that the smooth spaces arising from the city belongs to a world wide organisation. The counterattack is "sprawling, temporary, shifting shantytowns of nomads and cave dwellers, scrap metal and fabric, patchwork, to which the striations of money, work, or housing are no longer even relevant" (Deleuze & Guattari 2003:481). Cultural free states are proclaimed and demarcated, sociologists interest themselves in tribalisation – a false concept in this context because it is about a culturalisation on all levels. The city has proffered hiding places to persecuted groups for centuries, not least in London, Berlin and Vienna, and separatism in cities has been known since antiquity. Images of a multicultural city are given plenty of space in the media. It is the cultural diversity and segregation that characterises our time and gives perspective to the concept of postmodernity:

"Postmodernity may be interpreted as fully developed modernity; as modernity that acknowledged the effects it was producing throughout its history, yet producing inadvertently, by default rather than design, as *unanticipated consequences,* by-products often perceived as waste; as modernity conscious of its true nature – *modernity for itself"* (Bauman 1992:149f).

Power to exercise control in the city must be defended with rules. Even though the old still rules worked they still had to be replaced by new ones. Administration of rules shifts to an "exercising of will", which means that both the superior and the subordinate constantly find themselves within the limits of the system.

Power over the cities appears in new guises in the 2000s. Globalisation has meant that it has become more mobile and thus more difficult to localise. In spite of this, the majority of people are convinced that strong forces rule their lives. Pictorially we can liken people's identity to a particle in a magnetic field that takes up new positions as the energy is changed. The collective loyalty, a mutual understanding between individual and society, necessary to the success of the permanent revolution, has not appeared once and for all, but instead the actual energy in the feeling of society varies with time. There are influential nations, companies and political organisations, but none has the authority to reign supreme over the system with global cities. In this post-political world, to refer to Fredric Jameson, it isn't possible to discriminate between advertising, private initiative and the market's production of originals (Jameson 1994:183).

## Migration

In a world dominated by fast transport and the abolishment of distance, this cultural change was also perceived as motion. With their centres, districts, reserves and colonies, cities were captured in movements of varying direction. Only in the material world could culture stand still and be liberated from the quality that speed creates. Many of the concepts connected to cultural encounters, such as acculturation, disintegration, evolution, innovation, integration, devolution, revitalisation and survival, are related to movement. The idea of a union of cities, and attempts to neutralise the significance of culture and liberate people from their restrictions to place, had other consequences. Sometimes people have talked about the "ritual unconsciousness" that characterised the modernisation of Europe during the post-war period. Spaces for new creations also appeared. When the unspoken becomes more important than words, demonstration, play, theatre, light paintings, flowers and texts and moments of "cityness" are activated.

The 1950s reinforced the impression of rapid development – sometimes much too rapid. The work of sweeping away all traces of cultural prejudices aimed at dismantling the old society in order to level the ground for innovation and, in a broader sense, to teach the inhabitants to formulate their desires. This process became a reality for the millions of labour migrants that were recruited to the high-technological countries from the European periphery with dreams of a better life and a brighter future. State organisations were responsible for recruitment on the assumption that they would return home after a time of earning good money. It naturally followed that their civic rights would be limited. When it later appeared that they preferred to live on the periphery of the city, a European approach developed, based on a single-minded policy of trying to send immigrants back to their native countries. This official immigration policy was probably one of many factors that contributed to the racial riots that occurred in England at the beginning of the 1960s. At the same time, the conservative revival in Central Europe got new wind in their sails. In Switzerland, the state started to conduct campaigns against immigrants in 1964. The debate on "Überfremdung" – too many immigrants – was thereby sanctioned by the highest political decision-making body.

Signs of an increasing xenophobia appeared towards the end of the 1900s and spread to all levels of society, including the lower levels. Friction in the labour market increased. European cities were developed in other ways than during the large waves of technical and industrial innovation that characterised the post-war period. The culturalisation of cities and their inhabitants, the way of ascribing qualities and avoiding a social and economic understanding, mythologized the unequal distribution of welfare.

A prerequisite of immigration policy in the cities of Europe and the political administration of cultural minorities was the notion of one of the parties culturally amalgamating with the other – assimilation. Considering that Western society was readily described with the aid of metaphors collected from the natural sciences, offshoots from the apprehension of the 1700s on economic development according to nature's textbook, a similar system of ideas didn't seem strange in the context of cultural research. There was no hesitation in the idea that people were adaptable and could be moved like seedlings between greenhouses. Another was structural balance, originally one of functionalism's leading ideas. In the planning of city development it was important that different groups should be able to live in peaceful coexistence. This is how the concept multicultural came about. During the 1970s, multicultural was developed into a model of political democracy; a strategy for society's rapid change.

The term multiculturalism suggests that contemporary urban cultures somehow co-exist in a condition of mutual respect and possible equality. This remains far from being the case, although the role played by different ethnic groupings in shaping the development of cities across Europe has been immense. We see ample evidence of this in the essays included in this issue of the journal. For example, we learn about the changes that are occurring in cities as far apart as Barcelona, Berlin and Moscow. The term cosmopolitanism is also introduced in a number of the essays to describe the social and cultural infrastructures of many European cities. We believe that there is virtue in rescuing the term cosmopolitanism from its connotations of urban elites. In his original work on Rovere, Merton (Merton 1948) contrasted "locals" and their essentially narrow and instrumental concerns with "cosmopolitans" who lived in the "big society", as this description fitted that of the essentially urbane intellectual at ease in a number of societies. The social anthropologist, Ulf Hannerz (Hannerz 1980), has pointed out the elite dimensions of cosmopolitans in several of his works and has very successfully clarified the tensions between globals and locals on the world scene. The passage through a Nazi ideology – when the term became associated with Jewish groups and expanded into the understanding of Entfremdung – shows that, under certain circumstances, cosmopolitans challenge the other side of the coin, namely of being somebody in terms of a fixed national identity. The image is often conjured up of the middle-class European intellectual in the inter-war period moving easily across borders and between languages.

## Mixing Together

Multiculturalism as a term poses problems. It is discussed in many – if not all – the essays that make up this issue. In the European tradition, minority cultures were readily apprehended from an essentialistic viewpoint. American cultural scholars, such as the prominent figures of symbolical interactionism, Cooley, Mead and Dewey, put the emphasis on the social construction of deviation in a continuous present, its change and affluence. Interaction, situation and context were more important to them as instruments of analysis. Theories concerning the cultural organisation of diversity and multiculturalism had their foundations in functionalism. To put it crudely, multiculturalism, like so many other terms (such as community and social capital) is used in sociology in particular and the social sciences in general, and has connotations of "good" about it. It summons before us a notion of a socially, culturally and above all ethnically mixed society in which these different groups rub along together quite happily. It is almost as if the celebration of these differences enables us to overlook both the existence and practice of inequality between them. Multiculturalism can either mean that each group simply minds its own business and has little to do with the other, or that they participate in a common experience whilst drawing on their own cultural heritages in order to shape that experience. At worst, the notion of multiculturalism is a mask for good old-fashioned racism. There are examples of this across Europe today – not least in multicultural Britain where the British National Party has been remarkably successful in some of its cities in putting forward its own version of "separate but different". Elsewhere, however, there remains a notion of a "host society" into which all incomers are eventually expected to "assimilate". Scandinavia is a particularly good example of this perspective.

*Chicken Tikka Masala* is now acknowledged as one of Britain's choicest dishes, having been invented in the UK rather than India. The effect of half a century of sustained immigration into Britain is now accepted in many of its cities as a fact of life, and is perhaps indicative of the somewhat contradictory nature of British multiculturalism. A common notion conjured up among members of the majority concerns a population open to believing the worst of different ethnic and religious groups.

Even in multi-cultural Europe different ethnic groups tend not to mix, and often live separate lives in different parts of the city and nation. Sheila Patterson's book, *Dark Strangers* (1965:19), analyses the process of "absorption" into the "host" society in the following terms:

"In a homogenous and peaceable society, as opposed to a conquest society, social relations are harmonious and voluntarily ordered amongst the great majority of the society's members. Migrant groups entering such a society usually expect and are expected to develop more or less favourable relationships with their hosts. Such terms as 'adjustment', 'accommodation', 'integration', and 'assimilation' represent the goals recognised by both sides. 'Absorption' is the overall term for all stages of adaptation and acceptance used by S. N. Eisenstadt in his studies of Israel" (Patterson 1965:19f).

There is a hierarchy of absorption, from accommodation, via pluralistic integration, to its most complete phase of assimilation. Similar mappings can be found in Sweden, Denmark, Spain, Germany and elsewhere across Western Europe, which indicates that ethnicity has become much more fluid than it was. It used to be said that you could identify the latest ethnic group in town by the nationality of the taxi driver who drove you into Manhattan from Kennedy Airport. The same might now be said about much of Europe. Again, however, the picture is complex; Margaret Byron, for example, demonstrates in her essay in this collection that it is the group of migrants with the highest qualifications (Black Africans) which has the highest rates of unemployment.

The European labour market is facing a period of change and adjustment. The situation is not only characterised by complexity and national legislation, but also by the intervention of cities in economic policy. This is not so much the case in some areas of Europe where the situation in general is partly dominated by strong welfare traditions (such as in Scandinavia, Germany, Italy and France) (Esping Anderson 1990) and to a certain extent also because some countries, such as Britain, still have to subscribe to the provisions of the European Union's social chapter in full. Paradoxically, these constraints have increased the incentive to engage informal workers who can be hired for less and fired more easily as and when conditions demand.

Superficially, multiculturalism points to a society that is increasingly at ease with itself and in which "new" identities are being forged around the enjoyment of consumption. It can, however, also be some kind of a cover-up between the "have nots" and the "have lots" – those who earn a lot and those who earn very little, those with and without pensions, those with and without access to welfare, those with a settled or marginal status as immigrants, those who have a legal status and those facing precarious and undocumented realities etc. (Bales 2000). There is a strangely lulling effect in the warm glow of being called a "multicultural society". The consequences of a major (and seemingly inevitable) economic downturn and rise in unemployment remain to be seen. It seems likely that there will be a steep decline in discretionary spending on consumption in the leisure and entertainment sector which will hit casual and migrant workers particularly hard. At the same time, there will be greater competition for the jobs that are available, including those currently undertaken by informal workers. The potential for conflict and a definition in inter-ethnic terms is great. The unwillingness and increasing inability of state welfare regimes to deal with these problems will undoubtedly lead to greater pressure for active discrimination against non-citizens. There is already some evidence of this in the way in which some countries in the EU have excluded some of the new member states from the provisions of free labour mobility. In

Denmark, the government has already begun a policy of official discrimination against those migrants who have "refused" to integrate and become assimilated Danes. There is a potential across Europe for such policies to become mainstream in the event of either a serious economic downturn and/or an increase in Islamophobia or further major terrorist incidents in key European cities.

In a sense, ideas of being Italian, British, French or Spanish have always been tied to "others" in that it was an awareness of imperial power that made these countries great in the eyes of many of their citizens who had "served" their countries in some respect or other. The lack of a colonial history paved the way for other migration patterns in Scandinavia. Sweden, where it seemed that the "million homes" programme to build new high rise homes on virgin land in the fresh air and countryside around Stockholm, Malmö and Gothenburg was eschewed by young Swedes and became home to refugees from the world's conflicts simultaneously. This is graphically symbolised by the number of satellite dishes sprouting from the high rise flats in such places as Fittja on the outskirts of Stockholm as they pick up Kurdish broadcasts from native Anatolia, whilst the carefully restored traditional Swedish farmhouse that forms the community centre remains largely unused.

As has already been indicated, the new "multiculturalism" seems very different from the migration that took place in the 1960s and 1970s. Nevertheless, in some European cities there is now what might be termed an infrastructure of difference which has enabled this inflow to take place with relatively little sense of cultural disruption. The essays in this collection address the general theme of ethnicity and contemporary European urbanism in many different ways in a wide variety of cities and city pairings. What they have in common is a wish to explore the role that a contemporary merging of ethnicity and culture is having on the new urbanity that is now widely accepted as driving the new Europe. The effect is far greater than might be predicted from the relative social powerlessness of many of the bearers of these cultures. At the same time, existing urban processes continue to ensure the marginality of these groups. This latter point is well demonstrated in Miralles-Guasch and Cebollada-Frontera's essay regarding access to transport in metropolitan Barcelona. They show that there is an interaction between three groups – the young, women and recent migrants – in being unable to access private car transport which is becoming increasingly important despite Barcelona's well-deserved reputation for having built an efficient system of public transport. In a city which is probably more famous for its *Ramblas* than any other, the number of journeys by car is on the increase while those undertaken on foot is going down. Barcelona is also, like many large Spanish cities, no newcomer to in-migration, having hosted huge inflows from Andalusia during the post-war decades. In the 1980s, many refugees from South American dictatorships ended up in Barcelona. It is, however, only just beginning to come to terms with the new migration from the African continent, many of whom are illegal immigrants lacking both appropriate papers and an understanding of Spanish and Catalan culture.

In similar vein, Margaret Byron looks at what has been a longstanding flow of migration from the Caribbean to France and Britain, and how this has changed over the decades as a result of the change in labour market conditions in both those countries and, in turn, how this has affected senses of identity and citizenship. A labour force that was once directed into national reconstruction is now expected to perform a very different role in a neo-liberal, post-industrial environment.

Three essays focus on the ways in which new concepts of ethnicity are affecting London: two of which (Shaw and Karmowska and Eade) focus specifically on the Spitalfields area of London. Despite being located less than 300 metres from the City of London (Europe's richest region), until a few years ago Spitalfields remained resolutely ungentrified. Both essays point to the way in which regeneration and gentrification have taken place in the context of white residential gentrifiers and Bangladeshi restaurateurs trying to gain maximum benefit from the area. As Shaw and Karmowska show, on at least one occasion this led to the two groups coming to blows at a meeting trying to agree a development strategy. All three essays (the two already mentioned and Evans and Foord's), however, look at the way in which ethnicity now informs not only the meaning that is inscribed into many parts of London (and other British cities) but also (difficulties notwithstanding) what lies at the heart of many of the regeneration strategies which enthusiastically celebrate the "rich mix" provided by these areas with their globally connected but economically deprived populations. The Shaw and Karmowska essay develops this theme further by making a comparison with the former Jewish ghetto of Cracow in Poland.

Two essays take Sweden as their subject matter: Högdahl's account of the ethnicization of the Möllevången district of Malmö and Ericsson's account of life in two of Sweden's ethnoscapes. Högdahl sees how Möllvången's acquisition of immigrant-status has combined with that of being increasingly seen as a local skid row. She draws out complex lessons about the ways in which the minority groups and resident "drunks" negotiate their day-to-day existence, which she is also able to compare to the Long Lanes area of Cape Town. Ericsson looks at the ways in which many of these areas of Swedish cities acquire a reputation which is much more fearsome than the reality of everyday life, and how this affects all the groups who tend to operate according to the script supplied by the popular press and local social workers who bizarrely engineer moral panic. This contrasts to the inhabitants' lived experience of the area. Per-Markku Ristilammi discusses the transformation of cities into a static brand for a global market. The New Economy's insistence on constant change, coupled to the need for brand stability, was skilfully merged into the image of a stable bridge between Malmö and Copenhagen. Attempts to create a branded regional identity for the Öresund region seem of crucial importance due to the fact that the cities belong to two different countries. Ristilammi finds a paradoxical formulation of modern identity in the laying of the foundation of a specifically modern form of structured liberation. He argues that there is a need for metaphors that can challenge the monocultural vision of modernity. It is the multicultural that shows us a holographic future, and why it is so important to create symbolic spaces where the inhabitants of the region can be part of a project of mutuality.

Berlin is perhaps more symbolic than anywhere of twentieth century transitions from the wild and disreputable pre-Nazi days to the frontier of the Cold War and its subsequent denouement with the demolition of the Berlin Wall. Its emergence from this process as the capital of the new Germany is something that two essays (Färber and Gdaniec and Binder) reflect on, and in particular how it has been inflected by new concepts of ethnicity. Färber and Gdaniec do this by looking at an ethnic commodity – the shishna – and the symbolic importance that is attached to this in different parts of the city. They also draw a comparison between Berlin and Moscow and use the shopping mall to draw out some of the deeper significances of the city. Binder, on the other hand, looks at how two global issues (the war in Iraq and diplomatic festivals) have brought a sense of global cosmopolitanism to narratives of the "new Berlin".

A third essay with a German theme is Nora Räthzel's study of youth in Hamburg and the resulting ethnicised turf wars and their consequences for how the city, or at least parts of it, are experienced. Räthzel focuses on the common-sense view of youth in European cities and considers the significance of categories such as migrant and native when used in relation to each other. A comparison of two neighbourhoods leads to a revelation of striking differences.

This special issue has arisen as the result of a series of joint seminars conducted between the Department of Ethnology at the University of Uppsala in Sweden and the Department of Sociology at the University of East London, the Faculty of Social Sciences at London Metropolitan University and, more recently, the Department of Geography at King's College London. The first seminar took place in the shadow of the millennium shift in Uppsala, the second in London in September 2001, and the third was a travelling seminar that wended its way through Sweden from Uppsala to Malmö and arrived in Copenhagen in May 2004. The geography and timing are not merely incidental, as it was this iteration between Sweden and London's East End that enabled the themes addressed in this issue to emerge. The issues addressed here are broad and cover much of the new Europe from Barcelona to Moscow. All the essays address the issue of ethnicity – something that we believe is shaping the European city more than anything else and which, in turn, is shaping the new Europe. We draw comparisons in this introduction between London and Sweden as a device for illustrating the dissonances as well as the similarities in the forces that are now shaping the understanding of contemporary European urbanization. We have deliberately eschewed the term multiculturalism in how we describe these processes, largely because we believe that it obscures the realities of the power relations involved. We suggest that the cosmopolitanism that is recorded in so many of the essays included in this collection – and which is affecting the development of so many European cities – comes from below and often finds itself in conflict with the national and middle-class cultures of established social groups. This came out quite clearly in our recent travelling seminar to Sweden in which the highly ethnicised suburbs appeared to be far more cosmopolitan than the quintessentially "local" city centres. This contradictory situation is perhaps best illustrated once again by reference to Britain and Sweden.

## Culture Analysis in Transformation

The question emerges as to what images are produced by cultural research into cities? It wasn't easy for cultural scholars to explore a city during a century of radical change and investigate its modern odours, notations, sounds and image fragments, because the fieldwork assignment was formulated in different ways both nationally and historically. European ethnology dissected into fragments, while film and cinema audiences created an overall view. Ethnology was bound to national missions, museums and universities and created conditions for regarding folk culture in a similar way in different countries. European ethnologists tend to easily forget the spirit of the times. Perhaps it best comes to expression through literature, art and film. The spirit of the times contributed an understanding of cultural phenomena and brought them together in symbolic relationships and interactions. It also gave ethnology a place. The spirit of the times allowed the collective consciousness to function as a principle of unification.

The discussion on European ethnology and its transformation has been quite intensive during recent decades (Köstlin, Niedermüller & Nikitsch 2002). Here you also find advocates for a new cultural research that, among other things, explains what the future of city planning will look like – a question that is developed in order to avoid digging into the trivial technicalities. The trend of city planning that has come to be known as New Urbanism – that reduces the development of cities to a personal and artistic undertaking – has meant that questions concerning the city as an aesthetic object and as the trademark for the tourism and information market become ever more important: what gives the development process its drive and direction (Löfgren, Berg & Linde-Laursen 2000)? Will a European city ethnology continue to be rooted in the old society or will it dare to make prognoses, as Daniel Bell suggests, of a society that we haven't yet seen but that we can look forward to through interpreting the signs that are on offer. Will society of the future be aggressive, technocratic, masculine or culturalised to the point where technology and society can no longer exist as a uniting force field?

We wish to thank the Swedish Foundation for International Cooperation in Research and Higher Education (STINT) for financial support. The idea of bringing our Swedish-British universities closer together and the joint seminars in London and Uppsala became very successful and promising thanks to this important funding and finally this collection.

# References

Bales, K. 2000: *Disposable People. New Slavery in the Global Economy*. Berkeley: University of California Press.

Bateson, G. 1972: *Steps to an Ecology of Mind*. New York: Ballantine Books.

Baudrillard, J. 1988a: *America*. London; New York: Verso.

Baudrillard, J. 1988b: *The Ecstacy of Communication*. New York: Semiotext(e).

Bauman, Z. 1992: A Sociological Theory of Postmodernity. In: Beilharz, B., Robinson, P. & Rundell, J. (eds) *Between Totalitarianism and Postmodernity. A Thesis Eleven Reader*. Cambridge, Mass.: MIT Press.

Certeau, M. de. 1984: *The Practice of Everyday Life*. Berkeley: University of California Press.

Deleuze, G. & Guattari, F. 2003: *A Thousand Plateaus. Capitalism and Schizophrenia*. London: Athlone.

*Encyclopædia Britannica* 2005.

Esping Anderson, G. 1990: *The Three Worlds of Welfare Capitalism*. Cambridge: Polity.

Hannerz, U. 1980: *Exploring the City. Inquiries toward an Urban Anthropology*. New York: Columbia U.P.

Jameson, F. 1994: *The Seeds of Time*. New York: Columbia University Press.

Köstlin, K., Niedermüller, P. & Nikitsch, H. 2002: *Die Wende als Wende? Orientierungen Europäischer Ethnologien nach 1989*. Wien: Verlag des Instituts für Europäische Ethnologie.

Lefebvre, H. 1968: *Le Droit à la ville*. Paris: Anthropos.

Löfgren, O., Berg, P.O. & Linde-Laursen, A. 2000: *Invoking a Transnational Metropolis. The Making of the Oeresund Region*. Lund: Studentlitteratur.

Merton, R. 1948: Patterns of Influence: A Study of Interpersonal Influence and of Communications Behaviour in a Local Community. In: Lazarsfeld, P. & Stanton, F. (eds) *Man in the City of the Future*. London: Collier-Macmillan.

Morris, M. 1992: Great Moments in Social Climbing: King Kong and the Human Fly. In: Colomina, B. & Bloomer, J. (eds) *Sexuality & Space*. New York, N.Y.: Princeton Architectural Press: 389.

Patterson, S. 1965: *Dark Strangers. A Study of West Indians in London*. Harmondsworth: Penguin Books.

Sennett, R. 1978: *The Fall of Public Man*. New York: Vintage Books Random House.

Venturi, R., Scott Brown, D. & Izenour, S. 1977: *Learning from Las Vegas. The Forgotten Symbolism of Architectural Form*. Cambridge, Mass.: MIT Press.

Weiss, P. 1956: *Avantgardefilm*. Stockholm: Wahlström & Widstrand.

# Mobility and Urban Transport in Metropolitan Barcelona
## Accessibility versus Exclusion

*Àngel Cebollada-Frontera*
*Carme Miralles-Guasch*

Daily mobility and social exclusion are two areas that have become increasingly important in the social sciences, but which are often dealt with as separate issues. Nevertheless, recently published studies (Lucas, Grosvenor & Simpson 2001; SEU 2003) have demonstrated the direct relationship between the lack of territorial accessibility and the process of social exclusion experienced by certain groups of citizens. The purpose of this article is to follow this line of investigation in greater depth and analyse the relationship between both areas, highlighting the implications of a dominant mobility model based on private transport that fosters a process of social exclusion in the Barcelona Metropolitan Area (BMA).

Our working hypothesis is that the present organisation of urban territory favours an increase in daily travelling both in time and distance, increasing the costs that accordingly derive from this situation as well as citizen dependence on mechanical means of transport. This is a situation that places private vehicles in a dominant position with respect to other forms of transport and means that those citizen groups that do not have their own vehicle can encounter serious difficulties when it comes to access to certain goods and services, and can even find themselves excluded from the labour market.

In this article we will show that women, young people and immigrants are the citizen groups most vulnerable to this process of social exclusion which originates from the BMA territorial and mobility model and explain the dysfunctions experienced by the affected members of these social groups.

## Functional Specialisation and the Extensive Use of Territory

Since the middle of the 20$^{th}$ century, Europe has been building and consolidating an urban model of an extensive nature that uses up large spatial areas set up for a limited range of uses. This territorial model is based on long distances to such a degree that it is separating the different daily activities performed by citizens: place of residence from the work place or the shopping/leisure, factories far away from the established city networks and the shopping areas in the periphery spaces. This spread is accompanied by a growing specialised use of urban spaces and an increasing segregation of the social groups in the territory (Miralles-Guasch 2002).

One of the main inspirations for this urban organisation model is functionalism, a theory that allows for organising urban land space in different zones according to use, activities and densities, etc. The aim is to obtain an ordered and Cartesian urban territory, where added values are accomplished according to urban space classification and where conflicts and interference in usage are avoided. In short, it means organising the city as a space where each activity has its own place and each place is used for only one activity (Lopez de Lucio 1993).

A characteristic feature of the city model is the increase in the development of its land space, which favours occupying extensive areas of land setting it aside for the minimum number of uses. The formal expression of this urban model is recorded in urban and city planning documents, essential instruments for configuring a city's territorial space and which have been used to implement zoning when planning out urban areas. In addition to seeing the division of a city in terms of uses, one can also see city divisions in terms of social groups, since residential areas are organised around social, generational and cultural characteristics which are both homogenous and differing at the same time with regard to other co-citizens from other city neighbourhoods.

While new urban periphery operations are clearly founded on functionalism (industrial estates, shopping and leisure zones, low density neighbourhoods, etc.) the traditional compact areas that were characterised by, among other things, mixed use areas, are now going through a transformation which tends towards one of functional and social homogenisation (Marshall 2000). So, certain activities are being driven out from the urban nuclei and relocated in the new metropolitan outskirts.

The result is a city that is more and more functionally divided, socially fragmented and territorially diffused, where urban complexity is being weakened while the spatial distance between the different daily activities is increasing. In this new urban configuration the fast route (or motorway) is the new format that is taking over public space while the traditional road is losing protagonism and use in the urban setting (Miralles-Guasch 1997).

At the same time there is an increase in the seasonal cycles of the city brought about by transformations in production processes (just-in-time, trading hours, new production habits, etc.), which have lead to an increase in and flexibility of the hours set aside for working and consumption. Consequently, the number of people working during the night, on public holidays or who work irregular hours has increased significantly. Furthermore, looking from this perspective of time, one also has to take into account labour hired on a seasonal basis to cope with surges in production that are likely to occur at different moments during the year (Miralles-Guasch & Cebollada 2003).

## Mobility: the Basic Requirement to Link to Urban Territory

The increasing distances between urban activities has caused daily mobility to take on a central role since it allows for re-linking the different city zones and giving meaning to the daily life of its citizens. To become an integral part of the city means that its inhabitants need to be able to get to different urban areas. To be able to get to these places is a pre-condition for being able to participate in the city and, consequently, to gain access to job offers. Given this territorial frame, the present-day mobility of labour can be seen as follows (Miralles-Guasch & Tulla 2000):

– *An increase in the distances travelled*. The physical separation of different urban functions has brought about longer person trips: more and more people work further away from their place of residence.
– *Greater flow dispersion within the territory*. Travelling between the centre and the periphery of the metropolitan area has been on the decrease while parametrical journeys between metropolitan peripheries has been on the increase.
– *Wider time band for these flows*. As mentioned earlier, the increase in the number of hours dedicated to different job activities has brought about a flow diffusion not only in terms of territory but also in terms of time.

## The Role of the Private Vehicle

These new mobility characteristics have brought about changes in transport mode distribution, that is, in the means of transport used to negotiate the distances involved. The increasing distances to be travelled has meant a decrease in person trips made on foot, the most democratic means of transport because it is the one that is most accessible to everyone and the means which has occupied a dominant position within the panorama of transport modes (Pooley & Turnbull 1999). On the other hand, mechanical means of transport (those which rely on an exosotic energy source) are becoming more and more important. These can be summarised in terms of collective transport and the private vehicle. The former, despite being the most accessible to the population as a whole, do not cover the entire territorial area and are not available at all hours of the day, and so there are many places which are difficult to get to or leave from. In contrast, the latter are not restricted to the same limitations of in terms of schedules or fixed routes, but they are not accessible to everybody and therefore are of a highly selective nature.

Given this context, private vehicle used has increased steadily to the point where one can speak of a mobility module based on the car. In Catalonia in 1996 the private vehicle was the means of transport used most to resolve the question of getting to work (having increased from 37% in 1991 to 43% in 1996), while the use of the remaining means of transport fell. So, walking to work, which until then had been the most common mode, fell from 38% in 1991 to 33% in 1996 (Miralles-Guasch & Cebollada 2001a). This situation was the result of a move which has its origins in public policies based on a combination of road network construction and private enterprise.

Thus, we have a discernible territorial model for the use of the private vehicle where collective public transport, although open to improvement, has been conceptually assigned a secondary role.

## Accessibility or the Right to be Able to Get There

But, despite the increased use of the car to get to work, the fact remains that many citizens do not have independent access to this means of transport, either because they do not own a vehicle or because they do not have a driving licence (Ferri 2001). This situation means that there are limitations on their being able to get to the work place and this has a similar impact on being able to participate in the actively employed sector of society (Miralles-Guasch & Cebollada 2001b).

That fact is that an urban area's territorial and mobility models condition the chances of being able to get to places for different people, providing them with different degrees of accessibility to different urban zones (Burns 1979). However, in addition to being a territorial matter it is also a personal characteristic. Accessibility is not distributed uniformly across all citizens who reside in the same areas. Each person or group of individuals have their own accessibility space-time setting defined by the territorial organisation that characterises the spatial setting, but their relationship is also governed by income level and gender, etc. So, there is no generic accessibility for all citizens in a given place. What degree of accessibility is available for a persons who does not own or cannot drive a car when private transport is the only way of getting there?

So, we need to analyse access in specific and individualised spheres where the efficacy of the territorial organisation can be measured in terms of the various life projects and the possibilities open to each citizen. Effectively, this means adopting a position in contrast with analyses that are too generalised and which categorise spaces according to their accessibility without taking into account the diverse characteristics of the citizens. At the same time, this means re-thinking the analysis of accessibility in relation to the possibilities individuals have of participating in activities and making use of the goods and services available (Vittadini 1991).

## Those Groups who Experience Territorial Accessibility Difficulties

For citizens, the varying degrees of possibility to make use of a private vehicle provide them with varying degrees of accessibility to the territory as a whole. Within this range of possibilities there are those of a temporary nature such as illness, temporary driving ban, or the car being repaired. However, there is another range of possibilities which we can call structural that make it almost impossible for the individual to make use a vehicle. As regards this second option, accessibility is governed by characteristics peculiar to each citizen as follows:

- *Location of the residence* is a variable factor regarding access to places of work which depends on the coverage offered by public transport services. So, there will be areas where dependence on a car is greater than others.
- *Location of places of work* also determines whether it is accessible or not for the population as a whole. As in the previous case, the collective transport territorial services offerings in terms of routes and schedules mean that some areas are more accessible than others.
- *Household configuration* allows for establishing different strategies when it comes to organising and solving transportation needs to be able to get to work (Fox 1995).

There are three groups that, despite being quite heterogeneous, are at the biggest disadvantage when it comes to making permanent use of a car, and who are equally vulnerable to being excluded from the labour market because of a city and mobility model that requires them to use a means of transport which, for a variety of reasons, is outside their reach. These groups can be categorised as follows:

- *Gender*. Women have particular problems when it comes to making use of a private vehicle.
- *Socio-linguistic background*. This is a problem when it comes to obtaining the required driving licence to drive a car.
- *Age*. This puts young people in a paradoxical situation since they are entitled to work at the age of 16 but cannot obtain a car driving licence until they are 18.

## Women's Access to a Privately Owned Vehicle

The different gender-defined social roles have meant that women are linked in a particular way to a variety of daily activities. A similar distinction can be made regarding the use of different means of transport since women have less access to a privately owned vehicle than men; car ownership rates among women are below the average (Sabaté, Rodríguez & Díaz 1995). Even though it is becoming more common for women to obtain a driving licence, figures provided by the Spanish Ministry of Transport (Dirección General de Tráfico 2003) in their census of drivers in 2002 show that for every 100 people who held a driving licence, 62 were men and 38 were women; 73% of men over 18 had a driving licence as opposed to 43.6% for women.

Table 1. Breakdown of driving licence owners by gender. Spain 1980–2002.

|      | % Men | % Women | Total |
|------|-------|---------|-------|
| 1980 | 77.1  | 22.9    | 100   |
| 2002 | 62.1  | 37.9    | 100   |

Source: Adapted from Dirección General de Tráfico (Spanish Ministry of Transport), *Anuario estadístico general*. 2003.

Although clearly women do not represent a homogenous group and there are internal differences within this group depending on age and social scale, what needs to be emphasised here is that the rate of access to a private vehicle among women is always lower than their male counterparts, regardless of age or social scale (Díaz 1989). This means, for example, that women with higher incomes have more access to a private vehicle than women with lower incomes, but this is not the case for men from the same social categories. Figures for driver licence holders among students at the Universitat Autònoma de Barcelona is a further illustration of this fact. The difference can be seen clearly if we compare similar ages and socio-economic levels.

Table 2. Holding a driving licence by gender. Universitat Autónoma de Barcelona, 2004 (figures given in %).

|       | 1$^{st}$ cycle | 2$^{nd}$ cycle |
|-------|----------------|----------------|
| Men   | 57.5           | 79.0           |
| Women | 37.8           | 70.6           |

1$^{st}$ cycle students = Years 1–2 of undergraduate degree
2$^{nd}$ cycle students = Years 3–4 of undergraduate degree
Source: Miralles-Guasch 2004.

However, so far the data presented only makes reference to holding a driving licence, which does not automatically mean that these women have their own vehicle. Sanz (1996) calculated that by the mid 1990s the number of women in Spain who did not have independent access to their own vehicle was close to four fifths of adult Spanish women (this included both women without a driving licence as well as those who, despite having a driving licence, could not make daily use of a vehicle).

Women without a driving licence see their situation as something that is "out of the ordinary" given the dominant, and consequently symbolic, role played by a privately owned vehicle in our society. Consequently, they fall prey to feelings of lack of self-esteem, frustration, embarrassment and even guilt for not being able to comply with the canons of social normality. These perceptions are aggravated by the need to own a vehicle in the case of residents in areas where the public transport offering is poor, for complete social integration and particularly integration into the labour market (Cebollada & Miralles-Guasch 2003).

## Difficulties Faced by non-EC Immigrants when it comes to Obtaining a Driving Licence

The group defined earlier as "sociolinguistic" is becoming increasingly more significant in terms of numbers in Spain (Royo 2000). The lack of equality of opportunity for this group is determined by their ability to be able to get to the work places where their daily life activities take place. Non-EC immigrant groups, although they hold a driving licence issued in their country of origin, are required to take out a Spanish driving licence if they have been living here for a period greater than six months after "having previously fulfilled all the requirements and having passed the necessary tests laid out in the corresponding legislation" (*Boletín Oficial del Estado* 1997:3790).[1] In order to obtain a Spanish driving licence they are faced with two major challenges. First they need to obtain a residence permit without which they cannot work legally in Spain. Second they have to take a written theory driving test in addition to the practical driving test itself which means that it is essential for them to have certain minimum language skills in one of the languages in which the test is conducted to stand any chance of passing. Here lies the difficulty faced by members of social groups who come from countries whose language is neither of those used in the exam. In such cases, language becomes the main obstacle to obtaining a driving licence. The only exception is the case of countries who have bilateral agreements with Spain whereby their driving licences are mutually valid, countries such as Andorra, Argentina, Bulgaria, Columbia, South Korea, Ecuador, Japan, Morocco, Peru, Switzerland and Uruguay.

Thus, in addition to a territory conceived according to a functional space division, a mobility model based on the car, and the difficulties they face trying to find a place to live, the location of jobs open to this social group as well as the difficulties in being able to make use of a car makes social integration even more difficult for non-EC immigrants. For this group integration into the host society is measured in even more immediate terms as regards employment than any other of the groups mentioned here. The lack of alternatives to the car for resolving their daily travel needs makes it even more likely that they will be subject to social exclusion and find themselves driven along a path leading towards an illegal status.

For this group, the privately-owned vehicle in this urban context represents something that is a basic tool for their integration into the host society which they see as being fundamentally mobility and vehicle-oriented. But, they also see the driving licence, and in particular the procedure they have to go through to get it, as an obstacle to their integration. Consequently, their perception of the difficulties involved in obtaining a driving licence contrasts with their possibilities of obtaining a car (Cebollada 2003).

Given this situation, it is no wonder that the issue of obtaining a driving licence figures high on the list of major problems defined by immigrant associations that organise specific literacy courses in adult education centres under the title of "Reading skills: the driving licence" whose sole objective is help people to pass the much feared, yet essential driving test. Despite these efforts, according to data provided by the same people who run these centres and course, the rates for failing the driving test are very high.

## The Lengthy Process for getting a Driving Licence Faced by Young People

Age is the determining factor for the third social group regarding the relatively low chances of making autonomous use of a private vehicle. The concept of a young person as a social construct refers to the stage in the life of a person that is situated between infancy and adulthood. In order to arrive at a more specific definition of a young person, we will take the definition that defines them according to productive parameters, that is, "based on their productive capabilities and functions within the theoretical perspective of the social division of work" (Espluga et al. 2001).

Once again, Spanish Ministry of Transport figures for drivers show inequalities in car ownership rates according to cohorts:

Table 3. Breakdown of driving licence owners according to age. Spain, 2002.

| Age group | % |
|---|---|
| 18 to 20 | 29.6 |
| 21 to 24 | 59.2 |
| 25 to 29 | 74.7 |
| 30 to 34 | 78.3 |
| 35 to 39 | 79.5 |
| 40 to 44 | 78.4 |
| 45 to 49 | 75.9 |
| 50 to 54 | 67.3 |
| 55 to 59 | 61.5 |
| 60 to 64 | 49.0 |

Source: Adapted from Dirección General de Tráfico (Spanish Ministry of Transport), 2003.

As regards young people one must differentiate two stages in the procedure for obtaining a driving licence.
1. From 16 to 18 years old. During this stage a young person is not considered to be of full legal age and cannot obtain a car driving licence until the end of this stage despite the fact that they can begin working at 16. During this stage young people cannot make autonomous use of a private vehicle and therefore are not guaranteed access to the urban territory as a whole. So, how can they choose a job where, despite there being no prior experience requirement, the main conditioning factor is having access to a vehicle to travel to work?
2. From 18 to 30. This stage included the process towards complete "social maturity", that is, when a young person can cash in on his/her legal rights and culminates with their inclusion in the adult category. It is during this stage when a young person obtains a driving licence and, after 30, can form part of the largest car-ownership group.

Young people see the fact of having a driving licence as yet another stage in the gradual process of becoming an integral part of the world of adults. But, this is also a goal to be achieved because of imposed social pressure and the lack of alternatives to the car offered by the existing urban model to be able to reach the city in its entirety. Just as is the case for women, young residents living in areas with a poor offering of public transport also see the private vehicle as that tool a provides them with total access to the urban territory at any time of the day and thus experience the city more completely (Cebollada 2003).

The relatively late independent status of young people in Spain is usually seen as a reflection of the problems experienced by this community. It should be noted that parents are more likely to take care of the expenses generated by owning a car than the deposit for renting for a flat, which would at least contribute in part to allowing young people to become independent earlier. The fact is that, as perceived by Spanish parents, integration into Spanish society takes place, among other factors, through daily access to a private vehicle. How can one integrate into society and have the chance of a "good job" without a car; the instrument which gives us accessibility to the whole of the territory?

## Accessibility and Exclusion from the Labour Market

The following pages outline the dysfunctions experienced by the groups mentioned earlier regarding territorial access to work places via methods other than a privately-owned vehicle (Cebollada & Miralles-Guasch 2004). The following table provides a synthesis of the consequences of this situation.

If impact is examined from a territorial perspective the lack of transport reduces the job-seeking catchment area of those people affected. This is primarily linked to the location of their residence and, secondly, the availability of public transport to get to the desired location. This initial space can be extended for those who are able to resort to social support networks (be they family or from the vicinity) and get to work as an accompanying passenger in a car.

Working close to home is one of the possible consequences of the lack of transport and data for the Barcelona Metropolitan Area for 2000 (Giner 2002) provide us with an illustrative example of how the majority of women work in the same residential municipality as men. In addition, one can see in the following table, the differences in the number of men working in the same area where they work in contrast to

Table 4. Social impact due to lack of transport to get to work locations.

| Impact | Consequences |
|---|---|
| Territorially limited labour market | Work in the setting where one lives |
| | Specialised production according to local labour availability |
| | Decrease in possibility of access to a wide range of jobs |
| Inability to mobilise all available human resources | Curb on productivity |
| | Difficulties finding a job |
| Lost job opportunities | Jobs lost |
| Vulnerability of those affected | Unable to establish lasting/reliable mobility strategies |
| Adopting risk strategies | Long and unsafe itineraries |
| | Driving without a valid licence |

Source: Adapted from Cebollada & Miralles-Guasch 2004.

Table 5. Gender-sensitive representation of location of work place related to place of residence. Barcelona Metropolitan Area, 1995–2000 (figures given in %).

| Year | Men | Women | Difference |
|---|---|---|---|
| 1995 | 53.6 | 68.4 | 14.8 |
| 2000 | 44.9 | 62.7 | 17.8 |
| Percentage variation | -16.2 | -8.3 | - |

Source: Adapted from Giner 2002.

women: for 1995 the difference is rated at 14.8% while figures for 2000 provide a differential figure of 17.8%. Through the gender-related percentage variation we can see how the percentage of men working in the same neighbourhood as their place of residence has decreased by 16.2% as opposed to 8.3% for women.

A second consequence is that due to the impossibility of accessing the territory, people without a car have to adapt to the profile of job offers in the immediate surroundings of their place of residence, regardless of their education/training and preferences. Consequently accessibility to the territory as a whole also means limitations on their chances of personal development.

It is also the case that people without a car see their job options as being limited and thus job inequality is created between people based on each individual's relationship with the available means of transport. So it should come as no surprise that improvements in public transport are related to an increase in job opportunities for residents (Julià 2002). This constitutes the third consequence of a territorially limited labour market.

## The Impossibility of Mobilising all the Available Human Resources

From the point of view of a social group, lack of accessibility to work places for different urban groups means that it is not possible to make optimum use of the existing labour market in the region, resulting in impediments for those with profiles better suited to each demand.

The social groups most affected by the deficits of accessibility to the territory are those that demonstrate the lowest rates of activity and high rates of unemployment. This situation means that many employment policies are aimed specifically at these social groups. One example is illustrated by the local agreements regarding employment which often set as an objective the incorporation of women and young people in the labour market. But how can these objectives be met if there is no prior guarantee of the possibility of being able to get to the work place?

## Lost Job Opportunities

Those people who cannot make daily and continued use of a car have lost job opportunities during their productive life as has been demonstrated in various studies (Lucas, Grosvenor & Simpson 2001; SEU 2003).

Table 6. Employment and unemployment rates. Spain, 1st trimester, 2004.

|  | Total | Men | Women | Young People* |
|---|---|---|---|---|
| Actively employed | 55.38 | 67.37 | 44.07 | 47.18 |
| Unemployed | 11.38 | 08.38 | 15.71 | 23.00 |

* 16 to 24 years old

Source: Instituto Nacional de Estadística 2004.

This loss of job opportunities can happen for a variety of reasons which in addition can be defined in real and potential terms and can take a number of different forms. In the first place being a car owner as a pre-condition for securing a job. In these cases anyone not possessing a car licence is already discounted. Furthermore it can be found that following the selection process and when a firm offer has been made, an individual's lack of access is an impediment to getting to the workplace and consequently they are obliged to give up the job offer. Similarly this can happen while actively employed – on occasions a person may lose their current job because the strategy they have adopted to get to work is no longer possible (the person they accompany in a car can no longer give them a ride), or because the work place has been relocated and the new site is now inaccessible unless one has a car.

## Vulnerability of those Affected

The fact that there is no guarantee of an alternative means of transport other than a car is a further burden to those that cannot use a car and places them in a highly vulnerable situation in the event of any kind of change. In this way the inability to establish lasting mobility strategies in a context characterised by flexible production, seasonal work, constant changes in job situations combined with lengthy periods of unemployment act as an impediment to establishing lasting strategies for getting to work for those who do not have a car.

## Adopting Risk Strategies

Finally the last impact mentioned here is the adoption of risk strategies in which the members of social groups affected often have to resort to travel modes that carry a certain degree of risk as much to their personal integrity as to the group as a whole. There are two characteristic risk strategies:

In the first place long and unsafe itineraries when the distance between the resident and place of work has to be negotiated using inappropriate means, which can be due to the distance to be travelled, the lack of coordinated public transport or how the public space is designed. These trajectories can be further broken down as follows: Walking long distances, often around one hour. Trajectories through suburban areas where there is a lack of social control of the space which brings about a feeling of insecurity and risk, particularly among women. Travelling very early in the morning or at night, which further adds to one's perception of insecurity as mentioned above. Itineraries through spaces lacking an infrastructure for pedestrians who run the risk of being run over (using the hard shoulder, major cross roads etc.). A large amount of time spent using public transport due to the lack of coordination between the transport operators and the radial nature of the network.

Second, one of the strategies that imply greatest risk can occur when driving without a valid driving licence. This is a common strategy among immigrants who have a driving licence issued in their country of origin and who believe they are quite capable of driving a car to get to their destination. This practice means, firstly a risk of being fined by the authorities, but also a risk to society at large because there is a social group that makes use of a private vehicle without complying with established laws to do so (the requirement to be in possession of a valid driving licence and current insurance policy for the vehicle, etc.). In this particular case, immigrants have had to opt for this risk strategy due to the fact that it is not possible to get to the work place using collective means of transport and the difficulties on many occasions of being able to form travel support networks with "indigenous" members of the host society.

## Conclusions

It has been made clear throughout this article that giving priority to the private vehicle has not resolved the mobility needs of the majority of citizens. Not everyone has the same options or possibilities in terms of access and use of the car. Women, young people and immigrants are groups which are most frequently excluded from car use. This fact can seriously limit job opportunities for these groups and can impede the incorporation existing human resources to the labour market.

Furthermore, the increase of car use in the city will not be possible because of environmental and social constraints. The extension of equal opportunities and the increase in social cohesion necessarily implies reducing dependency on the private vehicle and requires the promotions of alternative modes of transport.

The integration into the labour market of the vulnerable groups mentioned in this article implies a public policy strategy of access which allows these collectives to reach the work place. It should be noted however, that the group most affected are immigrants given that access strategies not only affect the world of work but also the sphere of social integration precisely because immigrants are most vulnerable in terms of family networks as well as knowledge of their new social environment.

## Notes

1. "...comprobación de los requisitos y superación de las pruebas correspondients..." (*Boletín Oficial del Estado,* 1997 – equivalent of *Hansard* in the UK).

## References

Boletín Oficial del Estado 1997: Reglamento general de conductores. *Boletín Oficial del Estado* 135 (6 de junio de 1997): 3787–3826.
Burns, L.D. 1979: *Transportation, Temporal and Spacial Components of Accessibility.* Lexington, Mass.: Lexington books.
Cebollada, À. 2003: *La ciutat de l'automòbil, un model urbà excloent. Sabadell com a exemple.* Bellaterra (Cerdanyola del Vallès): Universitat Autònoma de Barcelona. Departament de Geografia [PhD Dissertation].
Cebollada, À & Miralles-Guasch, C. 2003: Hábitos y percepciones de la movilidad cotidiana de las personas sin permiso de conducir. In: Seguí, J.M. (ed.) *Los servicios, los transportes y las redes territoriales.* Palma de Mallorca: Asociación de Geógrafos Españoles.
Cebollada, À & Miralles-Guasch, C. 2004: Modelo urbano, movilidad y exclusión laboral. In: Manero, F. et al. *Entornos empresariales, capacidad de innovación y desarrollo territorial.* Valladolid: Asociación de Geógrafos Españoles.
Díaz, M. Á. 1989: Movilidad femenina en la ciudad. Notas a partir de un caso. In: *Documents d'Anàlisi Geogràfica,* no. 14, pp. 219–239.
Dirección General de Tráfico 2003: *Anuario Estadístico General.* Madrid (www.dgt.es).
Espluga, J., Lemkow, L., Baltiérrez, J. & Kieselbach, T. 2001: *Atur juvenil, exclusió social i salut. Recerques, experiències i accions institucionals a Espanta.* Bellaterra (Cerdanyola del Vallès): Universitat Autònoma de Barcelona.
Ferri, M. 2001: La mobilitat és un dels problemes més importants del país. In: *Mobilitat, transport públic i treball.* (Quaderns de l'Escola; 4), 2001, pp. 73–80.
Fox, M. 1995: Transport Planning and the Human Activity Approach. In: *Journal of Transport Geography,* 3 (2): 105–116.
Giner, S. 2002: *Enquesta de la Regió de Barcelona, 2000. Condicions i hàbits de la població.* Barcelona: IERMB.
Instituto Nacional de Estadística 2004: *Encuesta de Población Activa.* Madrid: INE (www.ine.es).
Julià, J. 2002: La mobilitat al llarg del segle XX. In: Vergés, R. (ed.) *Infraestructures de transport i territori.* Barcelona, Diputació de Barcelona i Societat Catalana d'Ordenació del Territori, pp. 25–42.
López de Lucio, R. 1993: *Ciudad y urbanismo a finales del siglo XX.* València: Servei de Publicacions de la Universitat de València.
Lucas, K., Grosvenor, T. & Simpson, R. 2001: *Transport, the Environment and the Social Exclusión.* Layerthorpe: Joseph Rowntree Foundation.
Marshall, A. 2000: *How Cities Work. Suburbs, Sprawl and the Roads not Taken.* Austin: University of Texas Press.
Miralles-Guasch, C. 1997: *Transport i ciutat. Reflexió sobre la Barcelona Contemporània.* Bellaterra: Servei de Publicacions de la UAB.
Miralles-Guasch, C. 2002: *Transporte y ciudad. El bimonio imperfecto.* Barcelona: Ariel.
Miralles-Guasch, C. (ed.) 2004 : *Hàbits de mobilitat de la comunitat universitària de la UAB.* Bellaterra (Cerdanyola del Vallès) : Universitat Autònoma de Barcelona. Vicerrectorat de Campus i Qualitat Ambiental.
Miralles-Guasch, C. & Cebollada, À. 2001a : Mobilitat i mitjans de transport: l'evolució del repartiment modal a Catalunya, 1991–1996. In: *Revista Econòmica de Catalunya* 41: 24–38.
Miralles-Guasch, C. & Cebollada, À. 2001b : Desigualtats socials en l'accessibilitat als llocs de treball. In: *Quadens de l'Escola (Mobilitat, transport públic i treball)* pp. 81–95.
Miralles-Guasch, C. & Cebollada, À. 2003: *Movilidad y transporte. Opciones políticas para la ciudad.* Madrid: Fundación Alternativas.
Miralles-Guasch, C. & Tulla, A. F. 2000: *Mobilitat Sostenible: innovacions conceptuals i estat de la qüestió.* Barcelona: Diputació de Barcelona.
Pooley, C.G. & Turnbull, J. 1999: The Journey to Work: A Century of Change. In: *Area,* 31 (3): 281–292.
Royo, E. 2000: *Libro Blanco de la Inserción Laboral de Refugiados e Inmigrantes.* Madrid: Comisión Española de Ayuda al Refugiado.

Sabaté, A., Rodríguez, J.M. & Díaz, M.A. 1995: *Mujeres, espacio y sociedad. Hacia una geografía del género*. Madrid: Síntesis.

Sanz, A. 1996: Los "sin coche" repercusiones ambientales y sociales. In: *Documentación Social* 102: 119–128.

SEU 2003: *Social Exclusion and Transport*, London: Office of the Deputy Prime Minister.

Vittadini, M. R. 1991: La cittá accessibile. In: Balbo, L. *Tempo di vita. Studi e proposte per cambiarli*. Milano: Feltrinelli, pp. 37–40.

# Labour Market Trajectories of Caribbean People in Britain and France
## Multi-ethnic Societies, Multiculturalism, or Assimilation

*Margaret Byron*

Western European countries suffered labour shortages in a number of economic sectors during the post-war reconstruction period. Immigrant labour made an essential contribution to the post-war reconstruction of Germany, Britain and France. Regardless of the receiving countries' original intentions, the migrants became settlers and the ethnic structure of many urban populations was consequently transformed.

This paper examines the labour market outcomes for Caribbean migrants and their descendants in British and French cities. Post-war France and Britain were similar in a number of ways, not least in having Caribbean colonies from which labour migrants eventually flowed to the metropolis. However, their national policies regarding the incorporation of the colonial populations differed significantly, and may have led to different experiences for the new citizens in the urban labour and housing markets.

## Migration within a Colonial Relationship

While labour migration became well established as a strategy for the socio-economic improvement of people's circumstances throughout the Caribbean, the post-war migration to Europe was unusual in a number of ways. Prior to the war, destinations for labour migrants had been limited to circum-Caribbean and North America. Moving to Europe therefore introduced a new dimension of distance, expense and time into the migration, especially as people were far more likely to spend longer periods of time in the destinations than had previously been the case. Settlement within the metropolis was arguably perceived as something less traumatic in that a shift across the Atlantic to Europe was a move within a particular geopolitical field, shared between source and destination and a result of the colonial process.

The years 1946 and 1948 were pivotal to the relationship between the Caribbean colonies and the metropolitan nations of France and Britain respectively. At these particular points, the departmentalisation of the French Caribbean colonies and the elevation of the population of the Island of Reunion from the status of French colonial subjects to that of citizens of the larger French state contributed to Caribbean peoples being incorporated into the metropolitan nations as citizens who had rights of entry and could settle and work without time restrictions. In addition, the British Nationality Act of 1948 provided all citizens of the UK, the British colonies and the Commonwealth (Holmes 1988; Solomos 1993) with unrestricted entry and the right to live and work in Britain.

The historical context is particularly important to this comparative study. Although Britain and France were experiencing labour shortages in the post-war development enterprise, a variety of discourses as to the 'desirability' of migrants from the Caribbean colonies as a solution to labour scarcity emerged (Freeman 1987; Miles 1990; Bovenkerk et al. 1991). The consequences of these legal changes in status for their Caribbean colonial populations were very different. Attitudes towards the Carib-

31

bean populations emerged from ideologies of inclusion and exclusion based on conceptions of what should or should not constitute the nation (Freeman 1987; Miles 1990; Hollifield 1992, 2000).

The legislation adopted by France and Britain in 1946 and 1948 respectively, created very similar statuses for those Caribbean peoples formerly under French and British colonial rule. However, as I will discuss in this essay, the apparent parallels in the nature and timing of this legislation belie the distinctly different discourses which had developed over time within these two European contexts. The organization of migration to France and Britain, and the integration of the migrants into the employment and housing structures of these two nations, reflect these contradictions.

## The State, the Nation and Post-war Immigration in Britain and France

State priorities in Western Europe shifted after World War II. An increased suspicion of foreigners both during and immediately after the war had led to resources being directed into border security. Immigrants were a potential threat. Immigration policy changed, however, as states recognised that their depleted labour forces could not meet the needs of their expanding economies and post-war reconstruction agendas.

Legislation of 1946 and 1948 represented the extension of the national borders of France and Britain into the colonial hinterlands. In France it was felt that such moves would increase the solidarity and security of the larger nation, and the same was true in Britain with regard to the Empire/Commonwealth. In deciding to departmentalise its island colonies of the Caribbean and Reunion, France achieved two objectives: labour shortages in France were reduced via the organized admission of French acculturated colonial citizens, and the population and unemployment pressure in the small Caribbean islands was lessened (Anselin 1995; Condon & Ogden 1991a, 1991b). In other words, this source of labour was seen as satisfying the assimilation agenda.

The extension of British citizenship to the colonial subjects in the Caribbean through the British Nationality Act in 1948 was not in itself aimed at creating direct access to the metropolis for the population of the colonies. From 1948 the population of the United Kingdom and Colonies had a shared citizenship (Dummett & Nicol 1990) that, by natural extension, could both reside and work within this realm. However, unlike the explicit and active recruitment which was organised and eventually institutionalised by the French state, labour migration from the Caribbean to Britain was the result of coincidence in terms of the return of ex-service personnel and their contacts to Britain following the 1952 US immigration legislation which deflected labour streams from the US to Britain and thus created an 'available alternative' for potential migrants in the Caribbean.

The migration outcomes for these two groups are inextricably linked to the circumstances of their acquisition of citizenship and their incorporation by the European state. French Caribbean people became culturally integrated into the cities and the urban economies as French citizens, albeit into quite specific sectors which, at that time, were experiencing a labour deficit. In contrast, the 126,000 Caribbeans who by 1959 were living in Britain (Dummett & Nicol 1990:171) were together with a growing population from India and Pakistan referred to as 'coloured' and increasingly identified and indeed problematised as 'immigrants'. "Within popular and political discourse, an immigrant is, by definition, a 'coloured' or a 'black' person" (Miles 1990:527). This 'othering' of many individuals in Paris and London as a result of their skin colour followed traditional class distinctions and in many ways became rooted in an already existing social complexity. Being incorporated by the 1948 Act as integral elements of the British population had close parallels with the association of the terms 'immigrant' and 'Jew' during the late nineteenth and early twentieth centuries (Miles 1990). Despite the evident desire of the British state to retain its imperial status within the global sphere, the definition of the boundaries of the nation state, access to citizenship and the resource distribution which would ensue, became a focal point for an exclusion that could readily be developed by demonising a particular immigrant group.

Despite the presence in Britain of ex-servicemen and women from British colonies who were culturally and linguistically closer to British society than most Europeans, the British state looked in preference to European workers to fill their labour needs.

Despite labour shortages, a significant immigration from Ireland and the recruitment of labour from displaced persons' camps in post-war Europe by the British state between 1948 and 1962, led to an increasingly vigorous debate at political level and in the media as to whether immigration from the New Commonwealth and Pakistan was desirable. These debates gave credence to the racism that was evident in the street. Instead of condemning such sentiments, representatives of the state and the media tended to direct the 'blame' for such attitudes to the growing presence of coloured immigrants, thus reinforcing these racist perceptions of cultural origin and the creation of barriers between the groups. The exclusion of Irish immigration from the restrictions imposed in the 1962 Commonwealth Immigrants Act institutionalised this racism. The 'good human stock' necessary for immigration (Royal Commission on Population 1949) did not include black or Asian people (regardless of their nationality and colonial experience). Instead the commission referred to Flemish and French protestant refugees who had settled in Britain in the past as groups that fulfilled these conditions. Incredibly, echoes of such sentiments are to be found in contemporary discussions of winning popular consensus on labour immigration policy. In an article published in the *Economist*, Cairncross (2002) proposed that, in Europe, the choice of culturally appropriate immigrants 'may mean giving preference to white, Christian, Central and Eastern Europeans over people from other religious groups and regions' (Cairncross 2002:15). This pre-imposes a very narrow, a-historical perspective on the current population of Europe. It is certainly not a 'multicultural' vision. It fails to consider how the population of countries such as Britain and France view themselves and the rest of the world after five decades of post-war immigration and integration.

## Caribbean Entry to British and French Labour Markets in the Post-war Years

Among the passengers travelling on board HMS Empire Windrush to Britain from Jamaica in 1948 (Lambeth Borough Council 1988) were several ex-members of the armed forces. The few hundred men and women who had previously served in the armed forces and military related occupations amounted to a small proportion of the nearly 300,000 migrants who subsequently travelled from the Caribbean to Britain. However, they constituted the critical pioneer group in what was largely a migration via social network contacts (Byron 1994). Spouses and other close relatives of the servicemen were soon to following their wake in search of work in Britain. By 1951 a total of 9,456 males and 6,732 females born in the British Caribbean were living in Britain (OPCS Census of Great Britain, Nationality and Birthplaces Tables 1953). The decision by the British public and private sectors to recruit labour from the Caribbean naturally followed from these 'connections' that had facilitated post-war migration from the Caribbean.

## Recruitment of Caribbean Workers by Employers in Britain and France

Recruitment of labour began on the Caribbean island of Barbados during the mid 1950s. In a rare and detailed account of recruitment of Caribbean migrants to Britain in the post-war period, Brooks (1975) highlighted the important role played by the colonial government in Barbados in sponsoring emigration due to the island's high population growth and increasing levels of unemployment. The 'safety valve' approach (Marshall 1987) involved the colonial state encouragement of emigration to reduce the pressure of 'overpopulation' and unemployment. Officials from Barbados went to Britain in 1955, documented employment prospects and contacted several large employers – mainly within the public sector – including London Transport and the Health Service. The Barbados Migrants' Liaison Service was subsequently set up in London to seek out further employment possibilities, liase with employers and monitor and assist with the welfare of Barbadian migrants in Britain. As a result, London Transport sent a recruitment team to Barbados which selected nearly 150 operative workers. It was decided that further selection and medical checks would be organized by the Barbados Labour Department. Brooks (1975) also notes that from 1959, candidates were required to attend preparatory evening classes prior to leaving the island. The Barbados government provided an interest free loan to cover the new recruits' fare to the place of employment, enabled many who would have otherwise been unable to do so to travel. In addition to London Transport, officials from the British Transport Commission, the British Hotels and Restaurant Association and the National Health Service visited Barbados with a view to recruiting labour forces. Some recruitment also subsequently occurred in Trinidad and Jamaica (Ramdin 1987). London Transport continued to recruit labour in the Caribbean until 1970. However, after the 1962 Commonwealth Immigrants Act, recruitment had to take place according to the voucher system introduced by that Act. That meant that every Commonwealth citizen with a passport issued outside the UK, and who wished to seek employment in Britain, had to obtain a work permit to secure entry.

Some obvious contradictions in colonial immigration policy emerged in the 1950s. The ambivalence of successive British governments and the at times open opposition to the migration of British citizens from the colonies during the post-war period has been well documented (Joshi & Carter 1984; Carter *et al.* 1987; Dean 1987; Paul 1997). It was claimed that colonial migrants could not be protected from the *public*'s discrimination (Dummett & Nicol 1990; Kershaw & Pearsall 2000; Paul 1997). Such a claim meant that the state "avoided the challenge"… to use its influence "to ensure racially equal practices and to play upon people's sense of fairness and dislike of a 'colour bar'" (Dummett & Nicol 1990:172). Meanwhile the colonial state, exemplified by the Barbados government, not only recognised the desperate economic conditions on the island, but actively approached a range of employers in Britain with the aim of finding employment for thousands of Barbadians. They saw this as mutually beneficial. Their perspective was shared to some extent by a limited range of employers. The very fact that London Transport continued to recruit workers in the Caribbean until 1970 (Brooks 1975) is evidence of the relative colour blindness prevalent in some ranks of British industry. While jobs were obtained by the colonial migrants, albeit in a restricted range of sectors, housing posed a different problem. Already a scarce commodity in British cities, housing became one of the greatest resource conflicts faced by colonial immigrants in Britain (Rex & Moore 1967; Smith 1989).

Recruitment of labour on the islands of Guadeloupe and Martinique was initially organised directly by public sector services such as the Post Office, Customs and Excise and the Health Service. Military conscription also constituted a major recruitment of migrants in the French Caribbean. In 1960 and onwards, about half of those born on the islands would carry out military service in metropolitan France. Although presented by Caribbean parliamentarians as an opportunity to receive technical training and make contact with the metropolitan people, the state agenda was to maintain law and order on the islands following disturbances there, while at the same time opening up the possibility of a long term migration to France (Condon & Ogden 1991b). In terms of an emigration force, this period of informal recruitment was not insignificant. Condon and Ogden (1991b) estimate that some 40,000 migrants from the Caribbean were living in France at the time of the 1962 census.

While recruitment was a critical factor in generating this migration flow, the importance of chain migration once 'pioneer migrants' had established themselves in France is undisputed. With their citizenship spanning transatlantic space, and a state that was positively inclined towards such migration, it is not surprising that many people in the French Caribbean chose to join relatives and friends seeking a higher income in the metropolis.

The period between 1955 and 1962 is one of considerable convergence in the patterns of Caribbean labour migration to Britain and France. In particular, there were significant parallels in the recruitment of labour from the Caribbean. In both cases, the public sector sent recruitment agents to the Caribbean territories. Both European countries experienced shortages of labour in these public sector industries, as local labour forces sought better paid jobs in the private sector (Peach 1968, 1991; Condon & Ogden 1991a). The ambivalence and contradictions in the British establishment's attitudes towards the migration of citizens from their Caribbean colonies contrasted with the French state's commitment to simultaneously reducing unemployment in the Caribbean while solving labour shortages in the metropolis. From 1962, as mentioned earlier, there was a very distinct divergence in state policy in the two cases. In that year Britain instituted legislation, the Commonwealth Immigrants Act, which effectively removed the right to live and work in Britain conferred on the residents of the colonies and other overseas territories by the 1948 British Nationality Act. Ironically, the French chose 1963 to instigate BUMIDON, the Bureau through which the institutional framework of organised migration was set up (Condon & Ogden 1991a, 1991b); migration being seen as the solution to overpopulation in the Caribbean and to job shortages in the metropolitan labour market. In short, France encouraged family migration, but Britain did not.

## Labour Migrants in Britain and France: Post-war to the 1970s

Over one third of both Caribbean males and females were concentrated in semi- and unskilled jobs in the manual employment sector. At the end of the 1970s, most Caribbean men were either still employed in the shrinking manufacturing sector or the transport and distribution sectors; almost one half being skilled manual workers or foremen. Socio-economic mobility was limited within this migrant generation, however, and few joined the ranks of professionals and employers. In the manufacturing sector they were directly involved in production and related activities, such as packing. There was a significant under-representation of black workers at the supervisory and management levels (Runnymede Trust and Radical Statistics Race Group, 1980). Night shift work was fast becoming increasingly unpopular with the white working class, and here black people's presence became disproportionately high (Smith 1976; Brown 1984; Fevre 1984), thus supporting Peach's (1968) assertion that immigrants from the New Commonwealth and Pakistan became a 'replacement labour force', filling sectors which were being shunned by the white working class due to the unattractive nature of the work. The occupation categories of Caribbean migrants were typical of these trends.

Caribbean women's ease of entry to the understaffed nursing and care sectors led to more than half of employed Caribbean women being classified as non-manual workers (Brown 1984). In addition, increasing numbers of British-raised daughters of Caribbean migrants were entering the labour market via the public administration sector. Nonetheless, over one third of Caribbean women were still in the semi- and unskilled manual sector at the time of this survey. Manufacturing industries employed many Caribbean women, and the contraction of this sector during economic restructuring thrust many such women into the lower levels of the service sector, where low paid jobs of caring for the elderly or as hospital auxiliaries were increasingly available.

It was noted that the low-skilled employment obtained by Caribbean migrants was, for many, essentially the outcome of a compromise decision to forgo the opportunity to undertake longer term skills training in order to obtain immediate low-skilled employment to meet their many obligations to young families in the UK and members of the extended family in the Caribbean (Ramdin 1987; Byron 1994). Nikolinakos (1975) and Harris (1987) posit that the post-war flow of migrants into European countries like

Britain was a contributory element to the process of capital accumulation. It was no accident that post–war Asian and Caribbean labour was channelled into those areas of British industry that were most vulnerable to future mechanisation and consequent large-scale redundancies. Their labour was cheap and expendable and, like most new immigrants, they were relatively less inclined to think of the long-term implications of employment decisions.

To summarise, Caribbean work experience in Britain from the 1950s to the mid 1970s was characterised by high levels of employment in the public service sectors and manufacturing industry. Subsequent developments in the British economy included the severe contraction of these sectors. For these migrants' descendants, who sought to enter the labour force from the mid 1970s onwards, the prospects were often grim.

Between 1962 and 1981, the Bureau set up to organise the departure of labour from the Caribbean to France, BUMIDOM, organised the migration to France of 160,300 people, of whom 85,863 were from Martinique and Guadeloupe (Condon and Ogden 1991b). Of these labour migrants from the Caribbean islands, 12,000 were in France as part of their national service postings, and chose to stay after their service to take up employment in France (Condon & Ogden 1991b). Migrants from the Caribbean were directed into the public sector, which had been hard hit by the movement of local white French workers into better-paid, private sector jobs. This sector was also particularly attractive to the Caribbean migrants due to the possibility of obtaining transfers back to the islands, the 'departments d'outre mer' after a period of work in France. Within the public sector, Caribbean workers were recruited into the Health Service and the Post Office in particular. Both of these large employers became heavily involved in organising the migration and training of workers from the Caribbean to France from the 1960s, and indeed were even engaged in recruitment prior to the formation of BUMIDOM in 1963.

## Assimilation or a Multiplex Labour Force? Who Does What in France

In the booming post-war years of almost full employment in France, the state sought labour from southern Europe: Portugal, Spain, Italy, its colonies and ex-colonies in West and North Africa and its Caribbean appendages. In turn, these immigrants were fitted into specific sectors of the economy, and to a great extent, this initial employment allocation shaped their socio-economic futures.

The 1999 French census data reveals something of a hierarchy of workers in France, largely linked to country of origin (Borrel & Boldieu 2001) as had been the pattern in 1982 (Condon & Ogden 1991a). Those born in France with French nationality occupy the upper sections of the socio-economic groupings, with nearly 40 percent of the males in this group in the proprietor or professional classes. There is a gender division of labour, with just less than 30 percent of French women in this socio-economic category. This is most marked in the top professions, where the proportion of French males is twice as high as that of women. During the period 1982 and 1999 there is a significant increase in the proportion of those employed in this economic category. There are a higher proportion of females in the intermediate professional categories, although women seem to be concentrated in the health and social work category, while there is a higher incidence of men in the technical sector. There has been a reduction of the industrial labour category, which in turn reflects the reduction of the manufacturing sector and a corresponding rise in the proportion of the population employed in the (mainly) service sector. Less than 40 percent of French-born men and 12 percent of women are employed in the industrial labour sector. Twice as many men are in skilled jobs compared to those in unskilled jobs. Although there are relatively few women in this sector, the majority of them are in unskilled work.

In relation to the majority French population, the work trajectory of the French Caribbean population seems to 'shift down a gear', particularly in terms of status. Their relative absence in the top two categories of proprietors and professionals/managers is noticeable. The proportion of French Caribbeans found in the intermediate professional category is half that of the wider French nationality group. Meanwhile, there is a high proportion of both men and women – especially women – in the public and private service sectors. Caribbean-born men are also concentrated in the industrial labour group – something of concern given the propensity of this industrial sector to decline over time. For example, a comparison of the 1982 and 1999 data reveals a decrease in Caribbean male employment of 24 percent in the service and labouring sectors. The small rise in the Caribbean presence in the top two sectors does not compensate for this loss, and it is clear that unemployment in the Caribbean-born population has increased between the two censuses. In a fairly discreet manner, the Caribbean French population has been assimilated compartmentally into the French labour market. The reduction of employment in the two major sectors in which this group is concentrated does not look promising for future job seekers.

The third sub-category of the migrant population under consideration consists of the large and complex group of foreign-born immigrants. While this group is under-represented in the professional categories compared to both the French-born population and the Caribbean-French group, there are signs of a growing class of proprietors from the main sending countries of Italy, Spain, Portugal, Algeria, Tunisia, Morocco and Turkey – and to a lesser extent the rest of Africa. This group is under-represented in the professional categories and also to a lesser extent in the public and private service sectors. The high over-representation in the industrial labour categories (both skilled and unskilled) and the personal services sector completes the pattern for this group.

## Conclusions

The ruins of Europe in 1945 provided, in many cases, the backdrop for a dramatic turn of social ideas, economy and work. Germany's big cities had been almost totally razed by the efficient weapons of war of the time. With regard to city planning, the situation was therefore an entirely novel one: the task was to plan a new future for urban life avoiding the consequences of a mass-society which had been so dreadfully demonstrated by Nazism. Although not quite as dramatic, similar issues also faced the rest of Europe, and the focus for social planning was predominantly framed in urban terms.

As I have shown, the consequences were not always the result of planning. I have stressed the impact of immigration policies and the fact that workers were desperately needed in an expansive labour market at a time of economic boom. The idea of regulation lay at the heart of European immigration policies – although, as revealed, it did not necessarily work out like that. In most western European countries, state authorities organised the recruitment of workers abroad after 1945. It resulted in waves of immigration to Britain and France and, after 1956, also to Germany. In the latter case, the postponement of mass immigration depended on the initial 'Wiedereinbürgerung' of refugees displaced during the preceding decades.

Despite these common preoccupations, national traditions exerted themselves during this period and affected the settlement of immigrants in their new countries. The influence on housing policies and the labour market differed from country to country, and triggered perceptions of the precise form of 'cultural otherness'. Caribbeans in Britain and France were no exception to this pattern. Even when they were accepted on the labour market – at least in specific sectors – their 'otherness' was rooted in the definitions made by the people living in other parts of the cities. Workplace cultures moved fairly rapidly into a more distinct pattern of ethnic divisions of labour.

The varying legislation and regulation of immigration into France and Britain resulted in a situation where migrants from the colonies solved the labour shortage problems in the metropolitan nation. While labour migration was generally accepted as a strategy for socio-economic improvement, my argument is that the post-war migration from the Caribbean to Europe contributed in numerous ways to changes in the view of urban areas. The city, or parts of it, became seen in increasingly ethnic terms. The result of the colonial process was, in many senses, the introduction of a global community to the city.

The problem has now become one of how to conceptualise the whole range of background factors in order to explain the links between city development, migration from new parts of the world, settlement and the labour market. Part of the problem is the variation in how migrants settled in different urban cultures, but also that the patterns of migration have changed so rapidly over the last fifty years. They have moved away from the classic patterns established in the late nineteenth and earlier parts of the twentieth century which formed the heart of the Chicago School of Urban Sociology. Due to guest worker regulations, immigrants had to live in quarters close to the factory gates in some countries of Central Europe. In general, while, migrants were attracted to cities due to the availability of employment and, over time, a concentration of members of their social networks, the city presented the migrants with numerous barriers to their spatial and socio-economic freedom. Factors which constituted obstacles included a severe shortage of housing in post-war Europe, the racial discrimination which influenced the allocation of this scarce resource, and their restriction to low level manual and public service employment in urban locations. Over the last four decades of the twentieth century these forces and their spatial and structural consequences gradually became embedded in the city itself. Ethnicity is now certainly an active force in the dynamic urban geography of Europe. Yet one has to avoid using ethnicity alone to explain the social geography of a city. People of common ethnicity and migration history often live in specific places creating niches for particular services, often supplied from within the group, which cater to the needs of the ethnic community. The 'ethnic space' evolves over time. Yet certainly among post-war labour migrants, their association with particularly localities was the outcome of negative housing forces and job proximity. Indeed the suburbanisation of many ethnic minority families in later years indicated a desire to escape the restriction of earlier times. There are different aspects to the discussion: the varying patterns of living in cities like Paris and London where otherness and cultural racism are either open or hidden; and the fact that Caribbean became a symbolic expression of being "immigrant" in Britain which, to some extent, related to skin and colour, as was the case for Algerians in France, Turks in Germany and Yugoslavs in Sweden. But a more precise analysis shows how the regulations and constraints of the labour market add a dimension of power and economy into the discussion which is often missing in more 'culturalist' approaches.

The oil crisis in 1973 marked a shift in attitudes towards migrant workers all over Europe. It has often been said, not at least by cultural scholars, that they use the past to explain the present. In this respect, it is important to emphasise that the past is a series of unforeseen events. Even when it seems that regulations and legislation represent a body of continuity, albeit with periods of change, the development of media discourses and city cultures are often interrelated. From the early 1970s, the image of migrants progressively turned into one of redundancy and unemployment. In a situation in which the labour market was being restructured, and the big corporations began to export production to other parts of the world, the otherness of the immigrants became charged with the perceptions of the majority of their alternative economies, and specific areas such as the back streets of London's East End and the suburbs of Paris. It might, however, be argued that in the longer term, those migrants from colonial areas such as the Caribbean, who had long-term familiarity with metropolitan culture and language, were better able to cope with the strains of change that have occurred in those societies in recent decades. An investigation of such hypotheses in relation to new migrants is therefore an important future assignment.

# References

Anselin, A. 1995: West Indians in France. In Burton, R. D. E. & Reno, F. *French and West Indian: Martinique, Guadeloupe and French Guiana Today*. London: Macmillan, pp. 113–136.

Borrcl, C. & Boldicu, J. 2001: De plus en plus de femmes immigrées sur le marché du travail. In: *Insee Première* no. 791.

Bovenkerk, F., Miles, R. & Verbunt, G. 1991: Comparative Studies of Migration and Exclusion on the Grounds of 'Race' and Ethnic Background in Western Europe: A Critical Appraisal. In: *International Migration Review*, 25, 2, pp. 375–391.

Brooks, D. 1975: *Race and Labour in London Transport*. London: Oxford University Press.

Brown, C. 1984: *Black and White Britain*. London: PSI.

Byron, M. 1994: *Post-war Migration to Britain: The Unfinished Cycle*. Aldershot: Avebury.

Cairncross, F. 2002: A Survey of Migration. In: *Economist* November 2nd, pp.1–16.

Carter, B., Harris, C. & Joshi, S. 1987: The 1951–55 Conservative Government and the Racialisation of Black Immigration. In: *Policy Papers in Ethnic Relations* no. 11. University of Warwick, Centre for Research in Ethnic Relations, Coventry.

Condon, S. A. & Ogden, P. E. 1991a: Afro-Caribbean Migrants in France: Employment, State Policy and the Migration Process. In: *Transactions of the Institute of British Geographers*, 16, 4, pp. 440–457.

Condon, S. A. & Ogden, P. E. 1991b: Migration from the French Caribbean: The Origins of an Organised Migration. In: *International Journal of Urban and Regional Research*, 15, 4, pp. 505–523.

Dean, D. 1987: Coping with Colonial Immigration, the Cold War and Colonial Policy. In: *Immigrants and Minorities*, 6 (3), pp. 305–334.

Dummett, A. & Nicol, A. 1990: *Subjects, Citizens, Aliens and Others, Nationality and Immigration Law*. London: Weidenfeld and Nicolson.

Fevre, R. 1984: *Cheap Labour and Racial Discrimination*. Gower: Aldershot.

Freeman, G. 1987: Caribbean Migration to Britain and France: From Assimilation to Selection. In: Levine, B. *The Caribbean Exodus*. New York: Praeger, pp. 185–203.

Harris, C. 1987: British Capitalism, Migration and Relative Surplus Population: A Synopsis. In: *Migration*, 1 (1), pp. 47–90.

Hollifield, J. 1992: *Immigrants, Markets and States: The Political Economy of Post-war Europe*. Cambridge, Mass.: Harvard University Press.

Hollifield, J. 2000: The Politics of International Migration: How can we bring the State Back in? In: Brettell, B. & Hollifield, J. *Migration Theory: Talking across Disciplines*. London: Routledge, pp. 137–185.

Holmes, C. 1988: *John Bull's Island: Immigration and British Society 1871–1971*. London: Macmillan.

Joshi, S. & Carter, B. 1984: The Role of Labour in the Creation of a Racist Britain. In: *Race and Class*, 25 (3), pp. 53–70.

Kershaw, R. & Pearsall, M. 2000: *Immigrants and Aliens*. London: Public Records Office.

London Borough of Lambeth 1988: *Forty Winters on*. London: Lambeth Borough Council.

Marshall, D 1987: A History of West Indian Migrations: Overseas Opportunities and "Safety-valve" Policies. In: Levine, B. *The Caribbean Exodus*. London: Praeger, pp. 15–31.

Miles, R. 1990: Migration to Britain: The Significance of a Historical Approach. In: *International Migration*, 29 (4), pp. 527–543.

Nikolinakos, M. 1975: Notes toward a General Theory of Migration in Late Capitalism. In: *Race and Class*, 17 (1), pp. 5–18.

Paul, K. 1997: *Whitewashing Britain: Race and Citizenship in the Post-war Era*. Ithaca: Cornell University Press.

Peach, C. 1968: *West Indian Migration to Britain, a Social Geography*. London: Oxford University Press.

Peach, C. 1991: *The Caribbean in Europe: Contrasting Patterns of Migration and Settlement in Britain, France and the Netherlands*. Research Paper in Ethnic Relations no 15, University of Warwick, Centre for Research in Ethnic Relations.

Ramdin, R. 1987: *The Making of the Black Working Class in Britain*. Aldershot: Wildwood House.

Rex, J. & Moore, J. 1967: *Race, Community and Conflict: A Study of Sparkbrook*. London: Oxford University Press.

Royal Commission on Population Report 1949: Cmnd 7695, p.124.

Runnymede Trust and the Radical Statistics Race Group 1980: *Britain's Black Population*. London: Heinemann.

Smith, D.J. 1976: *Racial Disadvantage in Britain: The PEP report*. Harmondsworth: Penguin.

Smith, S.J. 1989: *The Politics of 'Race' and Residence*. Cambridge: Polity Press.

Solomos, J. 1993: *Race and Racism in Britain*. London: Macmillan (2nd Edition).

# The Multicultural Heritage of European Cities and its Re-presentation through Regeneration Programmes

*Stephen Shaw and Joanna Karmowska*

In recent times, some cities in the UK and elsewhere in Europe have made explicit use of their 'multicultural heritage' as a theme to revitalise inner city areas. Places that were once regarded as forbidding and 'unsafe' for casual strollers are being re-imaged to attract visitors from the majority culture, and in some cases international tourists. Expressions of ethnic and cultural identity in the built environment, along with markets, festivals and other events in public spaces are being re-presented as testimonies to the historic contribution of immigrant groups to the life of the city. Commercial thoroughfares are being upgraded, refurbished and promoted as exotic backdrops for consumption, especially stylish restaurants, bars and nightclubs (Shaw, Bagwell & Karmowska 2004). From a Neo-liberal stance, this 'self-help' approach is a welcome development that enables ethnic minority and other entrepreneurs to capitalise on an expanding service economy, revitalising long-neglected urban landscapes. Nevertheless, others question the sustainability of initiatives to promote leisure and tourism as disadvantaged neighbourhoods become 'urban quarters': shop windows designed to appeal to the consumption practices of the emerging nouveau riche, their street culture commodified in contrived narratives of place (Zukin 1999; Bell & Jayne 2004; Chan 2004).

Such deliberate aestheticisation of places associated with past or present immigrant communities as an exotic spectacle can be seen in the broader context of 'place-marketing': an emerging body of theories and practices developed by city governments, especially in North America over the past decade (Ward 1998; Shaw 2004). From this perspective, the urban past offers a quarry of possibilities. In historic cities, the built environment and its associations with former residents provides raw material from which 'heritage products' can be extracted and assembled, usually in combination with contemporary themes. Through interpretation and promotion, diverse elements of urban life and urbanity are integrated to appeal to target audiences, positioned or re-positioned to establish a distinctive, if not unique brand (Ashworth 2001; Morgan, Pritchard & Pride 2002). In an increasingly volatile and globalized market, rival cities compete to attract target place-consumers that may include high-spending visitors, as well as investors, property developers and high-income residents (Karmowska 2003). Historic urban landscapes – chance survivals of earlier phases of a city's development – may be exploited as valuable resources that contribute to quality of life for urban elites.

In the early 1990s, some place-marketing theorists adopted a prescriptive, if not evangelistic approach, advising cities to formulate strategies that will secure them a sustainable competitive advantage. Notable advocates were Kotler, Haider and Rein (1993) who commended city governments in the United States that had demonstrated a flair for competitive niche thinking, defining or re-defining themselves as distinctive places with specific advantages to target stakeholders. The authors highlighted the importance of 'preserving the history of places, their buildings, their people and customs, the machinery, and other artefacts that portray history' (ibid.:209) in establishing a distinctive place-identity or 'brand'. Even 'difficult destinations' such as Harlem, New York can be re-branded (Hoffman 2003). Cities in Western Europe, with their more hierarchical systems of governance, have generally been less than comfortable with the idea that cities – and districts within cities – should compete with one another without reference to a national or regional plan. However, over the past two decades, UK cities across a wide political spectrum found themselves in an increasingly competitive 'market place', as central government reduced grant aid and encouraged 'municipal entrepreneurship' (Begg 2002).

Faced with the decline of older industries – especially mining, manufacturing and distribution – urban authorities and development corporations in the UK looked to North American models of leisure and tourism-led revitalisation, especially for derelict industrial and waterfront areas in regions that had experienced rapidly rising unemployment. As Urry (2002:107) observes, de-industrialisation created a profound sense of loss, both for old technologies and the social life that went with them. Furthermore, since much of this industry had been based in premises dating from the 18$^{th}$ and 19$^{th}$ centuries, a large stock of buildings became available for refurbishment and conversion to facilitate a 'heritage industry' that would trade, in particular, on nostalgic and patriotic images of 'traditional' working class life (Hewison 1987). Contemporary critics argued that images of continuity and national unity were thus being manipulated and projected by the New Right to legitimise the status quo, the reification of a stable, untroubled social order that the viewer was not encouraged to question (cf. Wright 1985; Walsh 1992).

Many present-day residents of inner city areas in the UK are, however, first or second generation immigrants, especially from former colonies; some are recent refugees and asylum-seekers. With the election in 1997 of a New Labour government committed to the principles of 'social inclusion' through a wide range of public policies and programmes, the heritage industry was encouraged to present cultural diversity as a positive feature of history and contemporary life in the UK. Nevertheless, there still remains a considerable gap between this policy intent and its translation into the practices of museums and other interpreters of heritage (Maitland Gard'ner 2004; Mason 2004; Symonds 2004). More broadly, across Europe the ideological turn from nationalistic discourses towards acceptance of a more pluralistic common heritage has been challenging, nowhere less so than in the post-Communist states of Central and Eastern Europe. To what extent is it possible to reconcile Neo-liberal principles of market-led regeneration with a celebration of multicultural heritage and social inclusion?

## Whose Place? What Time?

A decade ago, the European Union appeared to be making significant progress towards the pooling of national sovereignty; Ashworth and Larkham (1994) assessed the implications for the presentation of heritage by its twelve Member States that were soon to become fifteen. The authors argued that hitherto, the concept of the modern nation state had been underpinned by a national interpretation of cultural heritage that focussed in particular upon the built environment. An inherently selective process, some features had been selected for re-creation or preservation for the nation, some historical incidents emphasised, others forgotten. A more integrated Europe would, however, require a specifically European heritage interpretation. They noted, in particular, that little had been done to integrate the cultures of recent immigrants, from the Middle East, Africa, India and increasing numbers from other regions of Asia, all of whom were now citizens of Europe. Nevertheless, many were disinherited as their heritage was ignored, or not shown in a favourable light.

This article considers the implications of adopting a culturally and ethnically pluralist perspective at the *local* level, especially in the re-presentation of historic districts on the fringe of city centers as landscapes of leisure and tourism. In some cases, the very names of such localities have, for many years, signified the poverty of minority groups that have been marginalized, not only in the physical-spatial sense, but also socially and psychologically distanced from the brighter lights of the city centre (Shaw & MacLeod 2000). In public policy, there is however an increasing recognition of the special contribution of migrants to creative life of European cities. Landry and Bianchini refer to the historic examples of Vienna, Antwerp and Amsterdam as cultural cross-roads, while more recently in some areas of UK cities Asian businesses have helped create a 24-hour/7-day economy. They observe that such communities are outsiders and insiders at the same time: '[b]ecause of their backgrounds they have different ways of looking at problems and different priorities' (1995:28).

Within the framework of the system of governance that has been created by the dominant culture, minority communities adapt and invest in the built environment. In Europe, settlements where foreigners were allowed to live, work and trade in commodities and services necessary to the urban economy were generally located in districts symbolically outside the fortifications that surrounded established towns and citadels. As Europeans colonised other continents, spatial-symbolic hierarchies were reasserted in the pattern of urban development. With reference to European and Asian migration to Canada, Kay Anderson's (1995) one hundred-year longitudinal study of Vancouver, critically examines the hegemony of European (mainly British) settlers over 'Chinatown'. In the discourse of public policy, as well as in the local press, the district had long been regarded as a place of sinful and sinister activities. By the mid 1930s, however, some representatives on the city government began to recognise its potential as an exotic destination for sightseeing, like its counterpart in San Francisco. Today, with many of its sites preserved as heritage buildings, Vancouver's Chinatown features as one of the city's 'must see' attractions for cruise-ship passengers and other international tourists.

Arjun Appadurai (1997:33) has described such urban environments as significant features of contemporary cities that are receptors of complex and volatile cultural flows. He refers to them as *ethnoscapes:*

"landscapes of persons who constitute the shifting world in which we live: tourists, immigrants, refugees, exiles, guest workers and other moving groups constitute an essential feature of the world..."

Using the metaphor of weaving, he observes that the warp of stabilities is everywhere shot through with the woof of human motion. The suffix 'scape' indicates that multiple meanings are attached to such places through the subjective gaze of different actors. There are, of course, many historical examples of ethnoscapes: urban settings that were the product of diaspora that brought together diverse cultures and thus different ways of looking at the world, and two notable examples are given in the case studies of Spitalfields and Kazimierz below. What is new is the increasing ease with which people, capital, technologies, ideas and images can circulate on a global scale.

The self-conscious use of place-marketing to re-image urban landscapes such as those discussed above, is also a comparatively recent phenomenon. To make such areas accessible to visitors more affluent than local population, municipalities often in partnership with central government, landowners, developers and not-for-profit stakeholders – need to make a considerable investment to upgrade the public realm. Especial attention is needed to make the 'gateway' entry points from the centre more inviting for strolling pedestrians; in the case of larger cities, routes from public transport or parking areas. The influential economist Michael Porter argued that the thesis he previously set out in *The Competitive Advantage of Nations* (Porter 1990) was 'just as relevant to smaller areas such as the inner city' (1995:57). The role of the public sector should therefore move away from direct involvement towards facilitation of a favourable environment for business. Since competitive markets for investment and development operate within as well as between cities, businesses should exploit the strategic advantages of inner city locations, prime examples being proximity to downtown areas, entertainment and tourist attractions, and the entrepreneurial talent among their immigrant communities.

Porter's arguments had a particular resonance in the UK, where rising unemployment and the untenable financial circumstances of many inner city municipalities had encouraged them to nurture and attract expanding sectors of service industries, especially leisure and tourism. Built heritage and the vitality of contemporary cultural expression – for example in the creation of cultural quarters – could help to stimulate an urban renaissance (Evans 2001). Cities such as Glasgow (Paddison 1993) and Manchester (Schofield 1996; Williams 2003) adopted strategies for re-positioning that were widely acclaimed. Some aspiring world cities cultivated a cosmopolitan image through attractions and events that owed their existence to immigrants from elsewhere in Europe as well as from other world regions. Taylor (2000) discusses the development of Ancoats as an 'urban village' in Manchester's historic Little Italy. Urry (2002:144) describes a 'cultural re-interpretation of racial difference' in Bradford's *Flavours of Asia* to promote Asian restaurants and sari centres in tandem with wider understanding of Asian religions and the history of immigration to the city. Birmingham's ethnic diversity is celebrated in its promotion of music, food and drink offered by its Irish, Pakistani, Chinese and Afro-Caribbean communities (Henry, McEwan & Pollard 2002).

In post-Communist Central and Eastern Europe (CEE), the ideological shift from centralised master planning to place-marketing has been even more challenging. In Poland, Hungary and the Czech Republic, cities with rising unemployment and world class but neglected urban heritage, have nevertheless identified tourism as an important catalyst for regeneration and re-positioning to international markets. Indeed, in the rationale of public policy it has often been regarded as something of a panacea. For example, in his speech to the United Nations International Council on Monuments and Sites, the former Tourism Minister of Poland, Marek Paszucha (1995:44) expressed optimism for cities such as Cracow: 'Opportunities will present themselves for the care of historic buildings the creation of a higher technical standard, and also the possibility of the revitalization of the whole historic complexes...' He cautioned, however, that a *firm plan* would be necessary, since 'some threats to the historic places originate from the new economic situation of the free market'.

In the turbulent decade after the demise of Communism, the regulatory powers of city governments were weakened, and municipal finances were not in a strong position. In practice, their ability to plan and manage the growth of local visitor economy was somewhat limited. For example, in the Czech Republic, the attractions of Prague's built heritage stimulated rapid growth of international tourism. Despite strong local opposition, the municipality could do little to prevent over-development of hotels and other tourism facilities that displaced residents from the Old Town and heightened social polarisation (Hoffman & Musil 1999). Hall (2002) observes that the 're-branding' of some CEE destinations has been informed by a desire to portray 'Europeanness': a safe, stable and welcoming environment conducive to foreign investment, membership of the EU and tourism. Conversely, the presentation of national heritage has, in some cases, been manipulated by agencies of the state to disinherit ethnic, religious and cultural minorities. In the more extreme cases of Bosnia, Croatia, Herzegovina, heritage sites and museums were targeted in systematic programmes of ethnic cleansing by opposing factions (Maroevic 1995; Newman & McLean 1998).

As the European Union has expanded once more to include twenty-five Member States (2004), it seems appropriate to consider how the multicultural reality of European cities can be communicated to visitors. The article examines the role of urban governance in facilitating a climate conducive to leisure and tourism in such areas. Will promotion of a visitor economy based on multicultural heritage themes benefit low-income residents and small firms? Or will it cause their displacement? Will the process of re-imaging be a celebration of cultural and ethnic diversity? Or will the simplification that may be deemed necessary to re-brand a locality require de-selection, editing out, disinheritance of some cultures past or present? The authors reflect upon the continuity of migration in some historic European cities from medieval times to the present day, with reference to two case studies of Spitalfields in the East End of London, and the Kazimierz district of Cracow over decade 1992–2002.

## Spitalfields, East London

In medieval London, the settlements beyond the boundary of the city wall were outside the jurisdiction of the mayor and burgesses, as well as the powerful guilds that regulated craft production and other trades. These 'Liberties' provided physical space for marginalized groups and institutions whose presence was unwelcome within the city precincts. Thus, they accommodated successive waves of migrants from other areas of the British Isles as well as foreigners. Among the latter, some came at the behest of the monarch, and were tolerated because of the economic functions they performed. As its name suggests, Spitalfields developed in open land around a monastic foundation that cared for the sick, its location being just to the East of the important approach road through Bishopsgate, the main thoroughfare from the North to the river crossing at London Bridge. From the 14th century, cloth-makers from the Low Countries settled, originally at the invitation of King Edward III (1327–77) to improve indigenous textile production, but in 1381 their economic success and foreign customs made them the object of mob violence during the Peasants' Revolt (Cox 1994).

In the centuries that followed, other migrants arrived in Spitalfields (Shaw 2003). Many were escaping political and religious persecution or extreme poverty elsewhere in Europe. From the 16th century, the Sephardic Jews escaping the Inquisition in Spain and Portugal included some who prospered as moneylenders and merchants, but their safety was not guaranteed until the Commonwealth in 1649 (Porter 1994). Protestant Huguenots, expelled from France, gave the word *refugee* to the English language, and Spitalfields became their largest settlement. Their numbers greatly increased after 1685, and their contribution to the urban economy included silk weaving and fine instrument-making (Museum of London 1985). By the early 1700s, the area was by far the greatest centre of the textile industry in the capital (Inwood 1998), and their wealth was invested in fine Georgian town houses. After two or three generations, however, they ceased to be distinguishable minority, and industrialization made their skills redundant. Most moved away, but others took their place. The expression ethnic and cultural succession is well illustrated by the *Neuve Eglise,* built in the early 1700s, a non-conforming church that stands at the corner of Brick Lane and Fournier Street (Hebbert 1998:173):

"The original congregation declined as the French-speaking minority intermarried and became absorbed, until in 1809 the church was taken over by the London Society for Promoting Christianity among the Jews. In Victorian times, it served as a Methodist chapel until the influx of north European Jews to Spitalfields at the turn of the century. In 1898 it was converted into the Great Synagogue. From the 1960s, the Jewish congregation dwindled, and the building closed again. It was reopened in 1976 as the London Jamme Masjid, one of the largest mosques in the capital, with a capacity for 4000 worshippers in the prayer hall."

Until the 1950s, few architectural historians or preservationists acknowledged the merit of 18th century town houses (Delafons 1997). Nevertheless, the Survey of London (1957) reflected a growing recognition of the value of such built heritage in its assessment of *Spitalfields and Mile End Town*. It noted that the area's 'evil reputation' and lack of interest from developers meant that a remarkable number survived into the mid 20th century, albeit in a poor condition. Jacobs (1996:75) observes that these Georgian houses, with their trademark mansard roofs that accommodated silk weavers' looms, signified 'a more elegant, more prosperous and acceptably foreign' Spitalfields. Thus, it became desirable to recover something of the 'good society' of the Huguenots, known for their love of flowers, caged birds and intellectual pursuits. In 1969, using its new powers under the *Civic Amenities Act 1967,* LB Tower Hamlets, the area's local authority, designated three Conservation Areas covering the heart of Spitalfields around (but not including) the late Victorian fruit and vegetable market building.

In 1976, the Secretary of State upgraded the heritage status of Fournier Street to an 'Outstanding Conservation Area', thus confirming its national importance (LB Tower Hamlets 1979). Nevertheless, the continuing loss of the 18th century Huguenot heritage outside the Conservation Areas, as well as the poor state of many within them, prompted the formation of the Spitalfields Historic Buildings Trust (1977). A not-for-profit organization, it was founded by the Marchioness of Dufferin and Ava, and other eminent supporters of the influential 'Georgian Group' of preservationists. Between 1977 and 1987, the Trust bought neatly forty houses to be re-sold or leased to 'appropriate' buyers, and refurbished. Acting as an 'unofficial inner city development organization', the Trust claimed credit for successful restoration of nearly 80 per cent of the nearly Georgian buildings (Blain 1989:9).

As the Jewish population which had been the dominant community in Spitalfields and adjacent Whitechapel from the late 19th century moved away in the 1970s, Bengalis acquired some Georgian and Victorian residences that had established use rights as workshops for the textile and leather trade. Jacobs (1996:86) comments that the other new community of white, middle class gentrifiers, who desired a nostalgic return to a restored Georgian enclave, 'produced an environment that was bathed in a rhetoric of co-habitation, but was antagonistic to the Bengali occupation of the area… It was not surprising that the Trust's activities worked to squeeze Bengali garment workshops out of Georgian houses and into more "suitable" premises and places', with the aim of 'restoring' them to residential use. The Trust was not, however, wholly successful in their attempt to draw this sharp spatial divide, and a number of Asian businesses still occupy Huguenot town houses. The graceful affluence of these enclaves, by now inhabited by 'bohemian' white gentrifiers was, however, increasingly at odds with the squalor and visible neglect of the public realm in adjacent streets along and to the East of Brick Lane.

According to the Government's social indicators, Spitalfields in the 1970s and 1980s remained one of the most deprived neighbourhoods in the whole of the UK. Racial tension increased as white male activists of the right-wing National Front harassed and assaulted Asians in conscious imitation of the anti-Semitic Blackshirts of the 1930s, and Brick Lane became the focus of intimidation, which continued into the mid 1990s. The majority of the new immigrants, escaping famine and poverty in their homeland, found accommodation in low quality, often high-rise social housing. To address the severe problems of its inner city neighborhoods, LB Tower Hamlets successfully bid for £7.2 million government funding for a programme to revitalise Spitalfields and adjacent Bethnal Green 1992–97. In 1995, a further bid secured £11.4 million 1997–2002 to 'strengthen links with the City and encourage diversification of the local economy', especially into leisure and tourism. The vision for the 'Cityside' program would 'pioneer a new model of regeneration'. Its aims (LB Tower Hamlets 1996:1) were to:

i) establish the area as one of the most attractive and accessible business locations in the capital;
ii) develop opportunities between the corporate sector and micro and small firms;
iii) expand the tourism potential of the area in order to stimulate economic activity, drawing on London's strength as a world city;
iv) encourage greater integration of economic development in order to both harmonise and add value to existing regeneration initiatives;
v) break stereotypical images of local people by supporting their entry and progression into the corporate sector and related local employment fields.

In 1997, Cityside set up a 'town management' scheme whose remit included the organization and promotion of events associated with the local Asian population: Bengali New Year, Brick Lane and Curry Festivals. Businesses and residents from the area's diverse 'communities' were represented on the steering group, and it was through this more broadly-based forum that 'Banglatown' came to be used a brand for the area, especially to promote the new festivals and Asian restaurants. Although London's daily newspaper *Evening Standard* continued to run editorials and features that ridiculed the name (cf. Barker 1998), in time the name became accepted as a neutral place-descriptor, as Cityside's Director Andrew Bramidge (2002 personal communication) commented:

"There was a lot of sensitivity about 'changing the name of the area', but it was never about renaming Spitalfields – a distinctive locality since medieval times. Rather, it was marketing tool to get people to come and visit the area…A minority of people probably did want that – comparing it to Chinatown in the West End – but our view is that this was never an appropriate model. I think that it was quite an effective strategy because today you regularly get references to things happening in Banglatown."

A key aim of Cityside's vision was 'to achieve a quantum leap in the area's status as a visitor/ cultural destination' (LB Tower Hamlets 1996:13). Brick Lane was also identified as a 'Developing Cultural Quarter' by the City Fringe Partnership (1997–2002). It would thus be promoted to 'tourists as well as employees and business visitors, helping to enhance the City's reputation as the premier European business location' (City Corporation 1996:17). In this re-imaging of Brick Lane, special attention would be paid to the main 'gateways' or access points, including its pedestrian subways to improve perceptions of personal safety. The programme thus included the erection of Eastern-style ornamental gateways, signage and brighter street lamps the design of which incorporated 'Asian' motifs. Brick Lane's restaurants would be imaginatively promoted to non-Asian customers, especially businesspeople from the City. The vision recognised that the area would need at least one 'must see' attraction and identified two vacant heritage buildings from the Victorian era as suitable sites: Truman's Brewery and the nearby 'Moorish Market' (ibid.:14):

"[A] Cultural Heritage Centre will provide the area with its missing flagship attraction. It will foster a sense of pride amongst the local community and promote an image of London as an exciting and vibrant multicultural city…The unique and beautiful Listed building in Fashion Street, inter-connected with the above, provides almost 100,000 square feet and could provide a major 'bazaar/ souk'. This will act as a key motor to the local economy, providing the missing 'ethnic' shopping experience."

These two proposals were soundly based, but neither materialised during Cityside's five-year programme as the site owner had plans for more profitable uses. In 1992, Grand Metropolitan sold its redundant brewery to a local entrepreneur, who refurbished the buildings, gradually converting them to a lively mix of uses. Ten years later these include 250 studios for cultural industries, two bars/nightclubs, cafés, galleries, speciality retailers and an exhibition centre. The same businessman acquired the Moorish Market in Fashion Street, and has recently applied for planning permission to convert it to studios and loft-style apartments. A recent study by Maitland Gard'ner (2004) suggests, however, that neither the Georgian townhouses of that had been the subject of the Spitalfields Historic Buildings Trust's campaign for protection and restoration, nor more recent attractions aimed mainly at non-Asian visitors have much significance for residents of Bangladeshi origin. The latter group identified a very different set of areas, sites and buildings as important to their sense of identity with the locality. This anomaly raises fundamental questions concerning the ability of the statutory system of heritage protection to address the needs and aspirations of ethnic minority groups.

The commercial success of the converted Truman's Brewery site nevertheless exceeded expectations, as did the rapid rise of 'Banglatown' Brick Lane as a centre for ethnic cuisine.

A survey carried out for Cityside noted that in 1989 there were only eight cafés/restaurants in Brick Lane, with a few additions in the early 1990s. Between 1997 and 2002, however, this rose to 41, of which 16 had opened 2000–02, making Banglatown 'home to the largest cluster of Bangladeshi/"Indian" restaurants anywhere in the UK' (Carey 2002:12). All the restaurants (as opposed to cafés) reported that their clientele was 'overwhelmingly white', with a clear majority (70%) in the 25–34 age group and predominantly male (ibid.:4). The boom was facilitated by relaxed planning policies that allowed local shops to be converted to restaurants. Furthermore, the central area of 19th century buildings at the heart of Brick Lane was designated a 'Restaurant Zone' where restaurants, cafés, hot food outlets, public houses and bars would be 'favourably considered' (LB Tower Hamlets 1999). By 2001, however, street canvassing by waiters indicated an excess supply, a problem that became even more pronounced with the downturn after 9/11 and the reluctance of some visitors to enter a predominantly Muslim neighbourhood.

The Council called a public meeting on the issue at which some restaurant owners argued that licences should be extended beyond midnight to boost trade. However, a number of the white, middle class residents of the Conservation Areas to the west of Brick Lane argued that litter and anti-social behaviour by late-night customers was already a serious nuisance. Others argued that conversion to restaurants that commanded higher rents contributed to the loss of local shops. Unfortunately, a stormy exchange led to physical blows and required police attendance. LB Tower Hamlets then commissioned consultants Agroni (2001) to carry out a survey of over 1500 residents from 'all communities', which confirmed widespread opposition to the proliferation of bars and restaurants and to any extension of opening hours At the time of writing, the Restaurant Zone remains in force, but LB Tower Hamlets (2002) has recently used its planning powers to protect the southern section of Brick Lane as a 'Local Shopping Parade', a policy that is fully supported by Cityside.

The conversion of the previously run-down, mainly 19th century streetscape of Brick Lane to nightclubs, bars and restaurants has undoubtedly brought wealth to Bengali-owned businesses and job opportunities. Carey (2002) estimated that around 400 workers were employed in Brick Lane restaurants, of whom 96% were of Bangladeshi origin, 92% lived in the Borough, and 99% were men. Nevertheless, some problems identified in recent years have shed doubt on the wisdom of over-reliance on this sector. A third of restaurant owners expressed concern over staff turnover, and many felt that low pay and shifts made the work unattractive to younger Bengalis. Some said that it was risky to hire young local Bengali males who might be heroin or crack cocaine users, so they preferred to employ middle-aged men. Bengali women seemed extremely unwilling to work as waitresses, regarding restaurants as a largely male domain. Gender inequalities in the use of public space resulting from the visitor economy have also become apparent. Planning Officer Andrea Ritchie reported (2002 personal communication) that in a recent focus group facilitated by the Borough:

"Older Bengali women stressed the point that they had to be escorted by their husbands and that they could not walk along Brick Lane at all because there are just too many men there, with all the visitors and [restaurant] staff. So, although it is their area, they are socially excluded from it."

## Kazimierz, Cracow

Like Spitalfields in the East End of London, the present-day urban district of Kazimierz originated as a medieval settlement that lay outside the city wall of Cracow, Poland's former capital. However, in this case, it was a planned town in its own right. In 1335, King Kazimierz the Great founded the settlement that bears his name on a bend of the Vistula, physically separated from the royal citadel of Wawel and the established city only by an arm of the river. With all the privileges of a burgh including an impressive market, the monarch's aim was to make it one of the great trading centres of Europe that could compete with other cities, including the adjacent Cracow. Over the turbulent centuries that followed, the place incorporated both Christian and Jewish cultures, for under the *Oppidum Iudaeorum* it became one of Europe's largest and oldest continuous districts of legalized Jewish settlement. Czech, German, Spanish and Italian Jews migrated to Kazimierz to live alongside Roman Catholic Poles, developing their trades and crafts, especially wood and metalworking. Thus, they contributed to the area's wealth, as well as to its unique identity. Under royal protection, they established their communities with synagogues and prayer-houses, a few of which survive to this day. Now a World Heritage site, the historic built environment of Kazimierz reflects the richness of both traditions that co-existed for six hundred years, as well as its economic vicissitudes, one its most stable and prosperous periods being the 16$^{th}$ and early 17$^{th}$ centuries. Eventually, the end of the 18th century incorporated it as a district within Cracow, with the town walls demolished and the river-arm drained, it was physically united as a continuous urban settlement

In 1939, the Jewish population of Cracow was over 63,000 (about a quarter of the city's population) with a high proportion living in the Kazimierz district (Duda 1991), a presence that was to be terminated abruptly and tragically by the Nazi invasion. Kazimierz has now become a memorial site to the atrocities of the Holocaust, but it is also an urban district whose residents have suffered poverty and social disadvantage. In the post-Communist era of the 1990s, its potential was recognized as a special district requiring physical as well as social and economic revitalization, although sensitivity would be required to reconcile this with its complex duality and memorialization of the former Jewish inhabitants. As Ashworth (1996:59) comments:

"If the atrocity element was the only consideration then it would be relatively easy to accord a paramount status to the national and international memorial function. It was however such a widespread phenomenon throughout European cities even containing a majority of the population in some Polish cases that it merges into more mundane issues of the local revitalisation and renovation problems of inner city districts. It is the clash of the sublime and mundane, the sacred and the secular, the international and the local that provides much of the complexity now facing the city planners as they embark upon renewal in such districts."

During the Communist era, Kazimierz lost much of its former identity, and its built heritage deteriorated. Although it remained one of the most densely populated districts of Cracow, much of its housing was rented to its poorest citizens. Through to the 1990s, its physical environment was in visible neglect, and with rents controlled and set at a very low level, landlords had little incentive to carry out even the most basic repairs. Soon after the end of the Communist period, the need for a strategic approach was recognised. With funding from the EU, a team of planners and other officers seconded from the cities of Cracow, Edinburgh and Berlin carried out the specially commissioned study in 1993–94. The team prepared a joint report on the urban renewal and conservation of the built environment of Kazimierz, helping to identify the necessary legal, administrative and financial framework. The aim was to formulate a comprehensive program to revive the run-down but potentially attractive area, and for creating an effective balance of residential, commercial and visitor uses (Cameron & Zuziak 1994). The team produced the *Kazimierz Action Plan,* with short and medium-term horizons:

– 0–2 years (mostly marketing, partnership building and first regeneration works).
– 0–5 years (completions of landscaping of the selected sites, finalising particular regeneration projects).

Unfortunately, there was considerable uncertainty over financial support from the municipality and other public bodies, and it was difficult to set measurable objectives and milestones. Furthermore, the *Detailed Local Master Plan for the Historic Quarter of Kazimierz* (1987) adopted during the Communist era remained in force as the regulatory framework for land use planning. In practice, five years after publication of the Action Plan, few of its recommendations had been implemented (Brzeski 2000). Perhaps the main value of the project was to identify the potential factors that would be critical to the future development of the district, the role of public participation in this process, and the role which effective place-marketing would play. During the 1990s, several other EU-funded projects and proposals followed (including ECOS II and several seminars and conferences), but these had no more impact on the processes and pattern of development than ECOS I. As with Spitalfields, revitalization has occurred in particular enclaves within the district.

Over the past decade, organisations devoted to Jewish culture and heritage preservation have played an important role in re-establishing the district's former traditions, the 'Centre for Jewish Culture' being a notable example. Established in 1993 under auspices of Judaica Foundation, and with substantial financial support of the United States Congress, the local authorities and the Polish Ministry of Culture, this institute is housed in the former nineteenth-century prayer-house. The nearby Lauder Foundation was also established, its primary aim being to promote and cultivate the Jewish religion, traditions and celebrations in Poland. Unexpectedly, however, one of the most potent agents of change has been tourism inspired by cinema, as the area of Kazimierz around Szeroka featured prominently in Spielberg's (1993) film *Schindler's List*. In pre-war times, like Brick Lane, the high street of the Jewish quarter, Szeroka has thus attained celebrity status and readily included in itineraries of Poland from elsewhere in Europe and from North America, as well as independent travellers and participants in festivals and other events. Other sites and sights visited by international tourists include the Jewish cemetery, the synagogues and the mikveh (the old building of Jewish ritual baths).

Since the mid-90s, many other buildings in this part of Kazimierz, mostly dating from the 19$^{th}$ century, have found new commercial uses as 'Jewish-style' cafés, bookshops, restaurants and hotels. These prominently display signs in Hebrew, and some offer 'traditional Jewish entertainment'. Like the cultural institutions described above, however, nearly all are managed and staffed by Polish Catholics. A few minutes walk from Szeroka, the area around Plac Nowy has become a popular evening entertainment venue for younger Cracovians. With many bars and nightclubs, its somewhat studied decadence is therefore juxtaposed with memorialization of the 'Old Jewish Quarter'. A third sub-district of the World Heritage site has also been marked out on the contemporary tourist map around Plac Wolnica (the old market place of Kazimierz) and on the opposite side of Krakowska Street. Historically, the life of this predominantly Catholic part of Kazimierz took place around its splendid churches and the Old Town Hall (now ethnography and folk museum). Although these impressive urban landmarks feature in guidebooks, and are sign-posted by the municipality for the benefit of visitors, as yet there is little evidence of revitalisation in this area. Although this might be explained in rational terms, such as transport and relative accessibility, it appears that the development of urban tourism is subject to the vagaries of processes that are very difficult for city governments and other public agencies to anticipate or manage.

A key issue in the district is the number of heritage buildings that are of 'uncertain ownership' under the program of restitution. Most are properties that were owned by Jews who either died in the Holocaust, or else survived and left Poland, and whose descendants are entitled to reclaim them. As a result of disputed claims and uncertain ownership, some important historic buildings on prominent sites have not been maintained, and some are now in an unsafe condition. Despite this urban blight, and the district's previous reputation as a low-rent district, pockets of affluence emerged in the mid 1990s. Indeed, today some of the most expensive apartments in Cracow are in Kazimierz. Since the ECOS I report was published, there have been some significant changes in the social mix of Kazimierz, as tenants on low, controlled rents – especially the elderly and poor are often forced to leave the area. In recent years, this has accelerated, and in 2005 the rent controls are due to end. To some extent, the valorization of older property in Kazimierz has been an unintended consequence of a state-funded renovation program administered by SKOZK (Social Committee for Cracow Monuments Preservation). However, gentrification has not always resulted in the renovation of older buildings, as some of the most sought-after accommodation is in new-build low-rise apartments built to a high standard in a retro-style on infill sites.

The process of commercial, as well as residential gentrification has also been boosted by the voluntary efforts to improve the area by a local association of small businesses. Its initiatives have included a 'clean up Kazimierz' campaign to reduce garbage on streets and pavements, late opening of shops and galleries every first Thursday of the month, and a summer soup festival. As in Spitalfields and other inner urban areas of West European cities, the new residents include a mix of artists, scientists and young professionals, who are attracted by the accessible location, ambience and now fashionable address. Most of the district's former craft industries have also been displaced. Traditionally famous for its metal and woodworking, these have rapidly declined. Without effective planning control over change of use, or support from the state, craftspeople are now unable to pay rents comparable to restaurants and souvenir shops that have located here because of tourism. Thus, the ECOS plan for Kazimierz, with its emphasis on maximizing social and economic benefits – especially to its disadvantaged residents and to the district's established craft industries – has held very little sway. The Detailed Local Master Plan appears increasingly irrelevant to a post-Communist urban economy; the vagaries of market forces prevail.

Despite the overall lack of progress, one notable achievement of ECOS I was establishment in 1994 of the Local Kazimierz Office: an agency that has worked closely with the local community. Its activities have focussed in particular on social revitalisation. Its main strength was as a stabile point of contact for residents of the districts, as well as for potential investors. With modest support from the municipality, and from the Prince of Wales Foundation in the UK, it instigated projects that have been widely recognised as important for the community life of Kazimierz during a difficult period of transition. These included promotional activities, surveys to gauge public opinion, and public consultation on key issues that affected community life, educational projects that drew from the area's rich history, such as 'Future for the Past' that encouraged participation from young adults, in particular. In the late 1990s, the activities of Kazimierz Office received very little support from the City Council. Walczak (2002) concluded that, unfortunately, the Kazimierz Office was not functioning effectively. Its staff considered the organisation to be largely powerless and ineffective, with a budget sufficient only to support its own staff overheads and minor promotional initiatives (including newsletter), but without the authority or political support to implement the Action Plan and to achieve its community objectives.

In 2002 the Kazimierz Office was forced to close, but some of its volunteers have set up 'Friends of Kazimierz', an organisation that attempts to continue some of the initiatives, including a quarterly magazine *Kazimierz,* published in English as well as Polish. Other publications discuss local issues and promote events to visitors and to the local community. One issue of increasing concern is the effect of the booming 'Old Jewish Town' and late-night economy on the everyday lives of residents. Some pavement cafés and restaurants in Kazimierz are open long after those in the Market Square in Cracow have closed, and on warm summer evenings their customers tend to stay outside all night. At weekends, the pavements are lined with parked cars, and young people stand around, drinking and listening to the loud music from the cafés. In the daytime, the public spaces are occupied by groups of weary tourists, and mothers from the local neighbourhood have to walk some way from their homes to find a quiet area for their children to play. There are also wider concerns that the smartly renovated apartments and business premises will attract wealthy owners and internationally branded retail outlets, causing rents to rise well beyond the means of established residents. Those who are not displaced will also feel increasingly excluded, for example the new 'café society' will encroach upon and perhaps displace the area's local street markets. Ten years on, few of the objectives outlined in the ECOS I report have been achieved. Despite its status as a World Heritage site, and as a district identified for special treatment in the Master Plan, regulation has been ineffectual. And, as yet Cracow City Council has offered very little financial support for the local policies and initiatives that they, in principle, espouse. Market forces have thus prevailed, and the pace, location and type of investment by the private sector have been hard to predict. Only time will tell whether revitalization through leisure and tourism will renovate the historic urban landscape and provide the promised economic and social benefits for established residents and their small businesses.

The somewhat laissez-faire approach of the past decade has, however, produced a mosaic of 'scenes' within Kazimierz, sub-areas that cater for different segments of leisure demand: cheap bars for students, Jewish-style hotels and restaurants for international tourists, high class cuisine for the urban elite. Poland's unstable national economy and the current uncertainties over global tourism demand may also be compounded by the vagaries of fashion. The Friends of Kazimierz and other community groups express concern that at some stage, a downturn in some or all of these will leave the district's heritage buildings empty and neglected once again. Such concerns and doubts regarding the sustainability of leisure and tourism-led revitalization in the 'showpiece' district of Kazimierz had been partly addressed by the Mayor and City Council, elected on a programme of reform in November 2002. In the next few years, such concerns and doubts regarding the sustainability of leisure and tourism-led revitalization in the 'showpiece' district of Kazimierz will have to be addressed by the new Mayor and City Council, elected on a programme of reform in November 2002. By 2004, some preliminary work had been undertaken, most notably the submission of several projects for EU funding. A Task Team for revitalisation of the Kazimierz area has been established with five working groups: entrepreneurship and promotion; space of culture; social space; spatial economy; and housing. In the near future, the municipality plans to announce a competition for a 'complex and interdisciplinary study – conception for the revitalisation of the Kazimierz area, that would influence its economic and social activity' (Gorczyca 2004 personal communication). Whether or not this is the most appropriate way to address the problems of Kazimierz and its established residents and businesses will no doubt be the subject of considerable debate in the near future.

## Conclusion

The present circumstances of the two case study areas seem very different, but there are also some significant common themes. Both Spitalfields and Kazimierz have medieval origins as urban quarters where immigrant communities were permitted to settle and establish their trades. Over the following centuries, through the early modern period to the present day, this rich multicultural heritage has left its imprint on the urban landscape. In these and other European cities, such places have complex place-identities that contrast with the 'mainstream' image of the national heritage industry. For many years associated with the poverty of other cultural and ethnic groups, they may contain a large stock of heritage buildings, deemed worthy of conservation because of their architectural merit and/or historic value. Typically, however, there are serious problems of dereliction and poor maintenance. The public realm of streets, community facilities and other infrastructure is also worn out and visibly neglected, as the local tax base is low, and city governments have other priorities. Over the last decade, the opportunity to market and promote an emerging visitor economy has been seen as something of a panacea to revitalize such areas. Their built heritage has thus been exploited as raw material from which a distinctive heritage 'product' can be developed, the buildings saved and restored.

In the examples described above, particular places associated with one minority of a particular historical period – or else an exotic theme built around the contemporary inhabitants – are marked out, and promoted to appeal to target audiences. Within each bounded enclave, considerable effort is invested to create a safe environment for visitors; a suitable ambience conducive to leisure and tourism consumption. This 'monocultural' approach may help to establish a strong unifying theme that can readily be communicated to prospective place-consumers. An optimistic scenario is that the development of a thriving visitor economy generates badly-needed income and jobs for inner city residents, compensating for the decline of older trades, and raising business confidence. New leisure and tourism-related uses for vacant or under-used heritage buildings may facilitate the restoration of neglected urban landscapes. The creation of a tourism enclave also provides the rationale, and resources to upgrade the public realm, to the benefit of local users and visitors alike (Orbasli & Shaw 2004). Less tangibly, the process may raise 'local pride' in areas where low self-esteem has long been reinforced by negative stereotypes of inner city neighborhoods and their minority residents.

The case studies also serve to illustrate some difficult issues and problems for municipalities that wish to raise the profile of such disadvantaged urban areas through micro-level place-marketing to visitors. The significant cultural legacy of such areas may be far from obvious to the casual observer, especially short-stay international tourists. Likewise, the creative activities of current inhabitants may be hidden from view. From a marketing perspective, a strong and simple theme may be the most effective way of establishing a positive place-brand and playing down less favourable associations. But, as Judd (1999, 2003) has emphasised, with reference to urban tourism in North America, an essentially false reality may be created through re-imaging inner city areas as constructed 'tourist bubbles' where visitors move, as in a theme park: a process described by Zukin (1995:28) as 'pacification by cappuccino'. In both case studies, there is now an emerging 'mosaic' of enclaves: places presented as 'of' a particular time or group of migrants. Thus, the visitor crosses from the Roman Catholic ecclesiastical heritage of Gothic churches to a re-presentation of a pre-war 'Jewish ghetto'; from elegant Georgian terraces of the Huguenot silk-weavers and merchants to vibrant 'Banglatown'.

A less benign view is that the transformation of public realm into such visitor-oriented enclaves alienates those among established local communities who perceive little personal benefit, marginalising if not excluding some groups. In historic cities that have a heritage of immigration, there are essential difficulties of interpreting complex urban place-histories and territorializing ethnic-geographies that are seldom static. Like holiday resorts in less developed countries that become the playgrounds of more affluent foreign tourists, visitors and wealthy residents may valorize historic inner city areas. In this aestheticized urban landscape of multiple realities, the 'host' population may itself become the object of curiosity, a theatre of extras: actors whose role is to animate the scene (Shaw & MacLeod 2000). Ironically, the sign-posting and marking out of cultural and ethnic difference creates an anodyne homogenous landscape of 'pure consumption', disconnected from life of the local population. The unleashing of market forces may result in an unequal distribution of costs and benefits, and rising property values will drive out low-income residents and small firms, including local shops and craft industries that once provided a sense of place as well as utility and employment.

De-coupled from established systems urban governance and land use planning, urban tourism may take on momentum of its own. City governments and other public agencies may offer a clear vision of desirable outcomes, and some may invest in facilitating infrastructure, including the 'soft' infrastructure of place-marketing in its widest sense. Nevertheless today, in CEE as well as Western European countries, much depends on the commercial decisions of private-sector stakeholders, especially landowners and developers. In practice, policy-makers and planners can seldom predict with any certainty where, when or what type of investment will actually occur, far less its cumulative impact on the lives of local residents and communities. In a European Union of twenty-five Member States, the vision of an inclusive, pan-European heritage remains elusive. A culturally and ethnically pluralist perspective is far from straightforward, especially in divided cities where pasts as well as presents are deeply contested. However, without such sensitivity, there is a very real danger that urban tourism, while helping to save and conserve vulnerable built heritage, may exacerbate rather than de-fuse tensions in inner cities with turbulent social histories, where violent conflict has periodically re-surfaced.

## Notes

1. This article is based on the paper presented by the authors to the US/International Council on Ancient Monuments and Sites (US/ICOMOS) 6th International Symposium, *Managing Conflict and Conservation in Historic Cities: Integrating Conservation with Tourism, Development and Politics,* Annapolis, Maryland, April 2003. The authors would like to thank US/ICOMOS for sponsoring their presentation.

## References

Agroni 2001: *Brick Lane Restaurant Zone Consultation Report.* London.
Anderson, K. 1995: *Vancouver's Chinatown: Racial Discourse in Canada, 1875–1980.* Montreal/Kingston: McGill-Queen's University Press.
Appadurai, A. 1997: *Modernity at Large: Cultural Aspects of Globalisation.* Minneapolis: University of Minnesota Press.
Ashworth, G. 1996: Realisable Potential but Hidden Problems: A Heritage Tale from five Central European Cities. In: Purchla, J. (ed.) *The Historical Metropolis: A Hidden Potential.* Cracow: International Culture Centre.
Ashworth, G. 2001: Heritage and Tourism: Managing the Resource Crisis. In: Purchla, J. (ed.) *From the World of Borders to the World of Horizons.* Cracow: International Cultural Centre.
Ashworth, G. & Larkham, P. 1994: *Building a New Heritage: Tourism, Culture and Identity in the New Europe.* London/New York: Routledge.
Barker, P. 1998: London is no Place for this Ghetto Mentality. In: *Evening Standard.* 3rd August: 11.
Begg, I. (ed.) 2002: *Urban Competitiveness: Policies for Dynamic Cities.* Bristol: The Policy Press.
Bell, D. & Jayne, M. (eds) 2004: *City of Quarters: Urban Villages in the Contemporary City.* Aldershot: Ashgate.
Blain, D. 1989: A Very Brief and Very Personal History of the Spitalfields Trust. In: Girouard, M., Cruickshank, D. & Samuel, R. (eds) *The Saving of Spitalfields.* London: The Spitalfields Historic Buildings Trust, pp. 1–31.
Brzeski, W.J. (ed.) 2000: *Prospects of the Development of Kazimierz – What Hope for Revitalisation in the Future?* Cracow: Fundacja Krakowski Instytut Nieruchomosci.
Cameron, D. & Zuziak, Z. (eds) 1994: *Kazimierz Action Plan: A European Union ECOS Funded Project carried out by the Cities of Cracow, Edinburgh and Berlin 1993–94.* Cracow: Viator Co.
Carey, S. 2002: *Brick Lane, Banglatown: A Study of the Catering Sector,* final report, Research Works Limited, London. Prepared for Ethnic Minority Enterprise Project and Cityside Regeneration.
Chan, W. 2004: Finding Chinatown: Ethnocentrism and Urban Planning. In: Bell, D. & Jayne, M. (eds) *City of Quarters: Urban Villages in the Contemporary City.* Aldershot: Ashgate, pp. 173–187.
City Corporation 1996: *Revitalising the City Fringe: Inner City Action with a World City Focus.* London: City Corporation.
Cox, J. 1994: *London's East End: Life and Traditions.* London: Weidenfeld and Nicolson.
Delafons, J. 1997: *Politics and Preservation: A Policy History of the Built Heritage 1882–1996.* London: Spon.
Duda, E. 1991: *Krakowskie Judaica.* Warszawa: PTTK Kraj.
Evans, G. 2001: *Cultural Planning: An Urban Renaissance?* London/New York: Routledge.
Hall, D. 2002: Branding and National Identity: The Case of Central and Eastern Europe. In: Morgan, N., Pritchard, A. & Pride, R. (eds) *Destination Branding: Creating the Unique Destination Proposition.* Oxford: Butterworth-Heinemann.
Hebbert, M. 1998: *London: More by Fortune than Design.* Chichester: Wiley.
Henry, N., McEwan, C. & Pollard, J. S. 2002: Globalisation from below: Birmingham – Postcolonial Workshop of the World? In: *Area,* vol. 34, no. 2, June: 117–127.
Hewison, R. 1987: *The Heritage Industry.* London: Methuen.
Hoffman, L. & Musil, J. 1999: Culture Meets Commerce: Tourism in Postcommunist Prague. In: Judd, D. & Fainstein, S. (eds) *The Tourist City.* New Haven/London: Yale University Press, pp. 179–197.
Hoffman, L. 2003: Revalorizing the Inner City:

Tourism and Regulation in Harlem. In: Hoffman, L., Fainstein, S. & Judd, D. (eds) *Cities and Visitors: Regulating People, Markets, and City Spaces*. Oxford: Blackwell, pp. 145–166.

Inwood, S. 1998: *A History of London*. London: MacMillan.

Jacobs, J. M. 1996: *Edge of Empire: Postcolonialism and the City*. London/New York: Routledge.

Judd, D. 1999: Constructing the Tourist Bubble. In: Judd, D. & Fainstein, S. (eds) *The Tourist City*. New Haven/London: Yale University Press, pp. 35–53.

Judd, D. 2003: Visitors and the Spatial Ecology of a City. In: Hoffman, L., Fainstein, S. & Judd, D. (eds) *Cities and Visitors: Regulating People, Markets, and City Space*. Oxford: Blackwell, pp. 23–38.

Karmowska, J. 2003: Cultural Heritage as an Element of Marketing Strategy in European Historic Cities. In: Kozlowski (ed.) *Proceedings of the 5th. EC Conference, Cultural Heritage Research: A Pan-European Challenge*. Cracow, pp. 139–141.

Kotler, P., Haider, D. & Rein, I. 1993: *Marketing Places: Attracting Investment, Industry, and Tourism to Cities, States and Nations*. New York: The Free Press.

Landry, C. & Bianchini, F. 1995: *The Creative City*. London: Demos.

LB Tower Hamlets 1979: *Fournier Street Outstanding Conservation Area, Planning and Conservation Policy*. London.

LB Tower Hamlets 1996: *Eastside Challenge Fund Submission*. London.

LB Tower Hamlets 1999: *Brick Lane Retail and Restaurant Policy Review*. 1st March. London.

LB Tower Hamlets 2002: *Brick Lane Retail and Restaurant Policy Review*, 9th January. London.

Maitland Gard'ner, J. 2004: Heritage Protection and Social Inclusion: A Case Study from the Bangladeshi Community of East London. In: *International Journal of Heritage Studies*, vol. 10, no. 1, March: 75–92.

Maroevic, I. 1995: Heritage Wreckers. In: *Museums Journal*, vol. 95, no. 3: 27–28.

Mason, R. 2004: Conflict and Complement: An Exploration of the Discourses Informing the Concept of the Socially Inclusive Museum in Contemporary Society. In: *International Journal of Heritage Studies*, vol. 10, no. 1, March: 49–73.

Morgan, N., Pritchard, A. & Pride, D. 2002: *Destination Branding: Creating the Unique Destination Proposition*. Oxford: Butterworth and Heinemann.

Museum of London 1985: *The Quiet Conquest: The Huguenots 1685–1985*. London: Museum of London Publications.

Newman, A. & McLean, F. 1998: Heritage Builds Communities: The Application of Heritage Resources to the Problems of Social Exclusion. In: *International Journal of Heritage Studies*, vol. 4, no. 3: 143–153.

Orbasli, A. & Shaw, S. 2004: Transport and Visitors in Historic Cities. In: *Transport and Tourism: Issues and Agenda for the New Millennium*. Amsterdam: Elsevier.

Paddison, R. 1993: City Marketing, Image Reconstruction and Urban Regeneration. In: *Urban Studies*, vol. 30, no. 2: 339–350.

Paszucha, M. 1995: Managing Places – Cracow. In: *Historic Cities and Sustainable Tourism*, ICOMOS UK conference, pp. 39–53. Bath: ICOMOS.

Porter, M. 1990: *The Competitive Advantage of Nations*. New York: The Free Press.

Porter, M. 1995: The Competitive Advantage of the Inner City. In: *Harvard Business Review*, May/June: 55–71.

Porter, R. 1994: *London: A Social History*. Harmondsworth: Penguin.

Schofield, P. 1996: Cinematic Images of a City: Alternative Heritage Tourism in Manchester. In: *Tourism Management*, vol. 17, no. 5: 333–340.

Shaw, S. 2003: Multicultural Heritage and Urban Regeneration in London's City Fringe. In: Kozlowski (ed.) *Proceedings of the 5th. EC Conference, Cultural Heritage Research: A Pan-European Challenge*. Cracow, pp. 146–150.

Shaw, S. 2004: The Canadian 'World City' and Sustainable Downtown Revitalisation: Messages from Montreal 1962–2002. In: *British Journal of Canadian Studies*, vol. 16, no. 2: 363–377.

Shaw, S., Bagwell, S. & Karmowska, J. 2004: Ethnoscapes as Spectacle: Reimaging Multicultural Districts as New Destinations for Leisure and Tourism Consumption. In: *Urban Studies*, vol. 41, no. 10: 1983–2000, September.

Shaw, S. & MacLeod, N. 2000: Creativity and Conflict: Cultural Tourism in London's City Fringe. In: *Tourism, Culture and Communication*, vol. 2, no. 3: 165–175.

Survey of London 1957: *Spitalfields and Mile End Town, volume XXVII*. London: The Athlone Press for London County Council.

Symonds, J. 2004: Historical Archaeology and the Recent Past. In: *International Journal of Heritage Studies*, vol. 10, no. 1, March: 33–48.

Taylor, I. 2000: European Ethnoscapes and Urban Redevelopment: The Return of Little Italy in 21st Century Manchester. In: *City*, vol. 4, no. 1: 27–42.

Urry, J. 2002: *The Tourist Gaze: Leisure and Travel in Contemporary Societies*, second edition. London: Sage.

Walsh, K. 1992: *The Representation of the Past: Museums and Heritage in the Post-modern World*. London/New York: Routledge.

Ward, S. 1998: *Selling Places: The Marketing and Selling of Towns and Cities 1850–2000*. London: Spon.

Williams, G. 2003: *The Enterprising City Centre: Manchester's Development Challenge*. London: Spon.

Wright, P. 1985: *On Living in an Old Country: The National Past in Contemporary Britain*. London: Verso.

Zukin, S. 1995: *The Cultures of Cities*. Cambridge, Massachusetts/Oxford: Blackwell.

Zukin, S. 1999: Urban Lifestyles: Diversity and Standardisation in Spaces of Consumption. In: *Urban Studies,* vol. 35, no. 5–6: 825–839.

*References to Personal Communications*

Bramidge, A., Director Cityside Regeneration 2002: personal interview with S. Shaw, Spitalfields, London, 7th October.

Gorczyca, W. Department for Strategy and Development, Cracow Municipality 2004: personal interview with J. Karmowska, Cracow 28th October.

Ritchie, A. 2002: Planning and Community Liaison Officer, LB Tower Hamlets, personal interview with S. Shaw, Bow Road, London, 27th September.

Walczak, M. Vice-president Friends of Kazimierz Society 2002: personal interview with J. Karmowska, Cracow 27th November.

# Class and Ethnicity in a Globalising City
Bangladeshis and Contested Urban Space in London's 'East End'

*John Eade*

The recent focus on the global flows of capital, information, ideas and people and their implications for nation-state institutions (see, for example, Robertson 1992; Hall 1992; Lash & Urry 1994; Castells 1996, 1997) has highlighted the role played by different kinds of travellers, such as tourists, poor migrant workers and corporate elites. 'Globalisation' appears to challenge policies based around the nation-state since its boundaries cannot control these global flows. Indeed, national governments in W. Europe have adapted their welfare state provisions in response to what they perceive as 'globalisation' (Sykes, Palier & Prior 2001). A number of cities in the European region are now heavily involved in competing with each other to attract footloose global capital through their financial and business services and their success provides further evidence of the nation-state's limitations.

London is a prime example of these developments. Indeed, Saskia Sassen in her book, *The Global City* (1991), reinforced by her subsequent writings and her research collaboration with the Globalization and World Cities Network based at Loughborough University, has sought to establish the credentials of London, together with New York and Tokyo, as a dominant site for footloose global capital in a hierarchy of cities around the world. She detected the emergence of a new urban spatial order during the 1970s and 1980s through the massive expansion of financial and business corporations, high technology industries, information and media services. This new order was defined by a socio-economic polarisation between the extremely wealthy members of the business and financial elites, on the one hand, and the lowly paid providers of services to these elites on the other. Many of these lowly paid workers in London and New York were recent immigrants who were creating minority ethnic enclaves sometimes in close proximity to wealthy neighbourhoods and 'gated communities'.

The global city thesis has several limitations. Firstly, as Marcuse and van Kempen (2000) point out, the global city label suggests that a few places have reached the specific state of being global, thereby directing attention away from the more important phenomenon of globalisation as a process and its varying impact on all cities around the world. London, therefore, is only a particular example of how cities, generally, are shaped by changing patterns of global capital. Secondly, these globalising cities are not the sites for a new spatial order – rather they are places where earlier trends are reinforced in diverse ways around the world. In other words, the history of global capitalism is crucial to our understanding of contemporary globalisation, globalising cities and the interplay between global and local processes. Thirdly, several commentators have convincingly claimed that the emergence of global cities is not confined to a certain elite (see Smith 2002). In the UK, for example, political and economic elites in former industrial cities beyond London have pursued 'development' schemes, which have many of the characteristics associated with global cities (see Peck & Ward 2002). Fourthly, as Samers argues in a fine review of the global city debate, Sassen's emphasis on economic polarisation between global elites and those at the opposite end of the class structure ignores the crucial issue of social mobility as members of minority ethnic groups move up the ladder (2002:394).

This debate shows us that economic class still informs social inequalities as global/local processes transform urban life. At the same time, the Weberian tradition reminds us that there is no straightforward relationship between economic class and social status. Hierarchies of power and prestige are deeply influenced by economic markets but the latter do not mechanistically determine these hierarchies. If we look at the understandings people give their social situations, we see a complex interweaving of narratives where class distinctions and class solidarities jostle with other discriminations and loyalties. People's lives in London are shaped, therefore, not by a single agent – global capital – but by the interweaving of class and ethnic processes operating transnationally from above and below producing a complex world of multiple identities, imagined communities and transnational social movements (Smith 2001:188f). The relationship between economic class and social status is being reconfigured as people's lives are changed by new global/local dynamics. To understand such a situation we should use an analysis, which combines a structural, political economy perspective with postmodern sensitivities towards contingency, hybridity and emergent social and cultural identities.

## London's 'East End': Class, Ethnicity and Local/Global Processes

During the late 19th and early 20th centuries the rapid expansion of London's 'East End' saw the emergence of a self-conscious working class, as lower middle class clerks, supervisors and small businessmen moved further out into the expanding suburbs. A sharp social and economic boundary also separated this working class East End from the City of London's merchants and the aristocratic and upper middle class quarters in the West End. Although East London's working class neighbourhoods may have appeared at first sight to be homogeneous, they were riven by ethnic and racial differences as people arrived from the surrounding countryside, from other parts of Britain, from Ireland and from Eastern Europe.

Until the 1970s the local working class relied heavily on the Victorian industrial belt stretching round the City of London to the north and south, as well as the docks and their associated services. This mixture of manufacturing and dock enterprise linked the East End to the national economy and to a global economy shaped by colonialism. A distinctively working class culture was reflected in the rhythms of work and leisure. These occupational and cultural forces informed and were, in turn, shaped by the political changes of the early 20th century where the municipal socialism of the Labour Party was challenged by Communist, Ratepayer, Conservative and Far Right organisations (see Fishman 1988; Glynn 2000). After the Second World War the Labour Party established an almost undisputed position in response to local social restructuring, the physical rebuilding of neighbourhoods and global political developments such as the emerging 'Cold War'.

Working class communities had been severely disrupted by the 1940 'blitz' and subsequent rehousing. The development of 'new towns' beyond London after 1945 further weakened the working class in Tower Hamlets since they heavily recruited local skilled workers. However, the most decisive blow was delivered by the closing of the docks and their associated services during the 1970s and early 1980s. The establishment of the London Docklands Development Corporation in 1981 by the new Conservative national government initiated the restructuring of the dock neighbourhoods for high technology enterprises and business and financial services relocating from the City of London. A new workforce was drawn to 'Docklands' – middle class commuters and settlers occupying new private housing – while the old white working class continued to decline as its younger members continued to move out to the suburbs and new towns.

The restructuring of the global economy combined with national politics to produce a new urban landscape where those profiting from global flows of capital, technology and information now lived close to the remnants of the former industrial world. The old working class communities and the new middle class settlers are not homogeneous, of course. Differences of occupation and skill overlapped with ethnic and racial solidarities. Before 1939 dock labour was recruited predominantly from English and Irish families while Jewish settlers from Russia and Poland dominated the garment industry. Those employed in high technology enterprises and the finance and business services of 'Docklands' are largely white English newcomers. At the topmost levels of the finance and business services are the more transitory members of the global elites who are drawn from diverse nations, especially those in North America, the European Union and the Pacific Rim.

Other newcomers were Bangladeshi settlers who were employed mostly in manual jobs across the industrial and service sectors. A few, however, had entered white collar jobs in education, local government, welfare and social services and the professions. While their life chances were conditioned by their structural class position through jobs in education, local government, welfare and social services and the professions, their social identities were also shaped by ethnic differences based on continuing links with their country of origin and Islam. This interplay between class and ethnic identities was reflected in local political struggles where secularist and Islamist factions supported competing uses of local urban space (see Eade & Garbin 2001; Eade, Fremeaux & Garbin 2002).

## Secularists, Islamists and Contested Local Space

The juxtaposition of new forms of socio-economic division with remnants of the old industrial order is clearly visible in Tower Hamlets. The gleaming high-rise buildings of Canary Wharf at the heart of Docklands overlook the mean streets and dilapidated council estates to the north occupied by Bangladeshis and white working class survivors. The contrast between rich and poor in a borough so visibly shaped by global flows of capital, goods, people and information is a fertile ground for those who want to criticise the excesses of global capitalism. During the 1980s criticism in the localities dominated by Bangladeshis emphasised class divisions and class conflict but, more recently, these secular, socialist interpretations have been challenged by Islamists based at the East London Mosque, in particular. As a very large third generation of 'Cockney Bengalis' emerges with little prospect of gaining access to the new jobs, amenities and housing available in 'Docklands' or even jobs in the overcrowded ethnic enclave, the more attractive appear to be the Islamist critiques of western economic and political systems. Bangladeshi Labour councillors and other secularists have been forced onto the defensive since their policies appear to have made scant impact on the local ills of unemployment, drugs and petty crime. Islamist calls for the moral regeneration of Bangladeshi youth can also be linked both to political struggles between secular nationalists and Islamists within Muslim-majority Bangladesh and to issues confronting other Muslims around the world, especially those bound up with British involvement in Iraq (see Abbas 2005).

*Secular Nationalists and the Bengali New Year Celebration*
These different understandings were vividly illustrated in recent debates concerning the celebration of Bengali New Year (*Baishakhi mela*). The *mela* had been introduced in 1998 as a multicultural event financed by Cityside, a government-funded quango which promoted community arts in Tower Hamlets' western wards bordering the City of London. The *mela* was held in the Spitalfields – the heartland of the Bangladeshi settlement – and provided entertainment, which was intended to express the rich diversity of Bengali culture. Since music and dancing was frowned on by 'strict' Muslims, the organisers were careful not to offend the London Great Mosque on Brick Lane by noisy celebrations during prayer times.

The ideological significance of the New Year festival with regard to inequality and social justice was clearly presented in a guide for schools written by a Bangladeshi community group. The festival was associated with the Bangladesh countryside which, in turn, represented society as a whole:

"[t]he celebration of the Bangla New Year reveals the Soul of Bangladesh and pronounces the truth about the people and the country. [It] is free from class and caste...and is in the care of the entire society" (Khan 1990:115 quoted in Eade, Fremeaux & Garbin 2002:168).

This joyful mingling of a nation, united beyond the boundaries of social difference, also stretched implicitly across national borders to embrace a transnational Bangladeshi community around the globe. The festival reminded British Bangladeshis of the cultural heritage, which they shared with their compatriots elsewhere, but it also encouraged them to behave in an egalitarian manner free from the inequalities of caste and class – not only with other Bangladeshis but with all human beings.

We see here a utopian vision of a national community which implicitly reaches beyond Bangladesh to a transnational diaspora. This vision helped to establish a common platform between Bangladeshi secular nationalists and white secularists who dominate British state institutions at central and local levels. The New Year celebrations were also linked to other local multicultural events, which were shaped by an equally secular vision of a liberal multicultural locality. The 2001 advert for the event, distributed through the internet by a virtual community of British Bangladeshi professionals, for example, makes clear that the Brick Lane Festival placed Bangladeshis within a wider history of immigration and a contemporary mixture of cultural influences (see overleaf).

These two events were publicly funded on the grounds that they contributed to the multicultural character of the locality and to Tower Hamlets generally. This vision of a secular, liberal society, shaped by cultural mixture, was not shared by Islamist groups. These groups were encouraged, ironically, by secularist members of the central and local state, who wished to harness the resources of 'faith communities' in the delivery of policy issues. As Greg Smith points out in his provocatively titled article on similar developments in the neighbouring borough of Newham – "East London is no longer secular: religion as a source of social capital in the regeneration of East London" (2001) – local religious diversity provides a resource on which, since 1992, central government institutions have sought to draw. More recently, the Social Exclusion Unit attached to the Cabinet Office and the Home Office's Active Community Unit have discussed self-help in the following terms:

"Funders should recognise that faith groups may well be the most suitable voluntary and community organisations to deliver general community objectives and should be prepared to provide sustained financial support for this, learn with and from one another" (quoted in Smith 2001:147).

The ethnic and cultural diversity of 'faith communities' was acknowledged, as well as evidence that '[s]ome parts of communities are as disaffected from faith communities as they are from mainstream society'. However, the consultation paper argued that these factors did not 'minimise the enormous potential contribution which faith organisations can make to community self-help' (2001:147).

Local state officials were not so eager to recognise these 'faith communities' but, in Tower Hamlets, the purpose-built East London Mosque (ELM) had long been active in building alliances with local officials despite opposition from some secular Bangladeshis activists at least. Benefitting from the Brick Lane Mosque's refusal to engage directly with public organisations, the ELM's leaders presented themselves as members of the area's 'central mosque', encouraging outsiders to visit the mosque, providing help with local community schemes and generating finance to build an adjoining community centre.

Their position was further strengthened

after the attack on the World Trade Center on September 11, 2001 by media reports, which focussed on the mosque together with the more controversial centres in Finsbury Park and Shepherd's Bush (Garbin 2001:191). In a report on the ELM's role in cutting truancy within Tower Hamlets, *The Guardian* (August 2, 2002) applauded its determination to avoid "fomenting fundamentalism" and to "live in harmony with the wider non-Muslim community". According to the ELM's 'Director', the mosque "isn't just about praying...We want to see the well-being of our community, see children get their basic education and local schools perform better". The mosque's impact on local truancy was 'one of a range of progressive schemes at the mosque, including discouraging the practice of forced marriage and working with youngsters on issues of drugs and gangs'. The scheme was supported by public funds given to deprived local authorities and the local 'regeneration and external funding manager' welcomed the initiative on the grounds that 'conventional approaches..., such as home-school liaison workers and informing parents about the importance of attendance had not worked'. On the strength of this success the ELM leaders were going to explain 'how the scheme works to the Council of Mosques' in the hope that it might be adopted 'by other LEAs with substantial Muslim communities and truancy problems' (ibid.).

Members of the ELM management committee and the associated Young Muslim Organisation vigorously opposed the Bengali New Year festival and similar 'multicultural' events. Against the high-minded vision of an egalitarian national/transnational community the ELM's *imam* developed the vision of a pure Islamic local/global community. He argued that the festival was an unIslamic event which would only lead young Bangladeshis astray. A properly Islamic celebration was required which would help to counter the locality's socio-economic problems:

"Drugs, alcohol and the gang-fighting and all the other wrong things... unemployment and [the] unhealthy housing situation and the cultural gap between the older and the younger generation. Families are suffering. Marriages are breaking" (Interview with *Imam* of the East London Mosque, 2000, quoted in Eade, Fremeaux & Garbin 2002:168).

The imam proceeded to argue that the festival was promoted in both Bangladesh and Britain by a secular minority, whose enjoyment of fun diverted them from Islam:

"In Bangladesh they don't exercise... like this...[only a minority]...There is a secular trend and there are people who are purely having their own understanding about community, about culture...This was the culture of the Hindus...Nowadays some people are getting very much influenced by some other faith – that's why those people are away from Islam. They look for something fun – whatever it is, which culture, which religion – no matter" (Interview with *Imam* of the East London Mosque, 2000, quoted in Eade, Fremeaux & Garbin 2002:168).

This portrait of the new 'East End' clearly resonates with earlier constructions of London's dark 'Other' but the communities visualised are different. In Islamist discourse local Muslims are part of a global community (*umma*), which can be redeemed through the 'correct' observance of Islamic practices.

This interpretation of a global Muslim community defied Western ideological assertions about the primacy of secular culture in 'modern' nation-states. Indeed, in the *imam's* opinion, attempts by 'modernising' elites in Bangladesh to introduce secular nationalism were bound to fail because of the ways in which religion permeated everyday beliefs and practices. The efforts of the secular minority only resulted in the spread of Hinduism rather than secular nationalism. In other words, Bangladeshis could not escape the continuing struggle between Hindu and Muslim communities, which had determined politics in the Indian sub-continent through the partition of British India in 1946, the conflicts between India and Pakistan, and the tensions between India and Bangladesh after the latter's creation in 1971. However, what this deterministic vision failed to acknowledge, of course, was the role of both non-religious forces and contingency in this politics of identity. These conflicts were not inevitable and unchanging and what caused them could not be reduced to religious forces.

In spite of the tendency to present sharply contrasting visions of Islamic and secular communities, secularists and Islamists do not constitute homogeneous constituencies nor are they relentlessly opposed to one another. Not surprisingly, perhaps, individuals work pragmatically across ideological boundaries. ELM leaders forge alliances with white secularist officials in areas of common interests, while some Bangladeshi secularists are happy to work with particular Islamist leaders against their mutual opponents. A few secularists have rejected Islam as both a mode of practice and a set of beliefs but many more observe in various ways Muslim public practices, refusing to accept that Islam in Britain should be confined to the private realm of belief and domestic practice. Likewise, then term 'Islamism' covers a wide range of beliefs and practices which, in the political realm, are expressed in the differences between moderate and more radical groups such as *Al Mjujaharun* over how to pressurise the British government over its continued involvement in Iraq.

These pragmatic alliances are shaped by the competition for public funds. Since secularist Bangladeshis enjoy a far stronger position within local state institutions than those associated with the local mosques. They have been appointed to white collar jobs in the public sector, such as the National Health Service, education and the borough council. Secularists control the vast majority of community groups, clubs and law centres providing advice to Bangladeshis residents about how to gain access to welfare resources or leisure facilities to the third generation. They also dominate the various housing cooperatives, which became increasingly important during the 1990s as the borough council's housing role declined. Islamists are limited in their range of possible allies if they want to insist on the binary opposition between secularism and Islam. In practice, then, moderate Islamists have also sought to build alliances with non-Muslims involved in the distribution of public funds rather than remain within a narrowly defined Muslim enclave.

Consensus between these potential competitors for scarce material resources can be generated, however, through the language of community which emphasises the struggle by the 'community' against local economic and social problems. When Bangladeshi activists create such a consensus, they are applauded by white officials. When they frequently disagree among themselves about who should receive the funding (in ways which do not correspond to secularist/Islamist distinctions), the paternalism and sometimes implicit racialism of white official attitudes is exposed in their criticism of Bangladeshi factionalism (see Fremeaux 2002).

## Ethnicity, Class and the Local Impact of the Changing Global Economy

*Tower Hamlets*

These debates concerning community have a common focus – ethnicity. Secularists emphasise the ethnic boundaries between themselves and others shaped by language and the cultural heritage of their country of origin. Islamists are preoccupied with another ethnic boundary defined by religion. This focus on ethnicity is encouraged by outside funders, who want to celebrate 'multiculturalism' based on popular culture where ethnic communities could also express their 'unity in diversity'. In multicultural terms, Spitalfields is more than a British Bangladeshi heartland – it is a 'rich mix of communities both past and present' (see 2001 advert above). This emphasis on community as ethnicity is further strengthened by government support for 'faith communities'.

The effect of this interpretation of community is to direct attention away from issues of political economy and the local social divisions created by the changing global economy. Structurally the lives of Tower Hamlets' residents have been dramatically altered by the demise of local industries, the docks and their associated services but community representatives, government officials and 'development agencies' have usually avoided interpreting these dramatic changes in terms of class. Some Labour councillors and radical activists still emphasise the role played by class in the local social divisions created by global forces (see Jacobs 1996), but they appear to be increasingly out of touch with central government initiatives and the policies pursued by their own local government officials.

The shift in emphasis from class to ethnic interpretations of local society during the late 1980s and the 1990s is partly a reflection of political changes, of course. Conservative government claims that Britain was becoming a meritocratic, classless society in the 1980s have made some impact on popular understandings, while New Labour's insistence on community, consensus and 'third way' solutions to persistent national problems has also contributed. There are also many local factors at work. The decline of the old working class neighbourhoods has clearly been one major factor. Some of these neighbourhoods still survive outside the localities occupied by Bangladeshis and other minority ethnic settlers, as well as in Docklands. However, their post-Second World War political hegemony has been broken and they have to compete with others for such scarce resources as jobs, housing, health and welfare services on the basis of ethnicity. The Labour Party's recruitment of Bangladeshi activists and 'anti-racist' policies during the 1980s confirmed the ethnic terrain on which such competition had to be waged and led to a significant white working class backlash to the electoral benefit of the Liberal Democrats.

Competition on the basis of ethnicity has also been encouraged by the rapid expansion of Bangladeshi settlement in Tower Hamlets. Bangladeshi activists found it easier to mobilise support through appeals to cultural and religious traditions rather than class, especially after the demise of the radicalised Greater London Council and Inner London Education Authority in the mid-1980s. The manifold differences of income, education, language, status and village background could be minimised through an emphasis on what people shared as Bangladeshis. The availability of funds from Muslim-majority countries in the Middle East and South Asia also encouraged mobilisation on the basis of Islam; here people could unite not only on the basis of their ethnic ties as Bangladeshis but also across ethnic and economic divisions as Muslims.

People's awareness of their ethnic community ties is also encouraged by the heavy dependence on the ethnic enclave socially and economically. Tower Hamlets' western wards provided housing, jobs, education, information, social support and other resources for most Bangladeshis in the borough and even further afield. A few people from the second generation have broken out of this enclave into jobs and localities dominated by white people, but the paucity of their numbers indicate how difficult this is to achieve. The very large third generation is going to come on to the job market in the next ten years but many will still compete for jobs in an already overcrowded ethnic enclave economy.

*Bangladesh*

These factors go a long way to explaining why secularists and Islamists have paid scant attention to the dramatic gulf between Docklands and their own neighbourhoods. Docklands is not a place where they can successfully compete for scarce resources, whereas they can call on a wide range of economic, social, cultural and political links elsewhere. Another factor has also to be considered – the continuing links with Bangladesh. These links are forged by the changes in this country's political economy and cultural life as people engage locally with global flows of capital, people, goods and information.

Migration from Bangladesh to Britain was, not surprisingly, bound up with changes in global capitalism as colonial regimes collapsed after the Second World War. The first Bangladeshis to arrive in London had worked in British-owned ships as *lascars* during the colonial period. Although most settlers arrived after the break-up of the Indian Empire, they exploited links already forged with Britain during the colonial period. However, Bangladeshi migrants have also found work in other countries during the last thirty years, especially the oil-rich Muslim countries of the Middle East, while others have settled in European Union countries as well as in North America.

In Britain the vast majority of Bangladeshis come from one particular district – Sylhet – and from clusters of villages within that district. The local economic class structure shaped the pattern of chain migration to Britain as individuals raised the money needed for the journey from their families' position within the system of rural landholding. As Katy Gardner points out in her pioneering study of this process, the distinction between different forms of capital is required in order to understand a highly dynamic situation. Overseas migration:

"provides both economic and symbolic capital; being a migrant can command as much as social and economic power as owning land. It is not simply that migration generates valuable remittances; it also brings social prestige, knowledge, the 'cultural capital' of having been abroad, and the ability to be a patron" (Gardner 1995:130).

Although economic and symbolic capital are closely linked, the economic class structure does not determine the hierarchies of status and power in any mechanistic way. In the village where she undertook her research:

"status and power operate on many different levels and take many different forms. Often they are associated with economic class and economic capital but not always. Since status is never more than the way in which people perceive each other, it is never fixed, but continually changing" (1995:134).

The migrants' Muslim background played a key role in this dynamic situation since poor people could acquire high status through the public expression of their religious commitment. At the same time those prospering through migration could signify their distinction from their poorer co-religionists by subscribing to the beliefs and practices of a 'pure' Islam. They engaged with the revivalist teachings of Islamists who sought to eliminate the mystical, syncretic traditions associated with local saint cults ('pirism') and supported by poorer families in Sylhet (Gardner 1995:chap. 8). The transnational networks, emergent identities and multiple homes created through migration to Britain and elsewhere is clearly bound up with global debates concerning the essential features of Islam – a local/global process which operates within both Sylhet and Tower Hamlets and links the two locales together.

## Ethnicity, Class and Transnational Links: Changing Patterns of Marriage in Tower Hamlets

Some insight into this dynamic situation of transnational links and multiple hierarchies can be gleaned from a recent study on marriage choices (Samad & Eade 2002). The study was commissioned by the Foreign and Commonwealth Office to examine the issue of forced marriage through a comparison between Pakistanis in Bradford and Bangladeshis in Tower Hamlets. Meetings were held with twenty focus groups in each area. The groups were recruited on the basis of age, gender and class and the discussions were led by two Bangladeshi researchers (one male, one female) in English, Sylheti and standard Bengali.

While the aim of the research was to elicit people's views concerning forced marriage, the discussions considered the issue of marriage in general and a lot of time was given to the changing character of arranged marriage – the most common procedure within both communities. Implicit in any examination of how a particular group reproduced itself was the respective roles played by economic class, social status and political power. At the same time the diverse strategies pursued by British Asians were also influenced by outsiders, especially state institutions. The forced marriage issue highlighted the British government's involvement through immigration controls and the suggestion by the former Home Secretary, David Blunkett, that British Asians should abandon recruiting partners from their countries of origin.

A prime theme of the discussions was the future of arranged marriage in the British context. Demographic factors loomed large here since the Bangladeshi population was very young and in the next ten years a vast wave of third generation British Bangladeshis was going to hit the marriage market. Inevitably people debated the advantages and disadvantages of continuing to recruit partners from their country of origin. Frequent allusions to the 'generation gap' between older and younger British Asians were simplistic but generational differences did seem to influence people's views about transnational alliances. Bangladeshi male and female elders supported such alliances on the grounds that they strengthened family ties and reinvigorated cultural norms among their children. At the same time some elders noted the linguistic tensions inherent within such alliances. These tensions could become serious if individuals are unwilling to cope. As one elder explained, if a young woman brought up in Tower Hamlets married someone raised in Bangladesh:

"She'll speak English and he Bengali, so they'll have problems with language. Some will cope all right thinking they've no choice but others will not think like that" (Samad & Eade 2002:79).

Young Bangladeshis were even more adamant that satisfaction in a relationship depended on communication:

"The girl needs someone on her…wavelength. Someone she can interact with. She cannot spend the rest of her life with this person who can't even speak English" (2002:80).

Knowledge of English was closely related to both educational achievement and individual choice. As one young Bangladeshi student explained when comparing his parents' generation with what could happen to him:

"[People considered] where the partner's family was from, how wealthy they were, what was their caste background. My own wedding – the categories will be far more lengthy…It won't necessarily be just looking at status. I personally have my own preferences and I believe…that I can have these" (2002:82).

These comments about language, education and choice seem to indicate that the system of arranged marriages within patrilineal groups (*gusthi*) is being modified by settlement within London. However, one elder warned against any simplistic contrast between a changing Britain and a traditional Bangladesh:

"In Bangladesh changes are taking place, Previously…a hundred per cent was arranged marriage…Now it is increasing – ways other than arranged marriages; marrying according to individual wishes" (unpublished transcript, 2001).

So the key issue seems to be the ways in which settlement in Britain has affected the ability of families to maintain the caste-like divisions (*zat* or *jaat*) between patrilineages evident in rural Sylhet. The interviews did not explore this issue deeply but one elderly male contributor acknowledged the existence of a status hierarchy based on *jaat*:

"*Jaat* means someone is Choudhury, someone is Khan, someone is Talukder, someone is a Pir, someone is a Ghulam" (unpublished transcript, 2001).

Marriage between higher and lower *jaat* would cause problems. For example:

"[If] someone who sell scent [arranges] marriage to a person who sell fish [this] would not be right, because there will be problem in the future. There will be no balance in life because of this in relation to marriage. There has to be similarities on both sides" (unpublished transcript, 2001).

However, another elderly participant noted the familiar process of upward mobility where success in the economic class structure frees people from their low status:

"Today maybe…I have money. I have started a business – prior to that I might have been working in an office. I have changed this profession. Two days later I have not recognition as a fisherman. Then I can become a relative of an owner of [a] five star hotel – when my living standard goes up, when I have gained qualifications. When I become highly qualified then I would want my children's in-laws to be more qualified" (unpublished transcript, 2001).

Class is implicit in this contribution but, as in other discussions of social difference, class as a category was rarely used. Interestingly, when a young male student referred to class he associated class with *zat*:

"Some people are rich and some are poor. If a girl's going into a low class family than their children cannot get married to high class people. The Bengali word for class is *zat*" (unpublished transcript, 2000).

On the other hand, another male student did detect a difference between achieved and ascribed status, which could be linked to analytical distinctions between class and *zat*:

"Status? It's kind of ambiguous but meaning someone with money, someone with qualifications. Not status as in status given by, maybe, a handful of people – Bangladeshi elders" (unpublished transcript, 2000).

When the issue of Islam in arranged marriage was raised generational difference did appear to play a significant part. Older contributors were more inclined to see an interweaving of both cultural and religious factors. The elder, who earlier explained the differences between those selling scent and fish, justified the gulf in terms of Islam. Other considerations were also described as Islamic:

"Before marriage Islam says that you look at three things. First, religion. A person may be bad but the religion controls them. Second one is beauty and the third is wealth" (unpublished transcript, 2001).

Another elder attached great importance to the ethical behaviour of the young man:

"Only Muslim by name is not sufficient. One has to look at their ethical side. What is he like about his behaviour?"

Furthermore, the ideal partner should be close culturally and physically:

"When I arranged my sister's marriage, my daughter's marriage I visit them every week. But if I had arranged their marriage to [another] Muslim – a Saudi Muslim – I may visit because of my daughter but my wife or any other relative will feel very distant because they cannot talk to them. Language problem, cultural gap. There are many gaps. This marriage will not last for long."

Younger focus group participants were more inclined to distinguish between religion and culture and to entertain the idea that they could marry anyone as long as he or she was a 'good Muslim'. During a meeting with female students at a local F.E. college, for example, one of the contributors argued that devout parents would not object to their daughters choosing a non-Bangladeshi Muslim:

"If the family is properly religious – yeh? – they wouldn't care whether he was white or black as long as he was Muslim...But for some people it does matter – the cultural people...They get religion and culture mixed up – that's what leads to forced marriages and unwanted marriages" (unpublished transcript, 2000).

Other young participants were not so sure that religion and culture could be so easily distinguished in practice. As one of a mixed group of Bangladeshis aged between 16 and 21 explained:

"A girl can only marry another Muslim but a boy can marry someone from another religion. It depends on the family. The preference will be Bangladeshi, then another Muslim but this may cause problems. There could be confusion between culture and religion" (unpublished transcript, 2000).

The local debate about social dislocation found its way into these discussions. One of the Graduate Forum male contributors explained how forced marriage could be an index of such dislocation and parental attempts to control their daughters:

"If the girl go to different culture or something – say someone from Western culture or from [a] different background – [this would be] really frustrating to the community. For instance, if she got pregnant or something. It is very stigmatising…She should have known. She should have respected her parents' wishes as well. She shouldn't have a kid…She shouldn't be having drinks…drugs as well" (unpublished transcript, 2000).

## Conclusion

This paper has focussed on an area of London, which has been dramatically transformed through the redevelopment of the old dockland neighbourhoods and the settlement of Bangladeshi workers. This transformation appears to confirm a main theme in Saskia Sassen's global city hypothesis – the socio economic polarisation between global elites and those in the lower levels of the service sector. However, what is so striking about Tower Hamlets is the extent to which Bangladeshi settlers ignore the intrusion of these globalising forces, even though these forces are changing the landscape in which they live.

The debates about the use of public space and the issue of marriage suggest some reasons why the transformation has attracted scant interest among these global migrants. Bangladeshis understandably focus on what they can control and alter. The celebration of the Bengali New Year is a public event which they can shape in different ways and which is supported by outside funders. Marriage is a quintessential collective enterprise, which lies at the heart of debates about generation, gender and prestige. Both are bound up with how Bangladeshis can maintain and strengthen their presence in particular neighbourhoods where they can also find work and can relax. In other words, we see clearly the operation of an ethnic enclave sustained by the overlapping of cultural, social, political and economic processes.

The political-economy approach adopted by Sassen needs to be balanced, therefore, by careful attention to ethnicity. This is particularly important when addressing the issue of social mobility. Although our evidence does not provide any insight to the degree of social mobility among Bangladeshi settlers, it is clear that any movement across the economic class system will be shaped by notions of social prestige carried over from their country of origin. Most Bangladeshis can be described as 'working class' by virtue of their position within a local economy drastically affected by the global flows of capital, people and information but their notions of prestige are still shaped by the caste-like divisions of rural Sylhet.

Yet, as the differences between secular nationalists and Islamists over the uses of local space reveal, ethnicity takes various forms as people interpret the significance of Bengali language, Bangladeshi cultural traditions or religion in diverse ways. Furthermore, these diverse interpretations engage with debates beyond the ethnic boundary. As the British government responded to economic globalisation by privatising welfare provision, so community representatives were encouraged to take on roles formerly considered to be the preserve of the 'welfare state'. As majority images of Bangladeshis and other 'British Muslims' came to emphasise their Islamic affiliations rather than their ethnic background, especially since the late 1980s, so state officials could focus on the role played by 'faith communities' in the moral regeneration of impoverished urban locales. This insider/outsider engagement not only linked local debates and practices concerning 'multicultural celebrations' and 'forced' and 'arranged' marriages to the British nation-state but also to Bangladesh and to the wider Muslim world.

During the last twenty years political and academic fashions have moved away from debates concerning class towards a focus on identities based around race, ethnicity, gender, sexuality and age. This process has gone hand in hand with an often impassioned debate about what multiculturalism means in contemporary, post-imperial Britain. This debate is particularly relevant to London where the global flows of migration have resulted in producing the highest proportion of ethnic minority residents in Britain – 28.8% compared with 9% nationally according to the 2001 Census (see htpp://www.lsx.org.uk/news/page329.aspx, accessed 21/12/04). However, if we look beyond current preoccupations with identity politics to particular locales, we can see how collective identities are shaped by an interweaving of class and non-class allegiances where we need to draw on both political economy and culturalist approaches. In the context of London's locales, therefore, we can move not only beyond any opposition between these two approaches but also beyond Sassen's influential model of the 'global city'. As this paper has tried to demonstrate, we can do this by exploring the complex ways in which those at the lower end of London's class structure – in this case, Bangladeshis in Tower Hamlets – understand their everyday world and the manifold differences between themselves and between themselves and the wider world.

---

"The Brick Lane Festival captures the flavour and excitement of an area that has welcomed new Londoners for over 200 years. Taking place from 12 noon to 10pm, an amazing display of free music, dance and performance will celebrate
Spitalfields [sic] rich mix of communities both past and present.

On Brick Lane itself: pavement café's [sic], a craft market, Asian drumming bands, Caribbean DJ's, the London School of Samba and lots of mad Brazilians, jostle with stilt walkers, rickshaw rides, clowns and jugglers. In neighbouring Allen Gardens the main stage showcases top world music acts, alongside a children's entertainment area with fun fair rides, massive free inflatables, stilt-walking and dance workshops."

---

Highlights include:
Bangladesh's most popular band 'ARK' flying in to the UK to headline the main stage and performing a completely new globalised mix of 'Bangla Rock' influenced from the likes of Eric Clapton and Jon Bon Jovi. Completing the programme on the main stage is a mixture of Asian fusion, Funky jazz, East End rag time and Bengali dance all pulled together by 'Skorpio' an Asian compere, rap artist and poet '.

Carnival at Brick Lane's trendy Vibe Bar with live music percussion and DJ's concentrating on the sounds of Latin America, Trinidad, New Orleans and the West Indies.

Ballymore Bangla night @ Old Spitalfields Market from 7pm-10pm. The market owners fund a special Brick Lane Festival extension with a classical line up of music and dance from some of the UK's top Bengali performers.

More than just a good curry – this year's BLF launches the international Banglatown curry festival with speciality chefs from India, Pakistan, Nepal and Bangladesh preparing authentic regional dishes in the curry house kitchens for the whole month of September.

+ + + + History tours, international dance on stage and street, park games, fortune telling and much more.

Commenting on the day's activities Nicki Burgess, Event Organiser from the 'Ethnic Minority Enterprise Project' says, "This year the interest in the festival has gathered huge momentum and is 'taking off' on its own, it is fantastic seeing the whole community caught up in the process. Now we have Ballymore and Old Spitalfields Market involved, it is a real opportunity to pull the whole community together"

> For more information about the festival please call Nicki Burgess 020 76550906 Email nicki@emep.co.uk
>
> The Festival is organised by the Ethnic Minority Enterprise Project. The Festival is funded through a mixture of public and private finance. Main contributors are Ballymore the owners of Old Spitalfields Market and Cityside Regeneration Ltd; This is the sixth Brick Lane Festival and it grows in size every year."

# References

Abbas, T. (ed.) 2005: *British South Asian Muslims: A post-September 11 study*. London: Zed Press.

Alexander, C. 1996: *The Art of Being Black*. Oxford: Clarendon Press.

Alexander, C. 2000: *The Asian Gang*. Oxford: Berg.

Back, L. 1996: *New Ethnicities and Urban Culture*. London: UCL Press.

Baumann, G. 1996: *Contesting Culture*. Cambridge: University Press.

Butler, T. & Rustin, M. 1996: *Rising in the East?* London: Lawrence and Wishart.

Castells, M. 1996: *The Rise of the Network Society* (Vol. 1 of *The Information Age: Economy, Society and Culture*). Oxford: Blackwell.

Castells, M. 1997: *The Power of Identity* (Vol. 2 of *The Information Age: Economy, Society and Culture*). Oxford: Blackwell.

Church, A. & Frost, M. 1998: Trickle Down or Trickle Out: Job Creation and Work-travel Impacts of Docklands Regeneration. In: *Rising East* 2 (2): 73–103.

Eade, J. (ed.) 1997: *Living the Global City*. London/New York: Routledge.

Eade, J. 2000: *Placing London*. New York/Oxford: Berghahn Books.

Eade, J. & Garbin, D. 2002: Changing Narratives of Violence, Struggle and Resistance: Bangladeshis and the Competition for Scarce Resourecs in the Global City. In: *Oxford Development Studies* 30: 137–150.

Eade, J., Fremeaux, I. & Garbin, D. 2002: The Political Construction of Diasporic Communities in the Global City. In: Gilbert, P. (ed.) *Imagined Londons*. Albany: State University of New York.

Eade, J. & Mele, C. 2002: *Understanding the City*. Oxford, UK/Malden, Mass.: Blackwell.

Fishman, W. 1988: *East End 1888*. London: Duckworth.

Forman, C. 1989: *Spitalfields: A Battle for Land*. London: Hilary Shipman.

Foster, J. 1999: *Docklands. Cultures in conflict, worlds in collision*. London: UCL Press.

Fremeaux, I. 2002: The Strategic Use of the Notion of Community in Cultural Projects within Urban Regeneration Schemes. Unpublished PhD thesis, London Guildhall University.

Garbin, D. 2001: Politiques identitaires musulmanes et representation communitaire bengali dans l'Est End de Londres. In: *Journal des Anthropologues* 87.

Gardner, K. 1995: *Global Migrants, Local Lives: Travel and Transformation in Rural Bangladesh*. Oxford: Clarendon Press.

Glynn, S. 2002: Bengali Muslims: The New East End Radicals? In: *Ethnic and Racial Studies* 25 (6).

Hall, S. 1992: The Question of Cultural Identity. In. Held, D., Hall, S. & McGraw, A. (eds) *Modernity and Its Futures*. Milton Keynes: Open University Press, 274–316.

Jacobs, J. 1996: *Edge of Empire: Postcolonialism and the City*. London/New York: Routledge.

Khan, L. 1990: *Bangladesh Information Handbook*. London: Inner London Education Authority.

Lash, S. & Urry, J. 1994: *Economies of Signs and Space*. London: Sage.

Marcuse, P. & van Kempen, R. (eds) 2000: *Globalizing Cities: A New Spatial Order?* Oxford, UK/Malden, US: Blackwell Publishers.

Peck, J. & Ward, K. (eds) 2002: *City of Revolution: Restructuring Manchester*. Manchester: Manchester University Press

Robertson, R. 1992: *Globalization*. London: Sage.

Samad, Y. & Eade, J. 2003: *Community Perceptions of Forced Marriage*. London: Foreign and Commonwealth Office Community Liaison Unit.

Samers, M. 2002: Immigration and the Global City Hypothesis: Towards an Alternative Research Agenda. In: *International Journal of Urban and Regional Research* 26 (2): 389–402.

Sassen, S. 1991: *The Global City*. Princeton: Princeton University Press.

Smith, G. 2001: Religion as a Source of Social Capital in the Regeneration of East London. Rising East. *The Journal of East London Studies* 4: 124–153.

Smith, M.P. 2001: *Transnational Urbanism: Locating Globalization*. Oxford: Blackwell Publishers.

Smith, N. 2002: New Globalism, New Urbanism: Gentrification as Global Urban Strategy. In: *Antipode* 34: 427–450.

Sykes, R., Palier, B. & Prior, P. (eds) 2001: *Globalization and European Welfare States*. Basingstoke: Palgrave.

# Rich Mix Cities
## From Multicultural Experience to Cosmopolitan Engagement

*Graeme Evans and Jo Foord*

When I visit different larger cities in the European Union today I quite often get a feeling of being in several cities all over the world – at the same time and in the same place ... The diversity with respect to languages, urban architecture, cultural and social activities, shops, etc. makes our cities more interesting... today cultural diversity is also a necessity in order to make cities and societies more attractive and competitive in a global economy. There is no doubt that cultural diversity enriches our cities and societies with social, human and economic capital ... (Bertel Haarder cited in Hamburger 2003:2).

"The cosmopolitan perspective is an alternative imagination, an imagination of alternative ways of life and rationalities, which include the otherness of the other. It puts the negotiation of contradictory cultural experiences into the centre of activities: in the political, the economic, the scientific and the social" (Beck 2002:18).

The rich cultural mix of cities in Europe, as elsewhere, is beginning to be constructed as an asset. Bertel Haarder (Danish Minister for Refugees, Immigration and Integration) describes in the *Forward* to a manifesto on *Cultural Diversity in European Cities* (2003) a direct, personal experience of cultural enrichment. This is matched by an acknowledgment of the economic contribution migrants make and recognition of the potential 'ethnic' business has not only to revitalise urban economies but also to create attractive locations for global firms. Nevertheless this appreciation of cultural enlivenment is voiced against a backdrop of the poverty and social exclusion experienced by many migrants from within and beyond Europe's borders.

This paper looks at both the past influences on and present formations of this rich mix multicultural city. Our focus is on the impact of ethnic and cultural groups on the cultural and material landscapes of cities. These city landscapes, both semi-permanent (such as buildings, public spaces and cultural institutions) and transient (arts events and festivals) have been claimed as key signifiers of the 'new' multicultural urban experience and are becoming the objects of city planning, urban design, place making and (multi)cultural consumption (Christopherson 1994; Shaw, Bagwell & Karmowska 2004; Zukin 1996; Worpole & Greenhalgh 1999). Yet cities have their roots in a long, though often obscured, history of exchange and their landscapes have been, and continue to be, contested sites of cultural production and consumption. Much of this history can be excavated from the unacknowledged presence of cultural representations of 'Other' ethnic groups in the architecture, artistic movements and cultural institutions of cities. It can also be found in the hidden everyday landscapes of city life.

As the benefits of acknowledging cultural diversity are promoted, particularly across Europe, the underlying assumptions of a multicultural city remain unexamined. The term 'multicultural' is often used, somewhat benignly, to describe the increasing heterogeneity of city societies (in Europe particularly post 1945) and the result of global political economic changes and rapid migrations from former colonial regimes in Africa, the Caribbean and Asia. It also asserts cultural diversity as the norm and identifies a proliferation of relative cultural values. Whilst this may present a welcome challenge to exclusionary ideas of national (European) cohesion, this prescriptive version of multiculturalism does foster celebration of cultural diversity. It places ethnic identity, claims for rights and cultural acknowledgment at the centre of city politics. However it also creates a contest between relative cultural values – a contest that cannot be 'won' but which permanently pitches one set of values and practices against another. This postmodern relativism separates and isolates communities/social groups into cultural silos and, therefore, limits the potential for wholesale cultural transformation in which the 'the otherness of the other' can be acknowledged and used to generate transcultural exchanges.

In order to move beyond these limits of multiculturalism, this paper draws on the recently renewed debate on the nature of cosmopolitanism. As Beck (2002) argues, cosmopolitanism is a method for approaching how societies, especially urban societies, change from within through the influence of migrations. His concern is with the interplay of cultures and values – locally as well as globally – that create hybrid identities able to negotiate the contradictions of different cultures in everyday life. The cultural and material landscapes of cities are the sites of these everyday practices of cosmopolitanism.

In this paper we document the presence (and absence) of different cultural representations within the cultural and material landscapes of cities and explore the tension between on the one hand, the claims for the multicultural city to represent and celebrate diversity and on the other, diversity to be the basis of an active cosmopolitanism which facilitates the cultural interplay of strangers.

## The 'Other' in European Culture

Fontana (1994) has documented how the European identity, especially modern European identity, was constructed against 'barbarians' of different kinds and origins. Europe's self-image has consistently been defined in opposition to a mythical less civilized non-European 'Other'; and as Said points out: 'Most histories of European aesthetic modernism leave out the massive infusion of non-European cultures into the metropolitan heartland during the early years of this [20th] century' (1994:292). This is evident in the absence, camouflaging and erasure of non-European styles, references and forms in the histories of art and architecture, urban design and city planning, despite their undeniable hybrid influences (Jardine 1996). Kwesi Owusu contrasts the symbolic exclusion of the Black male in modern European art with that of the early periods and forms:

"Europe's collective identity is bound up with the cultures of the global south. It has always been thus. The ancients knew this and were particularly comfortable with it. Medieval generations came to accept it. In the paintings of the Adoration of the Magi, the image of the black magus attending the Madonna is dignified and expressive of human equality. Modern painters e.g. Van Dyke, however transformed him into a diminutive figure, either standing behind his mistress or kneeling at her feet. Such symbolic emasculation is a part of a recurrent phenomenon of misrepresentation and marginalisation in European history" (Owusu 1993:86).

However re-presentations of the European Renaissance (Gombrich 1950) do not acknowledge, as Owusu does, the acceptance of the Black 'Other' in medieval art. Rather a narrative has emerged of an internally coherent artistic process, devoid of any external influence or historical memory. This has reinforced a belief in Europe's deliverance from the cultural wasteland of the Dark Ages by the (secular) rediscovery of classicism. However, as further re-workings suggest:

"it makes more sense to think of the Renaissance as a culmination rather than a rebuttal of certain medieval tendencies…If no attempt is made to understand the mixed origins [Christian, Moorish, pagan]… then the richness and much of the beauty of its art will remain unappreciated and misunderstood" (Graham-Dixon 1999:13).

The linear model of European art history and visual styles therefore reflects the modernist propensity to forget its own history and reject whatever went before (Berman 1982). Writing about Vasari's 1550 seminal text *The Lives of Artists*, Smith (2000) notes that 'in order to exalt the art of his own time, (he) found it essential to derogate the Gothic that preceded it as the art of the barbarians who destroyed the classic Roman art he admired and his renascita revived' (2000:81). Similarly, the Dutch architect, Van Eyck has observed: 'Western civilization habitually identifies itself with civilization as such on the pontifical assumption that what is not like it is a deviation, less advanced, primitive, or, at best, exotically interesting at a safe distance' (1962:22).

This view of a hermetically sealed European artistic and cultural tradition, devoid of transcultural influence, is further taken up by influential commentaries on the history of cities. Notably Peter Hall's *Cities and Civilization* (1998) celebrates the creative milieu of European cities as central to the evolution of civilisation itself. Massey (1999) criticises Hall for his universal claims and, in particular, points out that the cities used as a basis for his evolutionary argument are both selective and Eurocentric. He not only largely ignores other civilisations from Mesoamerica to Eurasia, but also the reality of late-twentieth century urbanisation that has shifted south and east. These are the cities that are influencing cultural change now. Their expansion has its own dynamic, but at the same time they are integrally tied to Europe through global transnational migrations of people, ideas and aesthetics (King 1991, 2002; Conley 2002).

In a similar vein, Cohen argues that currently, 'the most prominent examples of cultural fusion in the arts do not come from global centres but rather from the world's periphery; they represent primarily an attempt at localization of global stylistic trends – the fusion of Western artistic styles or forms with local third or fourth-world cultural elements' (1999:45). For Werber (1999) the exchange goes both ways. For her migrants from the 'periphery' bring and develop a knowledge and openness to other cultures that creates new hybrid opportunities *within* the metropolitan core. Writing about the British Pakistani community, she argues that this cultural group has engaged in a complex traffic of 'objects-persons-places-sentiments' which has altered the perceptions of 'Britishness' and enabled the creation of a British Pakistani culture. Such transcultural exchange builds on long histories if interconnection between Asia and Europe.

## Multicultural City Landscapes

It is therefore immigration and settlement of people from the 'periphery' that represents the principal agent of cultural ex/change in cities. The comparative advantage of multicultural diversity in cities is dependent upon the continued ebb and flow of 'objects-persons-places-sentiments' (Werber 1999) between the 'periphery' and 'core' and between cities.

In talking about the creative dynamism of London, Philip Dodd, Director of the Institute for Contemporary Arts (ICA) however suggests that it is from within settled 'ethnic' communities that new artists are able to galvanise cultural capital, unite cultural practices and develop a creative edge through transforming art forms. He claimed that 'the second and third generation of Asians (are) the city's leading impulse, from music to street fashion, from new slang to video production...all high intensity economic activities' (cited in Biswas 2000:70). Speaking from within the ICA's neo-classical 'white' façade, Dodd appears to dismiss the cultural risks taken by first generation Asian migrants and their lasting impact on the cultural and urban landscape of London. These parents of the new artists were the shopkeepers and market stallholders, restaurant and sweatshop owners who transformed the retail landscape, inner city economies and culinary tastes of a nation. These early settlers were pioneers of cultural change. They adapted Victorian city premises and created new places (both temporally and spatially) for everyone to meet, shop and eat. They brought the corner shop – open all hours – and the local ethnic restaurant to nearly every neighbourhood. They infused moribund street markets with new energy and goods. This is the foundation of the everyday multicultural landscape of British and many other European cities (Rodgers 2002). Yet it is increasingly clear that even these well established 'ethnic' communities exist within cities that ignore their cultural participation and have no means of including their aesthetic contribution, personality and aspirations. As British-Asian architect, Rajan Gujral comments from Southall, west London:

"Ethnic communities are a permanent part of the society in the major cities of the country. There is no mistaking the areas favoured by the various ethnic groups; the writing on the shops, the rhythm in the streets, the faces, the dress. But somehow the communities live in spite of their environment rather than shaping it" (Gujral 1994:7).

The regulatory frameworks of urban planning, further restrict the claiming of space and transformation of place by migrants and ethnic communities. For example, in London, Birmingham and Leicester the extended family groups of some communities would benefit from the lateral conversion of terraced housing. However this runs counter to planning and building regulations, property market norms and mortgage company protocols.

This clash between the inventiveness of cultural innovation and institutional rigidity can be seen elsewhere. In Montreal, Quebecois three story houses where residents share social and domestic space accessed by external balconies and stairs (Gehl 2001:102) are no longer permitted by the city's planners. They are considered dangerous, particularly in winter weather. New housing must conform to an assumed norm with privatised, atomised and anonymous points of entry and exclusive domestic space. In New York, the South Bronx had been reduced to a frontier zone, culturally and spatially 'on the edge' and inhabited by the 'savages, the low, the Other' (Sciorra 1996:60). The areas' Latino and African-American working poor were largely excluded from the political and economic processes that shaped their daily life and physical living conditions. Responding to the growing number of derelict sites and buildings in the South Bronx, in neighbouring East Harlem and the Lower East Side, Puerto Rican residents appropriated municipal-owned land and property, cultivating community gardens and constructing wood framed shelters : 'These transformed sites serve as shelter for the homeless, social clubs, tenants associations, cultural centers, summer retreats and entrepreneurial ventures' (ibid.:63f). The three room *casita de Madera* constructed by *puertoriquennas* recreated the vernacular Caribbean form, raised off the ground with *balcon* (veranda). The repetition of this building form has created an urban village, *El Barrio* connected by walkways representing, what has been termed, 'landmarks of memory' (Lynch 1990:190).

However, such direct attempts to stamp identity and presence onto the urban landscape always takes place in opposition to dominant economic and political systems. Environmental and design professionals, who ostensibly claim to reflect and respond to community need, often resist or stereotype cultural influence and identity.

These embedded Eurocentric aesthetics and regulatory processes limit the active creation of state supported local ethnic cultural landscapes and institutions. Although the ethnic quarters of most European cities now have Afro-Caribbean and Asian cultural centres, Jewish museums and multi-cultural arts centres these spaces are predominantly independent and alternative to mainstream white-European cultural institutions. Few of these 'ethnic' cultural spaces are flagships in the manor of the established museums and theatres of high European art (one exception *might* be the 'Arab Monde' *Grand Projet* in Paris). As Owusu observes:

"For many black artists working in the city, the city itself is a terrain of contested spaces, and that changes the whole equation for many of

'Rainbow Theatre' – a redundant cinema and rock venue, in Finsbury Park, north London – now home to black evangelical group.
Photo: Graeme Evans.

them, because one does not assume one's own space within the city in the way that a white or European artist might" (Owusu in BAAA 1993:22).

Making a mark on the city landscape through cultural institutions, creative practice and community centres serves not only to fulfil a group's own needs but also to make that group visible. Wartime refugees from Poland and Czechoslovakia set up cultural community centres in London and other cities, which served as meeting places for existing populations and new arrivals, serving national food and drink, hosting gatherings, dances and events. Early centres were run in homes, only gradually moving to visible locations in the urban landscape. In time these more public settings became open to strangers, and today the Czech club and Polish centres in London generally serve their mixed locals communities. Irish, Chinese and more recently Vietnamese communities have established similar community centres, but many of these have become quasi-commercial

75

enterprises offering food and drink and entertainment for cultural tourists.

Other groups do tend to use their religious buildings as the location for community activity, artistic and cultural expression. Black (African, Caribbean, South American) evangelical groups now represent the only growing congregation in the Christian church with highly developed voluntary and cultural programmes providing front line services as well as meeting places. Yet, they generally occupy second hand buildings in marginal locations, rather than purpose built churches and meeting houses. Local mosques, again usually located in adapted industrial, cinema or church buildings, house cultural and education centres where languages are taught (English and mother-tongue), community, women's and children's groups meet, and political and cultural exchange takes place.

Many communities still repatriate surplus income to their places of origin, limiting capital accumulation for enterprises and cultural investment in their location of new settlement. This lack of accumulated resources further disadvantages such groups in public funding regimes where matched funding, sponsorship or support in kind (buildings or land) is often required. Only where diasporic groups are well-established or connected and can draw on community wealth can private support for cultural and religious projects be moblised. The largest traditional Hindu temple outside India – Shri Swammarayan Mandir – is located in Neasden in the Brent, north-west London. In the 1990s Brent became one of the first local authorities in the Britain to have a majority Black and Asian population. The temple was financed by the local Hindu community and is located opposite the local community school. Indian craftsmen and masons were flown to London to work on this sacred structure. They came on a pilgrimage but fell foul of local employment and planning legislation.

The development of cultural facilities by ethnic minority groups relies overwhelmingly on individual subscription, entrepreneur and community support. As a result, such facilities are marginalised and often linked to commu-

Hindu Temple, Neasden, north west London. Photo: Graeme Evans.

nity or religious activity and therefore excluded from the arts funding system. Moreover such provision is exposed to the whims of powerful individuals or a dominant group or caste. Relegating ethnic cultural activity to quasi-religious and community functions has several consequences that reduce the legitimacy and visibility of 'ethnic' cultural practice. First the association ensures that cultural expression remains hidden from public view and scrutiny; second professional and amateur cultural practice takes place in inappropriate and inadequate buildings; third such activity is neither recognised nor legitimated as creative (or professional) arts practice, and therefore, is denied both audience and appropriate resources for professional (and amateur) creative activity; finally communities risk isolation through a lack of engagement with others cutting off cultural exchange and potential sources of creativity.

This depiction of a multicultural landscape emphasises the hidden nature of cultural expression and a separation of cultural and ethnic groups. This has been reinforced by both state strategies and some of the self-help regimes adopted by communities to fill the void in cultural provision. It incorporates is ' a neat and well-established distinction between the private and the public, where you can say "Go and practise your religion, your cultural differences, your ethnic oddities and so on behind closed curtains. Once you come into the public sphere you have to obey a different regime'" (Hall 2000:46).

## Ethnic Festivals for the Multicultural City

Exceptions to these hidden, privatised cultural expressions are the growth of ethnic arts festivals building on religious celebrations (Diwali, Chinese New Year, Carnival Mas). Though promoted in tourist itineraries they are also opportunities for community celebration and display (Smith 1995). Nevertheless the growth and popularity of some of these festivals has created tension over policing and planning. These tensions have resulted in the re-scheduling and re-siting of some high profile festivals away from core inner city neighbourhoods. Such relocation breaks long held associations with and memories of place.

In New York weekend road closures for festivals had proliferated and a ban on new festivals has been enforced. The effect of this is felt most by new migrants who are less able to assert their claim to a festival than long standing groups with more power and influence. Authentic[1] cultural celebration and representation is perhaps most evident in the *carnival mas* carried out each summer in major cities with Caribbean populations. Two notable festivals are in London (Notting Hill) and Toronto (Caribana). The opportunity to shake off the European mask is taken with gusto:

"Since (Columbus) Africans have worn European clothes. We wear them to work, to school, to church, to the penitentiary and to bed. We dream in them. At Carnival time the process is inverted for you connect the silver line and make your own clothes. You make it special, load it with a baggage of your own treasures and make it speak your language. You make what you want and call it your own" (Owusu & Ross 1988:15).

The engagement of these increasingly large festivals with the city has however remained tense and fraught. Attempts to recreate them as benign sponsored arts festivals and as tourist events have failed. Their size and popularity have grown with their importance as places of cultural expression and identity formation. A festival event is the outcome of year long preparations and off-site cultural development within communities and schools. The meaning of a festival is negotiated and created through these preparations as well as in the performances of the festival itself. Such popularity has fuelled the tension with city authorities. They are perceived to represent a threat, yet are not compared with other more regularly violent mass popular ('white') gatherings (e.g. football). Indeed the handful of incidences are negligible given the degree of concentration of people in space and time.

In Toronto, the Caribana was relocated

in the early 1990s away from its city centre neighbourhoods and streets, onto an island in Lake Ontario, and spread over a week-long event, rather than a symbolic bank holiday. In London, the Notting Hill carnival will move in 2005 to Hyde Park, out of the narrow (now gentrified) streets of west London. The organising committee continues to be subjected to annual scrutiny, police interference, power shifts and pressure from funders. Such levels of surveillance are rarely experienced by white cultural organisations – even when they receive large state subsidies (Evans 2000).

The current social production of multicultural city space, represented in both the semi-permanent built environment and the temporary spaces of festivals, does not make cultural expression easy. There are few mechanisms available to ethnic minority communities to influence the design and form of city space and the opportunities to take control of its public spaces and streets are declining. Likewise the opportunities to shape everyday multicultural encounters, though street markets and in neighbourhoods with an ethnic identity have decline through regulatory controls and 'improvements' in the urban fabric. There is instead a growing trend in multicultural cities to create contrived ethnic quarters. By enacting planning mechanisms to regulate frontages and street furniture and insisting on the use of decoration embodying stereotypical symbols of particular ethnic identities (for example in Little Italy, Chinatown and Banglatown) *faux* neighbourhoods are created as business and tourist destinations. These spaces are often animated by staged ethnic festivals, funded or sponsored by local businesses, local authorities, lottery and other charitable grants. They are often presented as cultural showcases for visitors. Such interventions are a long way from the permanent cultural infrastructures and self-determined events to which communities aspire.

## Rich Mix Urban Arts

With these constraints it is no surprise that ethnic cultural expression finds its voice largely outside the material landscapes of the European

Notting Hill Carnival, London. Photo: Ian Watts.

city. This is out of necessity but also to some degree due to cultural preference and practice. Performance and display through music and the visual arts and crafts have become central platforms for self-expression and cultural exploration. Stuart Hall has noted that black young people are the 'dominant defining force in street-orientated British youth culture. Without them, white youth culture would not exist in the form it does today' (in Jaggi 2001:1). Popular culture in Britain has unquestionably been transformed by Black and Asian artists creating new musical genres, styles of fashion, language and food. While Black artists have sought out forms of expression and media that were more accessible and less susceptible to the gatekeeping control of others, they have been labelled by cultural intermediaries of aesthetic taste as 'natural', 'untutored' and 'primitive' or judged to be wholly responsible for the 'dumbing down' popular culture (ibid.).

Not all interventions from Black and Asian artists are in street culture. Many Black artists have worked within the disciplines of visual arts since the 1950s but they have been 'quietly written out of the record. Not British enough for the Tate, not international enough for Bankside' (Hall in Jaggi 2001). Similarly, Black novelists working in London in the 1960s and 1970s have been excluded from the current debate on role of the novel. Though Jaggi notes the increasing visibility of Black and Asian British artists and writers in the mainstream arts events held in London – the Booker prize (Salman Rushdie, Ben Okri, Zadie Smith) and the Turner Prize (Chris Ofili and Steve McQueen) – she also laments that they are still subject to restrictive value judgements which label them as ethnic artists and exotic adjuncts at the edge of British art.

Both the innovative creators of popular genres and those working within the visual arts and literature are faced by a cultural establishment that attempts to limit their creativity to documenting the assumed 'Africanness' or 'Asianness' in their British experience. In other words it wants to confine these artists to documenting the white establishment's black 'Other'.

Black and Asian British artists have also pursued the project of creating Black and Asian arts centres and cultural facilities. However this has been a particularly difficult endeavour. In the few cases where this has been possible, their marginal locations, fragile financial prospects and parsimonious or tokenistic state and charitable support has confirmed the secondary status of such projects in the arts funding system.[2] Where new or redeveloped ethnic arts centres have survived, they have done so with low levels of subsidy, in poorer, inaccessible locations, and in inadequate buildings by comparison with their white counterparts.

A comparison of two established arts organisations in Birmingham – the Ikon Gallery and the black arts centre, The Drum – illustrates this issue. Both projects won Lottery and European funds to relocate and upgrade their buildings (Evans & Foord 2000), but with sharply contrasting treatment and solutions. The former was re-sited in the downtown central business and entertainment district, with surrounding café culture; the latter in a less salubrious and non-central location, Newtown (2.5 km north of the city centre). The justification for these different location decisions 'reveals the need for micro-environmental factors to be taken into account when planning urban investment for White and non-White audiences' (Symon 1999:723). In this sense, the process of and eventual location strongly influences image, access/usage, markets and consequently the viability of cultural organisations. This therefore reflects the hierarchical values ascribed to certain cultural practices over others, even where they exist within the same art form or genre and within the same city and cultural regimes (Evans 2001).

There are several high profile examples of 'failed' Black and Asian arts centres in London including The Roundhouse and Brixton Village. These experiences only serve to confirm the prejudicial assumption that the groups themselves were not able to create and run viable major facilities, nor could they withstand market-tested demand.

This fragile history, which presents black and ethnic arts as terminally dependant and lacking the capacity to survive in cultural and commercial markets, has limited their physical development. Ironically this is at a time when the scope and scale of urban cultural diversity has been expanding – from both within established communities and through the relocation of new migrants. (This market failure is of course in contrast to the commercial mainstream success of black urban culture, notably music and associated fashion).

This legacy led one emerging visual arts group to resist the notion of a building base altogether. The Institute of International Visual Arts (inIVA) was formed in the early-1990s, with Arts Council funding, 'to promote the work of artists, curators and scholars from a plurality of cultural backgrounds' and 'to bring the work of culturally-diverse artists to the attention of the widest possible public' (ww.iniva.org). For the past ten years the organisation has led a peripatetic life, touring, curating and promoting, but without a permanent home. This pragmatic rejection of a fixed space has been reversed recently with a planned building to be located in the heart of London's new (Brit) art district of Hoxton/Shoreditch, in the city fringe (Evans 2004). Inevitably, the challenge of building a new and permanent home for inIVA has become a pressing and practical issue for the organisation and it also raises questions about identity, space and place that have been recurrent themes in inIVA's artistic programme: 'InIVA emerged from a particular historical and demographic context and a special relationship with London as a multicultural city. By locating our project in Shoreditch, we intend to build on these features and relationships and provide new channels of communication between the diferent constituencies – artistic, cultural, social and corporate – which currently rarely interact' (www.iniva.org). Whether this and other contemporary rich mix ventures can be successfully established and the spectre of past failures exorcised, tests the very notion of the multicultural city itself.

Another attempt to capture the multicultural city in physical form and place, recognising its absence and marginal position in the past – is seen in *The Rich Mix* cultural centre in East London. Located in the city fringe area of the borough of Tower Hamlets, which contains several of the poorest and most deprived neighbourhoods in the UK, and host to past and recent diasporas from Europe and Asia – a new build arts centre designed by Penoyre & Prasad aims to be a focal point for local communities, a meeting place, entertainment and educational centre (resonant of 19$^{th}$ century *People's Palaces* and 20$^{th}$ century *Maisons de la Cultures*/Arts Centres, Evans 2001). It will also seek to challenge and strive for creative excellence over a range of art forms, a crucial crossroads, dedicated to innovation and integration, working towards a new understanding of British culture. What is being unsaid here is the multicultural basis for this venture, which is only manifested in its multiscreen cinema combining mainstream and Bollywood films and home to a music training agency, Asian Dub Foundation. The centre's location (and funding) seeks to play a major role in the regeneration of its local area – an area that has been subjected to office and residential gentrification and development prior to the centre's formation.

This optimistic cultural development was based on *creative city* principles (Landry & Bianchini 1995, 2000), focusing almost exclusively on creative industries and related retail, hospitality (curry and balti houses, wine bars, designer retail and galleries), visitor attractions and street markets. The multicultural residential neighbourhoods have been neglected by this consumption-led approach, creating a socio-spatial divide with social programmes which promoted training in new media and patronising capacity building, but which ignored the local meaning and memory of place and the cultural knowledge, aspirations and skills of local residents (Evans & Foord 2003). The rich mix in this project has been reduced to a commodified landscape of street retail and entertainment – consumption opportunity for adjoining office workers, weekenders and the new urban professional.

This experience of practicing culture and attempts to claim space for Black and Asian art illustrates the contested nature of the production and consumption of culture in multicultural cities. Indeed Bhabha goes further by observing: 'Multiculturalism that is practised in most Western societies is at best only partial. Although there is always an entertainment and endorsement of cultural diversity, there is always also a corresponding containment of it' (in Rutherford 1990:208). The experiences of the multicultural city are therefore ones of limitation and restriction.

## Towards Cosmopolitan Engagement

For many, globalisation appears to threaten the diversity of cultural representation through an inevitable universalising of cultural reference points and practices. Featherstone (2002) however suggests that, in the wake of globalisation, there is currently a renewed interest in cosmopolitanism in reaction to the emergence of exclusive nationalisms and growth of market relations in every aspect of civic and personal life. This interest takes two forms: one expresses a hope that cosmopolitan groups/individuals will forge transnational values, institutions and lifestyles that will underpin the emergence of a global democracy in the image of European modernity; the other reviles the cosmopolitan identity as elitist and representative of a mobile middle class, cultural tourists dabbling rootlessly in a variety of cultures in a relentless search for new experiences, aesthetic stimulation and cultural novelty and unable to sustain a sense of local connection nor responsibility for the growing numbers of socially and cultural excluded. Beck (2002), in criticising both these interpretations, sees a more positive role for cosmopolitanism in a globalising world.

Globalisation through migration and the movement of ideas and goods also offers opportunities for the 'creolising' of cultural exchange through participation in different cultural practices, consumption and codes. For Beck (2002) this creates a cosmopolitan openness to strangers and ideas, to 'Others' and to the 'Otherness' within identities. Due to this openness, cosmopolitanism also means a breaking down of the internal and external borders which limit expression and identity formation. Whereas the notion of multiculturalism retains distinctions (and therefore borders) between cultures, cosmopolitanism actively works to blur distinctions between different identities. Cosmopolitan practice is therefore *trans*cultural rather than multicultural.

Cosmopolitanism is not a practice of an elite. International economic migration, transnational labour markets and flows of political refugees have created groups of people who have to combine the contradictions of different cultures within their everyday lives. Such groups cannot be part of a single nation state, indeed this dislocation is necessary for their survival. Beck comments: 'These groups, characterised by their in-between status, demonstrate that neither nation-state nor ethnic group has a monopoly on loyalty … there is an intermediate space where a set of alternatives might emerge, based for example on hybrid identities' (2001:50). He continues:

"Increasingly, people have biographies which relate to more than one place. We might say that a polygamous relationship to place is becoming the norm: and as one is in love with many places, one develops deep connections to more than one culture. Even when forced to be plurally located, affective relations may follow… This aspect of cosmoplitanization is very important… [and] concerns the integration and transcendence of contradictions between cultures, and at the same time, the preservation of commitment to localities…" (Beck 2001:50).

Importantly, such hybrid identities, for Beck, can emerge from within states (for example Black/Asian British identities) and these groups too can act as 'pioneers of cosmopolitanism' – a cosmopolitanism from below, from within the local.

Jacobsen also observes that there is a 'reinforcing bond' between local identities and international flows which exclude the state and '[t]hus, ethnic groups have secured, at least theoretically, international support in their jockeying for cultural recognition and political influence' (2000:22). This dynamic exchange can serve to bring international and other cultural forms and practices to a local audience, but also enable local artists to reach wider audiences and gain recognition for themselves, their art forms and their cultural practices. Cohen (1999:45) adds: 'The artists thus play an interstitial role, striving to bridge the disparate worlds between which they are suspended, without, however, losing their local voice and identity'. World Music captures this exchange, as has the growing interest in fusion foods and aesthetic styles.

Black and Asian British artists, as other minorities have done elsewhere (for example Native Americans, Australian Aboriginals and Maoris), self-consciously combine abstract and concrete symbols of 'Own' and 'Other' cultures. As Said reminds us: '... all cultures are involved in one another, none is single and pure, all are hybrid, heterogeneous, extraordinarily differentiated and unmonolithic' (1994:xxix). Rowe (2002) takes this further and assesses how artists effectively 'difference the city' through their work of combining aesthetic styles and creative processes. She cites the *Shamiana*: Mughal Tent – an intergenerational national and international textile project initiated by Shireen Akbar through the V&A Museum and exhibited there in 1997. This work united Asian women and children with women from a variety of other communities in the creation of textile panels. On these panels the women and children created representations of their everyday lives and landscapes. Working in groups in their communities, women learnt and developed textile skills from each other and through the V&A's collections. This artwork grew from a small project into one that was predicated on an exchange of cultures and artistic practices. The final result was 'a tent that covered the world' (www.vam.ac.uk/vastatic/shamiana).

Rowe sees in this work representations of London 'delineated by a landmark, a symbol of its authority, in this case Big Ben, yet that legibility is simultaneously reinscribed by the inflections of multicultural identities operating within the representational spaces of every day life' (2002:33). Through the creation of this piece the everyday lives of women, living in London, practising cosmopolitanism, are seen to disrupt an iconic symbol of colonial authority, appropriating its meaning for themselves.

It is this hybrid cosmopolitan practice and cultural fusion that Ulrich Beck, Stuart Hall and Pnina Werbner and others now maintain is (and maybe always was) the norm. It combines criss-crossing rather than one-way diasporic movements. If fluidity is the norm then resistance to the limitations imposed on cultural expression in the 'multicultural city' is to be expected – certainly while the 'Other' exists largely outside of the built environment, public amenities and legitimate (subsidised) arts and cultural facilities. Extrapolating from Beck, new global relationships and a transcultural vocabulary of cultural practices and symbols shapes this resistance and underpins the cosmopolitan city.

## Conclusion

Celebrating cultural diversity in the multicultural city – through the support of ethnic arts and festivals or the creation of ethnic quarters – tends to gloss over, or at least understate the real tensions between notions and realities of national(ism) and cultural identity. Instead they create palatable representations of different fixed identities and present these for consumption. All too often they become extensions of capitalisation and the realisation of property hope values through gentrification, heritage retro-fitting and civic and corporate place-making and branding (Evans 2003).

The experience of multicultural cities reproduces identities of 'Others' while hiding and dismissing the diversity of creative practice. British and other European cities, have not been seriously confronted by these issues, let alone resolved them through either cultural or social policy spheres. Those responsible for the development process and the professional imperatives of regeneration and cultural intermediaries (local, national, European/EU), have proven unable and unwilling to adopt pluralist (cosmopolitan) policies or practices, or to relinquish control over space and its built form. The continued use of multicultrualism – rich mix – as a rationale to guide (or spice-up) cultural/arts/planning policy limits the range and scope of subsidised interventions. It also permits complicity with the process of 'Othering' and therefore the exclusion of individuals/groups and their creative practices.

Adopting the openness to strangers of cosmopolitanism offers a way forward. Cities have long been the sites for trade and the mixing of people, commodities, ideas and cultures. In the cosmopolitan city 'it is imperative to abandon models of binary oppositions which impose fixed ordering and according to which cultural practices are classified in terms of Same or Other. And it is to this end that considerations of art cannot be separated from questions of politics' (Third Text, Ed. 1987/1:4, in Jordan & Weedon 1995:484). In the landscapes of the city this would manifest itself in what Lefebvre termed differential space, a 'space yet to come but which, in contrast to the homogenising powers of the abstract space of capitalism, will be a more mixed, inter-penetrative space where differences are respected rather than buried under sameness' (Borden 2002:114; Lefebvre 1991). Developing this theme further, cosmopolitanism goes beyond respect to active engagement.

In practice this cosmopolitan engagement already takes place *despite* the planned landscape and the limiting actions of arts and cultural professionals. It takes places in the ad hoc spaces carved out for cultural expression and creative endeavour. It also takes place through everyday encounters in the streets and informal public spaces, in mixed-use/mixed ethnic neighbourhoods of poorer inner city areas, in the streetmarkets and spatial concentrations of ethnically diverse food, fashion, entertainment and retail activity and in homes and playgrounds. These are the organic places of quiet everyday cultural resistance and cosmopolitan exposure.

## Notes

1. 'Authenticity' in a cultural sense is a difficult notion to distinguish in light of culture's natural shifting and fusion tendencies and the effects of 'staged authenticity' MacCannell (1984). Christopherson for example makes the distinction between 'genuine ethnic culture' and 'that which is manufactured for sale' (1994).
2. In London, after the abolition of the ("urban new left") Greater London Council in 1986, a number of "black arts" organisations were jointly-funded by the regional arts board (LAB) and successor regional funding quango, the London Borough Grants Scheme (LBGS). Between 1987 and 1994 and these two public bodies, the funding of such groups supported fell from 120 to 38. The then Director of LBGS observed: 'On the whole (black arts clients) were not established or mature organisations. Their resources were limited…systems were not all that they should have been, financially or managerially. Most were operating from poor premises which were usually rented' (Evans 2001a).

## References

BAAA 1993: *The Artist in the Changing City*. London: British American Arts Association.

Bhabha, H. 1994: *The Location of Culture*. London: Routledge.

Biswas, R.K. (ed.) 2000: *Metropolis Now*. Vienna: Springer-Verlag.

Beck, U. 2001: Cosmopolis and Risk: A Conversation with Ulrich Beck (Boyne, R.). In: *Theory, Culture and Society* 18:4, 47–63.

Beck, U. 2002: The Cosmopolitan Society and Its Enemies. In: *Theory Culture and Society* vol. 19:1, 17–44.

Berman, M. 1982: *All that is Solid Melts into Air*. London: Verso.

Borden, I. 2002: What is Radical Architecture? In: Miles, M. & Hall, T. (eds) *Urban Futures Critical Commentaries on Shaping the City*. London: Routledge, pp. 111–133.

Christopherson, S. 1994: The Fortress City: Privatised Spaces, Consumer Citizenship. In: Amin, A. (ed.) *Post-Fordism: A Reader*. Oxford: Blackwell, pp. 409–427.

Cohen, E. 1999: Cultural Fusion. In: *Values and Heritage Conservation*. Getty Conservation Institute, Los Angeles, pp. 44–50.

Conley, V.A. 2002: Chaosmopolis. In: *Theory Culture and Society* vol. 19:1, 127–138.

Evans, G.L. 2000: Measure for Measure: Evaluating Performance and the Arts. In: *Organisation Studies in Cultures, Organisations and Societies* vol.6:2, 243–266.

Evans, G.L. 2001: *Cultural Planning: An Urban Renaissance?* London: Routledge.

Evans, G.L. 2003: Hard Branding the Culture City – From Prado to Prada. In: *International Journal of Urban and Regional Research*, 417–440.

Evans, G.L. 2004: Whose Heritage is it anyway? Reconciling the 'National' and the 'Universal' in Québec City. In: *British Journal of Canadian Studies* 16:2, 333–347.

Evans, G.L. & Foord, J. 2000: European Funding of Culture: Promoting European Culture or Regional Growth. In *Cultural Trends* vol. 36, 53–87.

Evans, G.L. & Foord, J. 2003: Culture Planning in East London. In: Kirkham, N. & Miles, M. (eds) *Cultures & Settlement*, Vol. 3 of *Art & Urban Futures*. Bristol: Intellect Books, pp. 15–30.

Featherstone, M. 2002: Cosmopolis: An Introduction. In: *Theory, Culture and Society* vol. 19:1, 1–16.

Fontana, J. 1994: *Europa ante el espejo*. Barcelona: Critica.

Gehl, J. 2001: *Life Between Buildings. Using Public Space*. Copenhagen: Arkitekens Forlag.

Giddens, A. 1990: *The Consequences of Modernity*. Cambridge: Polity Press.

Graham-Dixon, A. 1999: *Renaissance*. London: BBC Worldwide.

Gujral, R. 1994: Opinion. In: *Architecture Today* 50: 7–8.

Hamburger, C. (ed.) 2003: *Cultural Diversity in European Cities*. Copenhagen: Ministry of Refugees, Immigration and Integration.

Hall, P. 1998: *Cities and Civilization: Culture, Innovation, and Urban Order*. London: Weidenfeld & Nicholson.

Hall, S. 1990: Cultural identity and diaspora. In: Rutherford, J. (ed.) *Identity*. London: Lawrence & Wishart.

Hall, S. 2000: Multicultural Citizens, Monocultural Citizenship? In: Pearce, N. & Hallgarten (eds) *Tomorrow's Citizens: Critical Debates in Citizenship and Education*. London: Institute for Public Policy Research, pp. 43–51.

Jacobsen, S. 2000: Indonesia on the Threshold: Towards an Ethnification of the Nation? In: *International Institute for Asian Studies Newsletter*, 22 June: 22.

Jaggi, M 2001: Dubious Divisions. In: *Guardian* 11/09/2000 www.guardian.co.uk.

Jardine, L. 1996: *Worldly Goods: A New History of the Renaissance*. London: Macmillan.

Jordan, G. & Weedon, C. 1995: *Cultural Politics: Class, Gender, Race and the Postmodern World*. Oxford: Blackwell.

King, A.D. (ed.) 1991: *Culture, Globalization and the World-System*. Basingstoke: Macmillan.

King, A.D. 2000: Postcolonialism, Representation and the City. In: Bridge, G. & Watson, S. (eds) *Companion to the City*. Oxford: Blackwell.

Landry, C. & Bianchini, F. 1995: *The Creative City*. Stroud: Demos/Comedia.

Landry, C. 2000: *The Creative City. A Toolkit for Urban Innovators*. London: Earthscan.

Lash, S. & Urry, J. 1994: *Economies of Signs and Spaces*. London: Sage.

Lefebvre, H. 1991: *The Production of Space* (trans. Nicholson-Smith, D.). Oxford: Blackwell.

Lynch, K. 1990: *What Time is This Place?* Cambridge, Mass.: MIT Press.

MacCannell, D. 1984: Reconstructed Ethnicity: Tourism and Cultural Identity in Third World Communities. In: *Annals of Tourism Research* vol. 11:1, 375–391.

Massey, D., Allen, J. & Pile, S. 1999: *City Worlds*. London: Routledge.

Owusu, K. 1986: *The Struggle for Black Arts in Britain: What We Consider Better Than Freedom*. London: Comedia.

Owusu, K. 1993: Which New Europe? A Dawn of Cultural Diversity or a Euro-Centric Paradise? In: Fisher, R. (ed.) *The Challenge for the Arts: Reflections on British Culture in Europe in the /Context of the Single Market and Maastricht*. London: Arts Council.

Owusu, K. & Ross, J. 1988: *Behind the Masquerade: The Story of the Notting Hill Carnival*. London: Arts Media Group.

Rodgers, A. 2002: Citizenship, Multiculturalism and the European City. In: Bridge, G. & Watson, S. (eds) *Companion to the City*. Oxford: Blackwell.

Rowe, D. 2002: Differencing the City: Urban Identities and the Spatial Imagination. In: Miles, M. & Hall, T. (eds) *Urban Futures. Critical Commentaries on Shaping the City*. London: Routledge.

Rutherford, J. (ed.) 1990: *Identity*. London: Lawrence & Wishart.

Said, E.W. 1994: *Culture and Imperialism*. London: Vintage.

Sciorra, J. 1996: Return to the Future: Puerto Rican Vernacular Architecture in New York City. In: King, A.D. (ed.) *Re-presenting the City: Ethnicity, Capital and Culture in the $21^{st}$-Century Metropolis*. Hampshire: Macmillan.

Shaw, S., Bagwell, S & Karmowska, J. 2004: Urban Explorers and Multicultural Neighbourhoods of European Cities. In: *Urban Studies* 41:10, 1983–2000.

Smith, B. 2000: Modernism in its Place. In: *Tate*, Tate Modern Special Issue no. 21. London: 79–83.

Smith, S. 1995: Where to Draw the Line: A Geography of Popular Festivity. In: Rogers, A. & Vertovec, S. (eds) *The Urban Context: Ethnicity, Social Networks and Situational Analysis*: Oxford: Berg.

Symon, P. 1999: The New Arts in Birmingham. A Local Analysis of Cultural Diversity. In: *International Conference on Cultural Policy Research*. Bergen, 10–12 November: 723–744.

Van Eyck, A. 1962: *Forum*. Amsterdam.

Vasari, G. 1550: *The Lives of Artists* (first published in Italian, enlarged version published in 1568, trans. 1970). London: A. B. Hinds.

Werbner, P. 1999: Global Pathways, Working Class Cosmopolitans and the Creation of Trans-Ethnic Worlds. In: *Social Anthropology* 7:1, 17–35.

Worpole, K. & Greenhalgh, L. 1999: *The Richness of Cities: Urban Policy in a New Landscape – Final Report*. Gloucester: Comedia/Demos.

Zukin, S. 1996: Space and Symbols in an Age of Decline. In: King, A. D. (ed.) *Re-Presenting the City: Ethnicity, Capital and Culture in the 21st Century Metropolis*. London: Macmillan.

# Urban Strategies and Loophole Tactics
## Claiming Space in Cape Town and Malmö

*Elisabeth Högdahl*

*David sits at a bar-table placed along one of the big windows in one of Long Streets many coffee shops. It is September and outside the rain is pouring down even though it should be spring and sunshine. Occasional pedestrians are passing by outside in Long Street, one of the most intense tourist streets in Cape Town CBD, central business district. David is only one of the many shop owners in the mostly Victorian houses in bright colours, with verandas and ornamented iron railings. Now he is telling the story about William. William is one of the street children who have become a more and more influential part of the street life together with street vendors, vagrants, beggars, thieves and informal parking guards. He used to hang outside the coffee shop, begging from the by-passers. Now and then David gave him some food, and he tended to turn up in the mornings when David was alone in the pub to prepare for opening the daily business. One morning David asked if William could help him by sweeping the pavement outside the door in the mornings. Then he would get breakfast in return, an arrangement that William seemed to accept and everything seemed fine for at short while. One day when David went to the bank, though, William was gone when he returned and the broom was lying on the pavement. William never showed up again at the coffee shop and a few weeks later David found him further downtown together with some other street kids, sitting in the street. They where sniffing glue and conversation was impossible. David tried to reach out to him, but was told to go to hell. After that incident, David never saw him again, and has no idea what happened.*[1]

This story about David and William that I was told during a fieldwork in Cape Town a few years ago, reflects a quite typical problem in the post-apartheid South Africa. The absence and presence in the cityscape has become an issue in relation to discussions on democracy and civil rights, as different citizens now conquer places from which they during apartheid was excluded.[2] The issue is closely related to processes related to power, and the dramatic South African context certainly can be used to clarify the issue also in a European context. Who has the right to be present in the city and under what conditions?

Raising this question, my aim is to discuss how streets and squares are not only physical places but also mental constructions in which categories, boundaries and attitude become important. Michel de Certeau has stressed the importance of viewing the city as both a *place*, basically the fixed physical setting, and *space*, created by the moving practices that makes the place become a living field of interactions and memory, creating certain rhythms and atmospheres (de Certeau 1984:117). From this perspective David and William are both constantly part of the creation of the city, bringing in their different thoughts, experiences and in their actions in the cityscape. They become part of the story of *how things are* in Cape Town, and this raises the need to discuss how people will be identified in the street and what concept will be created in interactions and narratives.

*How things are* can be seen both as an expression of personal attitudes, but also as a discursive statement on what is real and true

(Foucault 2002:133). The idea of reality is to a large extent an every-day political issue, where different issues appear in "the spotlight". The German philosopher Hannah Arendt describes how human interaction creates a *weave of relations*, where history and present as well as "inner feelings" are organised through different kinds of communication (Arendt 1986:74, 222). Arendt stresses that all power is created and maintained through legitimacy, and emphasizes the importance of consensus, whereby interaction may be seen as a form of negotiation to create both truth and reality. It is an issue on both *how things are* in the actual neighbourhoods and concepts on *how people are* in relation to this and they can be seen as socially constructed frames that puts up rules for interaction. In the streets agreements are reached to clarify roles and positions, but it is also important to show how people challenge boundaries and ultimately also bring about changes in the cityscape. The city seems to be a place of both order and chaos. Opportunities occur in both the physical environment and the normative network, making it possible to claim new places and to create new meaning. I will call these opportunities *loopholes*, a quite wide concept that to a large extent is depended on being "at the right place at the right time", and take advantage of the moment. Michel de Certeau calls that moment *kairos*, and it might at the end change both place and space (de Certeau 1984:85).

To clarify the discussion I will put the situation in Cape Town in relation to the European context by also using a fieldwork from the city of Malmö in Sweden,[3] and they serve as contrasting cases, rather than a comparative analysis. In Malmö I am mainly focusing on the area of Möllevången, which like many other old working class areas in Europe now is associated with a new ethnic mix and diverse lifestyles. The neighbourhood is also burdened with a reputation for crime, drug problems and welfare dependence. The landscape of crime and violence is of course very different between the two urban settings. At the present South Africa is plagued with extremely high crime rates and the crime-scene seems to have changed. From being close related to what is considered to be political violence connected to certain (combating) groups, to be more of an issue of every day politics, with violence originated from social and economical division, and that quite randomly might hit any South African citizen (Tshiwula 1998:8; Shaw 2002:53ff).[4] At the same time it is interesting how the districts of Möllevången and Long Street share the same problematic: they are both defined as "colourful neighbourhoods", they can be viewed as both an "appetizing" and "unappetizing" diversity – depending on the perspective. They both represent a balance act between order and a threatening disorder that can be found in many other urban settings. The street kids in Long Street in many ways symbolizes the "unwanted" and in Möllevången the down-and-outs gets a similar position. I will use these two groups to discuss how the processes of presence and exclusion might work in two different settings, in the specific framework of the story of *what it is like* in these different places, shaped by very different political and historical processes.

## The Vision of Long Street

The South African author Lawrence Green, describes Long Street as on of his favourite streets as he grew up in Cape Town in the 1920s, a street of free music entertainment, comic papers, doughnuts, sweets and the call of the waterfront (Green 1971:2). In the 60s Long Street became the favourite place of Cape Towns (mostly white) "alternative people" with anti-apartheid connotations (Bickford-Smith, Heyningen & Worden 1999:193). There are also stories of urban decline with shabby buildings, drugs and other unwanted business. With the growing critique of modern city planning during the 70s Long Street became a treasure, and efforts were made to make Long Street a *conservation area* in the late 1970s, something that became a reality in 1992.

This of course had consequences for Long Street, as it now also was declared as a historical setting. This affected shop owner David in his struggle to keep crime from Long Street as he, during my fieldwork in 1999, was in the process of forming a Long Street Committee together with some other shop owners. One important reason for forming the committee was to make Long Street a CID, a *City Improvement District*. By this they could become a part of a collaboration project initiated by the *Cape Town City Council*.

One of the ambition with the CID-project was to create an urban environment that could become "safe, clean, attractive and user-friendly in order to reinforce the area as a premier retail, business, cultural or entertainment destination or a combination of these" (City Improvement Districts Association 1999). Tourism is essential in the discussion, seen as a possibility to survival and development for local businesses but also as a way to become a part of the world-economy by making images of South Africa as a presentable part of the world. This process can be seen as an important part of an ongoing negotiation on reality, not only on how Long Street is but also how the future must be visualised. David and his colleagues were making up new visions for the street that included all these different stories on how things are in Long Street. They incorporated the Victorian houses, night-clubs, "ethnic" restaurants and smart clothing with hippie-style from the 1960s, flee market and junkshops, but also keeping some of the "old" stores still there. The crime situation was always in the centre of the discussions, though, and the shop owners were constantly surrounded with physical statements of the dangers. Burglar bars, alarms and guards are constantly present in contemporary Cape Town, and the city, now supervised by CCTV, has itself become a statement about unpleasantness and insecurity. David had employed a guard to protect his store, and the guard had his orders to operate in a gentle way, only to talk to the kids, never to hit them. David was afraid of some of the ideas that during the time appeared in Long Street, as some of the other shop owners wanted to have guards on horses.

It was clear that many of the shop owners felt quite trapped in the situation, and street kids like William became a part of the threat in keeping Long Street attractive to the other citizens and to tourists. When the modern city in the 1970s became a Long Street dystopia, it now seems like *people* have overtaken that threatening position. You cannot any longer control the presence of people, and if it gets really bad David believed it can turn out like Johannesburg, where parts of CBD are considered to be "no-go-areas" – at least for some people.

"In Johannesburg it's changed, the street vendors in all the streets, you can hardly walk on the pavement... Cause the street vendors are all over the place, you can't even see the *shops* for the street vendors. Town is *dead* from a business point of view, from a first world business point of view, it's become third world completely, and that's what we're trying to avoid here in Cape Town. Okay, we have a long way to go before we get, because Cape Town is different, cause here you have... I talk about skin colour, because I don't know how to describe people otherwise. You have indigenous people that live in Cape Town, who are browned skinned. We call them coloured people, they are *wonderful* people, 95 percent of them are beautiful, wonderful people. And they are the majority of the people in the Western Cape. So when they come to town they're like first world people. They are not poor and they are not out to rob and rape and steal, there are some of them who are, obviously in every society you have that, but the majority of them are really, really nice people. And I say the majority of the black people are also very, very nice people, but the percentage of the crucks is *unfortunately* amongst the poorer people. And the poorer people are the black people. And that's why in Johannesburg you have this huge problem. In Cape Town we don't have that, but we're still protecting... I want to back Long Street, Long Street must be a destination for people" (Interview with David 16/09/1999).

## First World and Third World Long Street

First world people! A street for people, but the right kind of people. In a way the argument seems simple. Poor people making disorder becomes black people making disorder, and obviously race is still central in the construction of reality. As David pointed out, the concepts of skin colour are so close related to human interaction that it is almost not possible to describe people or social issues without using them. *I talk about skin colour because I don't know how to describe people otherwise.* It is possible to translate Judith Butler's claim that "the body comes in gender" to "the body comes in race" (Butler 1993:ix; Steyn 2001:x). Race becomes a paradox hard to handle in the developing new truth of democratisation, and in this process concepts of first world and third world are creating differences more of behavioural kind than actual skin colour. They become a possibility to dismantle old concepts, but also creating new ones.

The discourse psychologist Kevin Durrheim claims that a rejection of the third world became a consequence of a peace talk strategy in the beginning of the 1990s (Durrheim 1997:38). Third world became synonymous with *non-peace* and the concepts of first world and third world can be seen as symbols of wanted and unwanted behaviour in South Africa (Lakoff & Johnson 1980). First world stands for not only the peaceful but also the productive, positive and winning, an utopia for what South Africa might be like, while third world symbolises the dystopia of non-development, or destruction of what is already accomplished. In Long Street the first world vision melts together with a sort of almost laid-back atmosphere, a particular kind of first world vision. The backpackers are quite typical for the street, young people travelling quite freely, not necessarily with a lot of money but with interest in interaction and the features of the street, hopefully honest, open minded and with friendly manners. Long Street appears as alternative also in relation to the traditional "white" South African administration, a part of an apartheid structure that is described as more related to a third world bureaucracy, stiff an inflexible. Long Street becomes a loophole for the shop owners, an alternative in-between the two third world metaphors of (black) third world deviance and (white) third world, "old-fashioned" business culture. The dichotomy of "first" and "third" world introduces en element of temporal lag in the categorisation of the social landscape. Some groups and behaviours represent the past.

The German historian Joachim Schlör pictures the city as a kind of laboratory for modernity, where new ideas are constantly challenging old ones, and Long Street can be seen as such a process, where apartheid becomes the springboard for profiling the new South Africa (Schlör 1998:18). The idea of the first world becomes part of a growing discourse that is creating a new cultural and economic front in Cape Town. Long Street becomes a laboratory with cosmopolitan connotations that reaches beyond the nation borders, with participants that are able to combine smart Rastafarian hairstyles with smart business. At the same time it is a shaky laboratory work, where you can (or want) no longer control the unwanted through deportation, as the same time as you're not sure about what to do instead.

"It's all democracy now, which is wonderful. I love it, it's great. But you find that people… You can't, *everybody* has the right, you can't say: "you can't stand here", because he *can* stay there if he wants to… but as long as he don't hassle anybody" (Interview with David 16/09/1999).

Even though most of the shop-owners in Long Street welcomes the democracy it is obvious that the changes also creates feelings of uncertainty. Fear is not only a feeling related to the crime situation, but also the fear of loosing control of the development process, manifested in the daily encounters with unwanted behaviour in Long Street. The third world becomes the "otherness", being part of something that you neither can nor want to identify with. First world behaviour becomes the "we do" and third world behaviour becomes "they do". So what do "they do" – the street kids for instance?

## Street Kids and Third World Behaviour

The kids are indeed just as present in Long Street as colourful shops and tourists. Different ages and different sizes they have one thing in common – they have all black or coloured skin. They are often described as dirty, dishonest, unpredictable and sometimes violent, the total opposite of what Long Street Committee wants to accomplish. At the same time they seem to be victims of poverty, bad education, bad parenting and racial division which call for sensitivity and rescue.[5] A way of dealing with the issue represents *Homestead*, a hostel for boys a few blocks away from Long Street.[6] One day when I joined Max, one of the shop owners, to visit the shops in his block to try to get more shop-owners involved in the Long Street Committee, we bumped into Jonah. Jonah was living at the Homestead, and for the moment he was begging for money outside Seven Eleven on the top of Long Street. When he recognised me from visiting the hostel he quickly withdrew his hand, looking a bit embarrassed. They were not supposed to beg when they stayed at the hostel, and this was indeed a bit confusing. Why did he ask for money when he got food and clothes at the hostel? One hour later I found Jonah and a friend further down Long Street and as they did not seem to disagree I joined them in their walk down Long Street.

Jonah did not know that Long Street is Long Street. To him it was just the "street below there", a place to go where things happens, not really a street you have a special love for or considering to be *home*. To walk with him and the other Homestead boys made it clear that they had a strong sense of using the place, walking in groups in the streets and pedestrians, crossing the roads by cruising between cars in a total, as it seems, lack of fear. Almost like it was unconscious, a well learned lesson about the relation between body and environment. They seemed to get around the whole city; you could find them here and there, always streetwise and careless. But if you asked them for a street by using its name, many of them seemed to have a hard time to understand what you talked about. Later in the same afternoon I met some of the other boys, a small group between maybe seven and ten years, as they were sitting on the pavement at a street corner in a state of total boredom.

"Nothing happens, they declare. One of the boys eats a cookie. He takes small pieces to make it last as long as possible. They do not want to be at the Homestead today. It is boring. Nobody is there. One of the small boys is pulling the lattice to the well in the street. The other boys look a bit amused for a short while. Then it is boring again. When I ask the boy if he knows people in the shops he nods his head. He got the cookie from the café behind us.

–And in that butchery you get pieces of biltong...

Explains the boy as he is pointing at one of the shops on the other side of Long Street. Now he seems a bit amused, like this conversation makes more sense to him than questions about places and street names" (Walk-about with Max, Jonah and friends 04/12/1999).

It seems clear that places to these children were a tool to get in contact with people. Even though these boys were on their own, they still interacted with and depended on others. Cape Towns street kids become formed by the interaction, but also of the city in itself, as they gather at places where things are happening and leave when the city gets empty. Boredom becomes an essential part of life, more of a state of nothingness than the temporality you feel when you have more interesting future plans to stage. *People* definitely seems to be more central in the spatial organisation than the place in itself, they probably get around better in the central Cape Town than most of the citizens – only from another perspective. It is hard to imagine Jonah talking about the Long Street as a place with a certain, emotional value, or create realistic visions about what to do there next week or in ten years. To have a perspective on both time and place you need both skills to plan for the future and be able to create emotional bounds both to other people and the place you live in – skills that very few of the street kids have had possibilities to develop.

Michel de Certeau uses the concepts of *strategy* and *tactics* to clarify different kinds of actions. Strategy is connected to institutions, and a particular form of management of power, something that makes forms and frames for other peoples possibilities to use the city, like city planning, traffic regulation, law making, security and surveillance cameras. Tactics, on the other hand, becomes what happens when people improvises and uses these condition in a creative way, not necessarily like it was meant to be (de Certeau 1984:xix). The street kids are to a great extent using the latter aspect to take place in the city, and this can also be related to Alberto Meluccis discussion on time. Melucci makes a division between the inner "floating" time with dreams and associations, and the socially organised time with beginnings and ends, repeated cycles and frames for interaction (Melucci 1996:18). These concepts seem to be related and it is symptomatic that learning how to tell the time is one of the first skills to conquer in the Homesteads informal school *Learning to live*. To *learn to live* is among other things to be able to make concepts about socially constructed (strategic) time and eventually be able to create stable frames for social interaction that other people can relate to. Being incorporated in a general idea about *how things are* but also develop emotional bonds. Important in this process is to be able to *place the time*, to settle personal experiences and memories as well as socially organised conceptions in the city, and as a consequence make places and people meaningful in a more permanent sense. In a way the kids in Long Street seems to live in a floating time situation, with no clear beginnings and ends. More than creating permanent relations, they seem to live in a different world, where random opportunities become not only the tool to survival but also the reality in itself. In a way it creates a different reality, a different city and a different Long Street. It became clear when we walked down the street that the reason for begging was the game shop further down the road. A perfect example of how to use opportunities that turns up. Begging is a quite easy thing to do, if you are used to it, just put up your hand and hope for the best – a random event.

The street kids hanging around Long Street can be seen as tactics to the extreme, living in a ongoing improvisation to estimate and take advantage of the situations that occur but with no skills to relate to strategic formalisations, neither according to time or place In that sense the story about David and William appears different. What David *really* offered was hard for him to relate to, handling it from *his* perspective – like another random event, like a temporary loophole. Probably appreciate it but with no skills to make the situation permanent, something that for David, more familiar with strategic thinking, was very difficult to handle or to even understand. He did not know what to do.

## Balancing Concepts I

If we relate this discussion to the two concepts first world and third world behaviour, it seems like the street kids very well fit into this concept of "otherness" and the dystopia of third world behaviour. This is a threat to the vision of creating an attractive Long Street as a part of an attractive Cape Town, but the solution is perhaps not totally rejecting third world. It was quite obvious that the members in the Long Street Committee somehow tried to incorporate third world people informally. Quite often I could see poorly dressed men sweeping the street, or just sit to keep an eye on what's going on. It is clear that a number of "poor" or even "homeless people" was quite integrated in the life on Long Street in a permanent sense, becoming employed by the shop owners to do different kinds of work. When I walked with Max it was interesting to see how he greeted and talked to a lot of people, from other shop-owners to men sitting in the street. And he did not necessarily see them as a problem or a threat:

"I don't have any objections to street people, I just object to laws that prevent them from working and allows them to only exist by committing crime. If they would be allowed to polish shoes, if they were allowed to carry delivery, you know, as you can do in any other third world country" (Walk-about with Max, Jonah and friends 04/12/1999).

From Max's perspective we get another angle of the third world concept. If you can incorporate the third world concept into the first world vision, making it productive in a sense, it becomes a part of the street without destroying the vision of Long Street. Proper third world behaviour is in that context to subordinate first world values, and to use it in a way that encourages it rather than work against it. Steeling and begging is typical examples of improper third world behaviour, as well as polishing shoes and sweeping the street becomes the opposite. The biggest problem with the kids is not necessarily their poverty, but the bad impact they have on the streetscape, using it in an apparently active way and taking threatening advantages of different situations. It seems like the idea of first world and third world also have to do with *balance* between these concepts, and that the two lifestyles might exist side by side as long as the third world does not undermine the foundation of the first world vision. Keeping *third world* in control rather than totally rejecting it. But it is also a critic of the strategic, rulemaking government as the actual *creator* of the negative outcomes of third world. By not being able to adapt to the new situation in Cape Town they are making it hard for people to survive, making them commit to crime or informal business. Maybe becoming what has already happened in Johannesburg. The members in the Long Street Committee were stuck in-between the wish to get rid of the problems and the urge to solve them. It is a negotiation process that in the post apartheid society seriously challenges old borders and old conceptualisations, putting people in painful uncertainty on *how things are* and *how people are*. And it makes the issue about presence in the street very obvious, putting conflicts and negotiations at the frontline, conflicts that also exist in Malmö. Where to be, when and how to behave – in the mutual agreement on *how things are* in the streets of Malmö – and Möllevången which indeed, just like Long Street, represents a possibility for different lifestyles.

## Perspectives on Möllevången

Möllevången is seated about two kilometres from the centre of Malmö, and was mainly built 1900–1940 with quite traditional block of flats and some factories, quite many of the buildings with brick facing. In the centre of the area is a square, Möllvångstorget, seated, in many ways also the most common representation of the area. Möllevången became a place for working class movement during the 1920s, with a number of well-remembered conflicts between workers and factory owners. It was an area that seemed to manifest a kind of "working class pride", a kind of brief indication of the long time rule of the Social Democrat Party that was to come. But Möllevången was already in the 1940s considered to be in a state of declination, and many of the more well situated workers moved into the new parts of the city where open functionalistic style became a manifestation of the "modern folk home"(Billing & Stigendal 1994; Ristilammi 1994). In the 1960s the area more and more, just like Long Street, became a possibility to develop "alternative" lifestyles, but also a rising rate of drug addicts and social problems. In the 1970s Möllevången was seen as a quite dilapidated area from the authorities point of view (and many inhabitants of the city as well). In many ways placed at the backside of Swedish modernity, honestly more in interest of social workers and the police than seen as a possibility to represent a positive view of the city of Malmö (Högdahl 2003:66).

Today the picture of Möllevången has changed a lot, as industry is gone and the visions of the city are symbolised by the new bridge crossing Öresund to Denmark and the rest of Europe (Idvall 2000). Even if considered to still having a lot of problems with drugs, unemployment and social deviation, Möllevången is seen as a mixture with options in the new Sweden, as a part of the world rather than the homogenised and isolated (but modern) folk home. In for instance tourist books, the description of Malmö has been changed from the functionalistic modern city to a cityscape focusing more on the chaotic, mobile and messy in a positive sense (Andström 2000; Lundh & Sandblad 1950). In frontline of this new position are to a large extent the immigrants, very visible in Möllevången by the many small groceries and gift shops with imported products from all over the world. This have been incorporated in the old setting and the alternative lifestyle has partly transformed into a new modernity of tolerance, with more obvious smartness, often reflected as for instance festivals, carnivals, pubs and different kind of music events. The market at Möllevången square has become one of the most popular pictures in the marketing of the city of Malmö, providing with a kind of "unswedish" touch. In this sense the vision of the colourful immigrant also provides with an opportunity to challenge the traditional picture of the Swede – as being to rational, to stiff, to quiet, to shy and to boring. This is indeed a springboard for launching of the new *cosmopolitan Malmö* – a city with tolerance, spontaneity and ability to reach out, both to different parts of the world and different ways of living. In that sense the situation reminds a lot about Long Street in Cape Town, South Africa. As well as in Long Street there are also fears, and Möllevången appears as a polarisation, with tolerance and positive diversion at one side, and deviation and criminality on the other that sometimes melts together with concepts of "otherness" in the negative sense. Möllevången becomes a challenge to ideas on *how things are* in Malmö, a kind of quite positive representation of tolerance that also raises question about presence and under what circumstances this might be done. As well as Long Street Möllevången appears as a balancing act, and if the immigrants often are viewed as a positive contribution to the cosmopolitan lifestyle, it is harder to include the down-and-outs in this picture. During my fieldwork I followed some of them, trying to understand the concept of third world in a Swedish context.

## Perceiving the Down-and-outs

The down-and-outs, often referred to as "drunks" in daily interactions, are indeed a group marked by long time ambivalence in the city. Similar to the street kids they are seen as both disturbing elements and victims of circumstances. Not so often seen as direct cause of serious situations of violence, but definitely hard to transform to an appetising presence in the street, as they are marked and conceptualised by filth, unpredictability and outbursts of bad behavioural manners. They represent, as well as the street kids in Cape Town, a category that is quite hard to relate to and to handle from both authority and the other people in the street. Like the street kids the drunks seem to basically conduct what de Certeau calls *tactics of the weak,* where they have to take advantage of opportunities with the obvious risk of getting rejected (de Certeau 1984:xix). Even though Möllevången is considered to be a place of tolerance, it is obvious that there are certain limits. A few years ago the benches close to the square were removed. Åke, one of the homeless men I interviewed in Möllevången, claimed it was the "drunks" own fault, behaving improper by being there to many at the same time, yelling, drinking and bring in weapons. Especially Åke who had lived a big part of his life in the area had a strong sense of the environment and street life. For him, as well as the other inhabitants, Möllevången was a living field of memories where different places symbolised different phases in his own life. As Michel de Certeau has pointed out, memory is indeed a very important part making *space* in the city, as memory makes the places become haunted with meanings, and de Certeau claims that *haunted places* are the only ones possible to really live in (de Certeau 1984:108). To Åke Möllevången was definitely haunted with personal memories not only of the life as a homeless but also of normality. The flat he used to live in with Eva before they moved out in the street and the playgrounds where his children used to play. They had, among other memories, become time markers of Åke's personal life, which made it possible to create time tables of his life which creates possibilities to orientate in reality. This also creates a strong sense of what is normal behaviour and when these borders are crossed over. The Swedish "drunks" are aware of a more obvious consensus on the discourse of *how things are*, where they themselves are able to put up limits for their presence in the street. A little park at the outskirts of the area, called Jesus Park (for a reason I have not really been able to figure out) becomes a perfect loophole.

Usually the drunks meet there to drink and talk, and in summer they periodically almost live in the park, sleeping at the benches or in the bushes. As time has passed Jesus Park in storytelling has become a "messy" place to many people living in the area. By using *kairos*, being in the right place at the right time, the "drunks" has transformed the park into another kind of normality, a permanent place for the down-and-out community. Other places are not so easy to transform. A more attractive place represents the Triangle Square a few blocks away, quite close to the very centre of Malmö. This place, though, has more obvious conditions as it is to be shared with the other inhabitants in the city.

## Claiming Space in The Triangle

The Triangle is visualising another kind of physical landscape than Möllevången, with multiple stores and a small square with a hot dog stand. The people who pass by uses a sort of rounded pedestrian along the side of the square and the two areas are divided by a small wall. Along this wall you can also find a lot of park benches, following the division line on the open "square side", with quite good view of the activities going on and in convenient distance to the liqueur store about one block away. Åke and some of the other drunks usually met there during the weeks when the liqueur store is opened, always sitting on the bench furthest away from the sausage store and the pedestrian. Åke explained why they choose this particular bench:

"– I know Tomas who has the sausage store and well, he's said that don't sit in front of it, so we sit over here and then we can sit here and drink too.

– As long as you hold your mouth and take it easy it is no problem. But as soon as somebody starts to scream and yell and things like that, then somebody always gives a roar, says Per, a friend of Åke.

A few meters away Åke has made a picture in blue with crayons at the pavement and nobody seems to have any objections to this. But what is important is to not *pee* or in other ways make a mess. Tobbe, another friend, explains that he usually uses a hamburger store on the other side of the square, well known for a tolerant attitude to the homeless people in the area, and he also tries to look after for the others behaviour.

–I usually cleans here as well, if he pukes I'll take care of it...

It is not always easy to keep up the good shape, though, even if most of them know the limits for proper behaviour, the escalating drunkenness introduces chaos into the good intentions and it might sometimes be hard to remember behavioural orders. Today one of the men is too drunk to go to Stippes and he pees openly at the side of the bench. No one of the bypasses says anything, some of them are gazing at the activity taking place and a lady is staring with harsh eyes. Some people are respectfully looking down, pretending like nothing unusual is going on. The critical gaze as well as sound protests definitely becomes important in defining the improper behaviour and Tobbe looks a bit embarrassed as he sits on the bench. Some activities, though, definitely passes the limits of the acceptable. Åke, in a state of complete drunkenness, wants to move to another bench in front of the sausage store.

—Come, lets sit in the sun...

—No, I don't want to go to the sun.

—But over there, it's only...

—Only what? I will warm you, come on Åke, put on your jacket, I don't want to go there. Over there everybody is sitting with prams and everything. Should we sit there and drink?

—No, not there, on the first bench...

—But there are two old crones sitting there...

Children, families and "old crones" have priority to drunks, Olle knows that and so does Åke, even though he has forgotten for the moment. You can't occupy a place already taken, there is no loophole there to use, and eventually it could lead to loss of the already accomplished permanency of the other bench" (Interview with Åke and friends 04/12/1999).

It was obvious that the drunks, like the street kids in Long Street, could reach a kind of presence which seemed to call for restrictions. But it is also important to point out that there is a negotiable line between total acceptance and rejection, and that ideas about vulnerability, citizenship rights and visions of tolerance in some case have been in advantage for the drunks. One day in the Triangle a man approached Åke and the others on the bench, giving him some folded up bills.

"– Here you have 60 crowns...
– Hello...
– I've been down there myself, so...
Åke is almost interrupts the man in his eagerness and then he is giving Henrik instructions to go to the liqueur store, probably not what the man had in mind.
– I've been living in Celsiusgården (a place for alcohol treatment), he tries.
– Yes, hi brother, I'm Åke... Thank you brother, have a nice day... it was so nice of you...
– I know what it's like...
And Åke does not have to beg this day and he is enthusiastic.
– They feel *sorry* for you, Åke, *they feel sorry for you*...
Henrik says with a humorous irony in his voice" (Interview with Åke and friends 16/09/1998).

## Balancing Concepts II

Both the drunks in Möllevången and the street kids in Long Street might be related to the concept of *floating significants*, as the content of their presence is not related to an overall fixed meaning, and their presence seems to be inscribed by a manifold of values, depending on who was talking and under what circumstances (Winther Jørgensen & Phillips 1999:35). Different discourses and different statements were manifested, and how the place was considered to be was of big significance for how the people were allowed to be. It is quite clear that the drunks as well as the children in the every day life might be connected with feelings of unpleasantness, something that might result in rejections but also possible to use as a loophole to gain advantages. It is also obvious that they were operating in a different context and with different skills. Even though the difference is of course also a result of young age, it was quite visible that the drunks were more aware of the strategic aspects in the places. The drunks were in comparison more skilled to make up plans in relation to the condition of the places and the people in a more "ordered" sense. The children, on the other hand, seemed to operate from a totally tactical point of view with no real knowledge of the strategic aspects of the city. They were constantly breaking the rules without really knowing it and became unpredictable in their total tactical behaviour. They did not know what de Certeau refers to as *the law of the proper* in different places (de Certeau 1984:21). The drunks in Malmö seemed, unless they were too drunk, to be more skilled to carry out the (Long Street) vision of a proper third world behaviour, as they seemed to subordinate (first world) normality values. By doing so they were to a larger extent than the street kids, able to use *kairos* to make a more permanent occupation of a place without getting rejected. It makes certainly an interesting perspective on tactics, and what it means to be streetwise in a successful way. It is clear that Åke and his friends have been able to incorporate themselves into the order of the city, knowing not only their obligation but also their rights. The street kids seem impossible to incorporate in the vision for Long Street, impossible to transform into neither first world people nor proper third world behaviour.

## Conclusion

The reason for me to pick up the concepts of first world and third world from the shop-owners in Long Street and use them to discuss presence in the street in Cape Town and Malmö, is not to claim that Sweden has a problematic in the same sense as South Africa. My aim is not to discuss uneven distribution of resources in a global sense; I rather want to view them as "folk concepts" in the everyday life. Above all they represent a time and space dichotomy between the past and the future, and they also represent a power relation where people enters the everyday negotiation with different legitimacy and therefore have different options to make an impact in the streetscape. The problems of South Africa might seem far away, but the power related every-day negotiations are as well present in our own backyard. It is not only the "drunks" in Möllevången that are accused of being out of place and time. "Third world behaviour" is also now and then affecting the immigrant community, and it could also possible to view the discussion in the context of gender. Such processes of inclusion and exclusion is possible to observe in many European urban settings, as certain neighbourhoods balance between the "colourful" and the "disorderly". Some of these urban areas are, as well as Long Street, moving towards a "touristification" with problems of gentrification – others are stuck in being seen as unmanageable problem areas.

The conditions for people taking place in the city certainly put de Certeaus concept of *space* into a different view. If "space is like the word when it is spoken" one might wonder whether people can, may or want to speak even the same language (de Certeau 1984:117). Narrative is definitely an important element in the process of doing the street, with texts, personal experiences, and hearsay all filling their specific functions at different levels. From this perspective it is interesting to consider if *other people* are invited to be participants, or to become in order. How we "make" people and interpret human presence creates notions not only about *what people are like*, but also about *what it is possible for them to do*. This affects city life and its rhythm in that it ultimately leads to conditions of emptiness, presence, silence, or noise. This also gives a broad understanding of the concepts of discourse and power, since discourse ranges far beyond the world of language and power can scarcely be seen solely from a "top-down" perspective. In fact, it includes every aspect of everyday interaction and it is communally legitimated by those who ascribe the same kind of knowledge. The idea of *what things are like* is a kind of habituated point of departure for the interpretation of existence, but it is obvious that this is in constant change.

The city and its inhabitants are in a constantly ongoing learning process through which mental maps are drawn and redrawn.

The possibility of using loopholes is an important reason for the constant shifts which take place in everyday life and which can also lead to permanent change. The loopholes are an important part of what could be called *the democracy of the city*, a potential to negotiate in a public dialogue that seems rather informal but scarcely non-political. South Africa under apartheid has made clear the very serious consequences of preventing people from establishing loopholes, since the vision of the racially segregated city made it almost entirely impossible for a large share of the inhabitants to change their private life situation or to question the prevailing order. Repressing people who have no chance of participating via dialogue or negotiation generates obvious feelings of powerlessness, while also risking that acts will be performed outside the "legitimate" negotiation arenas. Limits have to be made to keep the street and the city somehow in order, but in this process we constantly need to question the conditions by which the public dialogue is carried on. Particularly those elements that are taken for granted, and it is important to ask oneself by what techniques it is created and whose interests it actually furthers.

## Notes

1. This text is created from an interview with David 16/09/1999. I am using pseudonyms in this article, for all people interviewed.
2. This was carried out especially through the legislation of *Group Areas Act* where the population was divide in different race groups and forced to live in different parts of the city. The legislation from 1950 divided Cape Town, as well as other South African cities, into separated race group sections, that by the geographer John Western are referred to as the developing of *etno-city*, a kind of apartheid modernity vision (Western 1996:64). Categorisation of race combined with exclusion was of course the most effective way to implement apartheid, even though it never was legitimised through the whole population as the defeat proved in the beginning of the 1990s (Levett 1997:3).
3. I used both these areas as empirical examples in my PhD-dissertation *Doing the Street. On Borders and Loopholes in Möllevången and in Cape Town* (Högdahl 2003).

4. Big squatter camps had since long time ago developed at the outcast of Cape Town, as desperate black people saw the city as the only possibility to make a living. Often to be sent back to the places they came from in the countryside or to the constructed homelands that had been set up by the National Party government in an effort to solve the issue of the unwanted part of the population. (Beinart & Dubow 1995; Reynolds 1989; Unterhalter 1987; Western 1996).
5. According to social worker Heather Parker Lewis, stereotyping and labelling the children is one way of coping emotionally with the feeling of uncomfortable guilt (Parker Lewis 1998:14; Rock 1997:14f).
6. Some of the children at Homestead stay there for quite a long time, go to the informal school and finally move to the children's home and hopefully become a part of the "established society", but a majority of them stay there only for a short while. Spring and summer are the best seasons for a street kid with a lot of tourists to beg and steal from, entertainment and warm nights to sleep outside.

# References

Andström, Bobby 2000: *Malmö – stad i världen*. Malmö: Författaren och Anders Rahm Bokproduktion.
Arendt, Hannah 1986: *Människans villkor. Vita activa*. Göteborg: Röda Bokförlaget.
Beinart, William & Dubow, Saul 1995: *Segregation and Apartheid in Twentieth-century South Africa*. London/New York: Routledge.
Bickford-Smith, Vivian, Heyningen, Elizabeth & Worden, Nigel 1999: *Cape Town – in the Twentieth Century*. Claremont/Cape Town: David Philip Publishers.
Billing, Peter & Stigendal, Mikael 1994: *Hegemonins decennier. Lärdomar från Malmö och den svenska modellen*. Malmö: Möllevångens Samhällsanalys.
Butler, Judith 1993: *Bodies that Matter. On the Discursive Limits on "Sex"*. London/New York: Routledge.
*Cape Times,* Top of the Times 28/02/1997.
de Certeau, Michel 1984: *The Practice of Everyday Life*. Berkeley/Los Angeles: University of California Press.
City Improvement Districts Association, Cape Town 1999.
Durrheim, Kevin 1997: Peace Talk and Violence: An Analysis of the Power of "Peace". In: Levett, Ann (ed.): *Culture, Power & Difference. Discourse Analysis in South Africa*. Cape Town: UCT Press.
Foucault, Michel 2002: *Vetandets arkeologi*. Lund: Arkiv förlag.
Green, Lawrence G. 1971: *A Taste of South Easter*. Cape Town: Howard Timmins.
Idvall, Markus 2000: *Kartors kraft. Regionen som samhällsvision i Öresundsbrons tid*. Lund: Nordic Academic Press.
Högdahl, Elisabeth 2003: *Göra gata. Om gränser och kryphål på Möllevången och i Kapstaden*. Hedemora: Gidlunds.
Lakoff, George & Johnson, Mark 1980: *Metaphors we Live by*. Chicago: The University of Chicago Press.
Levett, Ann 1997: Introduction. In: Levett, Ann (ed.): *Culture, Power & Difference. Discourse Analysis in South Africa*. Cape Town: UCT Press.
Lundh, Gunnar & Sandblad, N. G. 1950: *Malmö – ett bildverk*.
Melucci, Alberto 1996: *The Playing Self. Person and Meaning in the Planetary Society*. Cambridge: Cambridge University Press.
Parker Lewis, Heather 1998: *Also God's Children? Encounters with Streetkids*. Cape Town: Ihilihili Press.
Reynolds, Pamela 1989: *Childhood in Crossroads. Cognition and Society in South Africa*. Cape Town/Johannesburg: David Philip Publishers.
Ristilammi, Per-Markku 1994: *Rosengård och den svarta poesin. En studie av modern annorlundahet*. Stockhom/Stehag: Symposion.
Rock, Brian 1997: *Spirals of Suffering: Public Violence and Children*. Pretoria: HSRC Publishers.
Schlör, Joachim 1998: *Nights in the Big City. Paris, Berlin, London 1840–1930*. London: Reaktion Books.
Shaw, Mark 2002: *Crime and Policing in the Post-Apartheid South Africa. Transforming under Fire*. Cape Town: David Philips Publishers.
Steyn, Melissa 2001: *Whiteness Just Isn't What It Used to Be*. New York: State University of New York Press.
Tshiwula, Lullu 1998: *Crime and Delinquency*. Pretoria: Kagiso Publishers.
Unterhalter, Elaine 1987: *Forced Removal. The Division, Segregation and Control of the People of South Africa*. London: IDAF Publications Ltd.
Western, John 1996: *Outcast Cape Town*. Los Angeles: University of California Press.
Winther Jørgensen, Marianne & Phillips, Louise 2000: *Diskursanalys som teori och metod*. Lund: Studentlitteratur.

*Interviews*
Åke and friends 16/09/1998
David 16/09/1999
Walk-about with Max, Jonah and friends 04/12/1999

# Haunting Experiences of Images
## Blind Spots and Fantasy-Frames in the Mass Mediated Suburb

*Urban Ericsson*

In the early sixties, the Social Democratic party launched the so called million-programme. It aimed at addressing the housing shortage. Instead of maintaining worn out inner-city apartments, new suburbs were designed to house a million people. This specific political ambition was achieved. But during the construction of the suburbs, and in the aftermath of the project, the public reacted and questions were asked. The suburb thus became an arena for political controversies. Up to this day, the suburb is host to narratives about society. The million-programme was supposed to mean housing for all, and represent "Folkhemmet" – the welfare-state – as defined by the Social Democratic party. At the beginning these areas were national symbols for ideas about "Swedishness" and the future. It wasn't only a housing programme, but a reform programme that aimed towards and prepared to take Sweden into the future. Nature and natural elements were used to build the self-image of Swedishness into the very architecture of the new housing. The suburb was portrayed as a national event – even though similar high-rise buildings and large scale neighbourhoods were also springing up in many parts of Europe.

Critics thought that the high-rise buildings were anonymous and created a hostile environment. Certain suburbs were soon singled out by the Swedish press, and connected to certain stereotyped images. Major city suburbs were represented in the mass media as places were unemployment, criminality, anonymity and other alarming social tendencies could be witnessed daily. The suburb thus became a problem. In addition, migrants living in these areas became increasingly represented by the mass media as images of the Other. As a result, the suburb no longer represented Sweden's future but an attempt at integration into Swedishness. The geographical positioning of the suburbs – on the outskirts of a city – had become metaphorically associated with outside societies in terms of Immigrants and Ethnic groups. Such images had previously been reserved for the working class, but from the late seventies and early eighties, the ethnic element became increasingly emphasised in mass mediated narrations. It had become a place for the Other.

The concept of Otherness is built into the definition of a city, in that people who pass each other in the street are strangers. The mass media has therefore been important in that it enabled people to get to know city areas they had no connection with. Narratives about other parts of the city can, on the one hand, lead to a feeling of intimacy with the stranger, although on the other hand, such representations can also have the opposite effect. I have therefore analysed the imagery of the Swedish suburb with this in mind.

In this article I will use Slavoj Žižek's notion of the *fantasy-frame,* together with Avery F. Gordon's discussion about *blind spots* and *haunting experiences,* to explain the representations of the Swedish suburbs in the mass media. It all boils down to what it is like to live in the shadow images of the stigmatised suburb and how such images are dealt with. These experiences are dealt with in different ways, depending on the relationship to the suburb and the relationship to the mass media. In this article, the examples of Maya, who lives in Gottsunda, a suburb in Uppsala, and the football player, Zlatan Ibrahimovic, from Rosengård in Malmö, illustrate different ways of dealing with the suburban fantasy-frame – something that they face daily. I will describe how both the viewer and the portrayed articulate relations of power in mass mediated images. The article also focuses on the observer's production of the suburban space. By using this approach I hope to show that the mass media confronts both the observer and the portrayed with images that become real in the sense that they have to be dealt with. Media becomes practice.

## The Haunting Experience of Emptiness

Looking through a window is a peculiar form of mixing distance with closeness and is, I think, like reading a newspaper or watching TV, in that short and fragmented glimpses of life appear before the reader or observer. The pane of glass allows you to see everything, and in that respect everything seems close, although there is no actual opportunity to take part in the activities outside. The window is a filter that divides seeing from doing and inside from outside, with distinct boundaries between text and practice. But these dichotomies are too simplistic if one is to take account of the multitude of relationships that exist between viewer and performer. What happens on the other side of a pane of glass – the reality that the viewer beholds – can be described in terms of Žižek's *fantasy-frame*. Drawing on Hitchcock's *Rear Window,* he outlines a concept for an understanding of the attention that recognises the power of seeing and the techniques of perception. A fantasy-frame involves a scenario where the performer has to act in line with the spectators' expectations in order to become visible and recognised. James Stewart's character in *Rear Window* is physically connected to his apartment in that he has broken his leg and there is nothing else to do but look out at the backyard activities of his neighbours and into the daily lives of people living in the other apartments. This occupies all his time, and one night, he suspects that a neighbour kills his wife. This window becomes his fantasy window. Everything that he sees through the window captivates his hopes and his desires. The window becomes the media for seeing and that self-made filter becomes a prerequisite for seeing. At first, no one believes in the story. His girlfriend, played by Grace Kelly, at first doubts his speculations. She wants him to stop imagining things and instead concentrate on their relationship. Her wish to develop their relationship becomes a hindrance to him and a spot that disturbs his view, as she does not fit into his fantasy. In order to get into his life and evoke his desires, she has to act within his fantasy. She does that by leaving the apartment and crossing the backyard, thus becoming visible to Stewart's gaze through the window. Her absence and re-appearance then fit into his fantasy-frame. It all became possible when she became a part of the scenery, or the plot, that he had invented (Žižek 1989:139). This sequence in Žižek's analysis is important, I think, in connection with the mass mediated narratives of the Swedish suburb and the portrayal of the immigrant as a stereotype character within that blind field of Otherness. The suburb can, when looked at from a window, or on mass mediated screens, be regarded as a space and frame, and thus comparable to Stewart's character looking down at the backyard. One of the major features in Stewart's character is that he has to keep and make a distance so that he can come close. It is very much like Boorstin writing about the tourist and the tourist's relationship to the exotic and foreign. The tourist's appetite for what is foreign is satisfied when the preconception of foreignness is verified (Boorstin 1992:109).

I will now describe a recent event that made me conscious of the importance of mass mediated images – and will use this scene as an introduction in examining the impact of mass mediated images and how the understanding of Otherness is created by the observer's imagination of the Other.

*Looking at the Blind Spot*

Maya and I were standing in her daughter's bedroom, looking out across Stenhammar Park. Pine covered slopes and children's playground areas were visible. The houses surrounding the park could be discerned through the leafy tops of the trees. Children walked along one of the footpaths, busily looking into each other's bags of sweets. Just in front of the window was a rather big lawn. Two girls came running to fetch a forgotten football.

Such suburban views always take me by surprise. While these ordinary, or trivial, scenes of what is happening outside a window in the reality of everyday life in the suburb catch my attention, I am aware that something is missing. On this occasion I found myself waiting, rather intensively, for something to happen. Even though things were happening in front of me, there was something missing. This "waiting for something to happen" feeling made me curious. It made me think about how different happenings are associated with different spaces, and if "nothing" occurs it is signal that the viewer lacks the ability to see. It is as if the viewer is blinded by his, or her, own way of looking at an event. Every window is an invitation to see. This view of nothing, or emptiness, triggered my expectations and in doing so also made me see my preconceived notions of this particular space. I had this reflection in mind when I started to talk to Maya, who was still looking out of the window. I told her that this view supposedly took in one of the most crime-ridden areas in the neighbourhood. She said:

"Yes I know, but it is hard to understand. I've been living here for over a year. I moved to this apartment last spring and I have never seen or heard anything. I'm never afraid to walk along the pathways at night. I think this is a beautiful neighbourhood. It is close to the day nursery, and only a few minutes walk to the centre where all the services are. Hopefully I'll get a job there. That would be great. I know this area has a bad reputation, but I don't know why. I haven't seen anything."

While looking out of the window, Maya and I were sharing a view that was not ours but a kind of *re-memory*, recalling something we had never seen (Morrison 1987:36f; see Gordon 1997:165). It was as if we had already created an image which was not there, even though we were standing there talking about it and relating to it.

In her book, *Ghostly Matters,* the sociologist Avery F. Gordon sets out on a ghost hunt. She takes ghosts and haunting seriously, as they have real importance in both social life and sociological research. "Being haunted draws us affectively, sometimes against our will and always a bit magically, into the structure of feeling of a reality we come to experience, not as cold knowledge, but as transformative recognition" (Gordon 1997:8). In conjunction with Roland Barthes' reflections on photography, Gordon writes about blind spots and blind fields. In Barthes' terminology, these fields are called *punctum*. A detail in the picture disrupts the harmony and, in Gordon's analysis, it means that, paradoxically, invisible fields visualise or evoke a kind of seeing and understanding. Punctum is not an individual aesthetic experience, Barthes writes, but it manages to activate the dynamic in the blind field. "It is what I add to the photograph and what is nonetheless already there" (Barthes 1981:55; see Gordon 1997:107). These blind spots accentuate punctum, and are a way of making the invisible visible: "… when we catch a glimpse of its endowments in the paradoxical experience of seeing what appears to be not there we know that a haunting is occurring" (Gordon 1997:107).

Looking out over Stenhammar Park was a haunting experience. Maya and I were still talking about the neighbourhood and the positive things she felt about the suburb when she suddenly told me that she didn't want her daughter to grow up in this suburb, and they'd have to leave. I thought that was a surprising statement. She felt that she had to leave this beautiful place even though they both enjoy their living there. The statement came out of the blue. On the basis of what she had told me earlier, I thought that there was no real reason for this impatient desire to move. When asking her about that, and why she felt that way, she couldn't give me a direct answer. Maya did not agree with the dark images of the suburb, telling me that these images were mass mediated and didn't represent what it was really like to live there. Her eagerness to move away wasn't related to her actual experiences, but to the mass media's haunting images of crime, insecurity and bad reputation. This reflection can also be observed in other interviews with people in Gottsunda and relates to a daily and recurring questioning of the mass mediated images (Molina 1997:209). My waiting for something to happen was a waiting for the stereotyped mass mediated images of suburbs and immigrants to be played out in front of my eyes. In order to bring together both mine and Maya's feelings of the haunting emptiness of reality, and Gordon's theoretical approach to that same feeling, I will describe an event where a social worker talks about the suburb of Gottsunda in Uppsala, and especially the surroundings of Stenhammar Park – the very same park that Maya and I observed that afternoon.

*Mapping the White Spot*

The suburban scene was already set when we climbed the stairs from the vestibule to the conference room. Our guide talked about the shootings that had taken place a couple of months earlier. Someone had fired two shots into the hall, at night. She pointed to bullet holes in the wall. Perhaps the social worker was responding to the expectations of her audience. I couldn't help thinking that these holes in the wall were a kind of trademark for the social workers: a visit to a suburb known through the mass media for its problems with crime should contain these images. It was like a suburban ready-made.

The audience at this information were students and scholars who were there to listen to

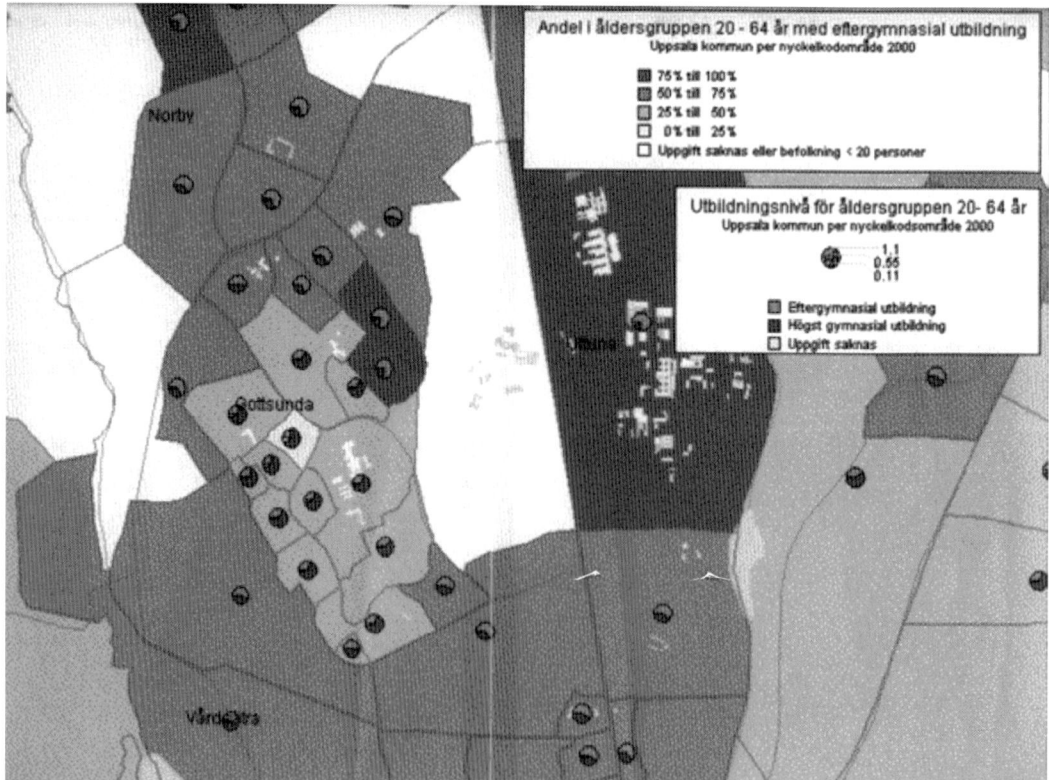

Fig. 1. Scanned copy of the original map. The area of Stenhammar Park and "the white spot" can be seen underneath the text, Gottsunda.

and learn about the demography of the suburb and how the area was to be integrated into society by different projects. The social worker began her presentation by showing us a local map. The map showed the distribution of the levels of education in the area. Different shades of green represented the education levels in the suburb – the deeper the green, the higher the education level. A white spot in the centre of the map immediately attracted our attention.

Benedict Anderson writes about the map as a technique of representation. The colouring of the map – where the imperial states portrayed the colonies in different colours to indicate ownership – emphasised the authority of the empire (Anderson 1991:175). The white spot on the map in the lecture room reflected another relationship to the state, and evoked a vision of Otherness. Even though some members of the audience wanted to unpack the notion of criminality and look into the underlying structures of the area, we could not get away from that white field; the blind spot that, paradoxically enough, couldn't be explained in any other way than that it didn't exist. It was like an invisible magnetic field that captured all our attention. Attempts to talk about something else were impossible. Even though the uncertainties were great, or just because of that, the gossip started. We heard about drug addicts' needles being found in the children's sandpits – the same story that was told in the suburb of Rosengård a couple of days later when another social worker gave a similar "suburban talk".

The map's borders, frames and colours brought matters to life. While the white areas represented very low education levels, it soon came to be understood as an area that neither the social workers, nor the local population had any knowledge about. The social worker explained how some efforts had been made to "come in" to this area. To those of us at the seminar – including the social worker – the configuration of the map seemed to represent a haunted space. Making maps and framing the suburb is an act of recognition. In the case of the white or blind spots of Gottsunda, it was a recognition of the lack, or absence, of knowledge. An intense emptiness was materialised in the map's white spot, as there was no expression or representation of people's informal space or what kind of education they had received before coming to Sweden.

The white colour functioned as a metaphor. In most narrations, the colour white evokes an image of innocence and purity. In this case, however, it signalled a desire to turn white into green. In a sense, it functioned as a visual technique to expel the feeling of being blind, or haunted.

## Displacing Emptiness – Making the Invisible Visible

Staging the suburb through the mass media does not just concern images of criminality and barren concrete environments, even though these aspects might lurk in the background (Ristilammi 1997; Dahlstedt 2004:4). In poets' docu-fictions, in musicians' lyrics and in mass mediated interviews with well-known individuals (all in some way identified with their migrant background and their relationship to the suburb), there are traces of another understanding; an active struggle with emptiness (dreams, fantasies) and an attempt to relay that emptiness to the viewer.

In typecast settings, where the suburb is the scene and the fronting individual performs or relates to that scene, the individual is described as a creative representative of the suburban culture. In such settings, the mass mediated suburb becomes the place where multicultural feelings are exposed to the viewer through entertaining dances, carnivals and flavours. In this kind of staging it is crucial to separate and disconnect the suburb from the surrounding society in order to make it viewable (see Stallybrass & White 1986:126ff). The multicultural is made separate and exclusive to the suburban space. The multicultural thus becomes something that those outside – in "normality" – look at but don't participate in (Ericsson 2001).

Graham Huggan writes about *staging the margins*, and asks whether articulation from the margins is a way to social change – and whether it can be called resistance or just reproduces the mainstream culture. Sometimes, representation from the margin is a result of a political and self-designated task, while at other times it is a designation from the mass mediated representatives. In both cases, however, it is the ones who stage the marginality that risk losing their credibility. Judgement is in the hands of the media and the spectator or reader (Huggan 2001:85). Every now and again, the mass media represents the long awaited suburban voice that finally gives a true picture of the suburban way of life. In these representations, the fantasy-frame is evident through the narrating structure of the mass mediated articles. The mass mediated images and texts about a celebrated Suburban Immigrant is a way of talking about Otherness in praise-filled articulations (see Marshall 1997). The fantasy-frame confirms the spectators' expectations by the way the individual is portrayed. Many of these celebrated individuals have to act against a haunting emptiness of Otherness (Ericsson 2003). Their doings are measured and understood in terms of results and shadows of their suburban past. Alexandra Pascalidou, writer and journalist, writes about her experiences of media in her book, *Frontkick*:

"As soon as the media expeditions came along to portray 'the suburb's losers', we knew what they were after. We therefore invited them to the spectacle they expected – or the opposite. When they started filming, my boy friends who were hanging around in the town centre, suddenly started to fight or shoplift to secure a few moments of fame on the TV screen. We either had to fight in order to be seen or mount a counter attack to glorify our existence. 'Rinkeby is best – no protest!'" (Pascalidou 2003:158).

The mimetic practice, as explained by Pascalidou, corresponds to the viewers' blind spots. It doesn't have to be as abstract as a white spot on a map, as these white spots or blind fields can be found in other sequences, as is shown in the above quotation, or in interviews where the focus is on the questions as well as the answers. Every question is, in a way, an attempt to fill the emptiness of not knowing. It is where, in the imagination (emptiness) of the observer, the scene is set. It leaves the performer or actor without any power other than to act within the viewer's fantasy frame, and paradoxically it is this portrayal that makes the fantasy real. The subject seems to be entangled in the stereotypes made for her/him. In order to discuss this power relation, the rest of the article will consider the footballer Zlatan Ibrahimovic's articulating strategies, and analyse the *media-graphy* surrounding him.

## Embodying the Suburb

The following headings are included to give a quick overview of the media narratives:

Zlatan Ready for Success (*Sydsvenska Dagbladet* 05/09/2002)
Zlatan's Magic Night (*Sydsvenska Dagbladet* 14/06/2004)
With Zuper-Zlatan the Team Will Never be out of Count (*Dagens Nyheter* 18/06/2004)
Zlatan Can be the Difference (*Expressen* 22/06/2004)

The footballer, Zlatan Ibrahimovic, who plays for the Italian football club, Juventus, is one of those highly recognised and celebrated individuals surrounded by a distinct fantasy-frame. In the Swedish mass mediated biographies, his immigrant and suburban background constantly reappears. In 1999 he made his debut for Malmö FF (FC) and, together with his team mates, took the team back to highest division after a short spell in the second division. Ibrahimovic became known as the person who made it all possible. The journalists made out that his brilliant footballing skills were a result of his suburban background. Just as place and the individual intermingle, Ibrahimovic's ascribed characteristics were, and still are, to be understood in relation to the stereotype of the suburb and the Immigrant. Otherness performs in the name of the hero and saviour when he scores for the national team. These representations thus involve a kind of racism, or Othering, which to a certain extent contain the encouragement and approval of difference.

*"The Hunt for the New Zlatan. In Zlatan's Backyard*

Unemployment. Widespread crime. Social segregation. Rosengård, the neighbourhood that spreads itself over the south-eastern parts of Malmö, is a tough world to live in. Here 50 languages are spoken, but only one is common to all. It's a language that connects all cultures, crosses all borders and breaks all barriers. It's the language of football. Come with us on a journey to the land where sand turns to gold and talent grows on trees. Come with us to Zlatan's world" (*Expressen* 29/05/2002).

Several elements recur in the media's coverage of these biographies. The above quotation represents a colonial discourse. In line with journalistic strategy, the story is told in terms of a journey. The chance to break loose from the background that binds him is in the hands of Ibrahimovic, as long as he is ready to sacrifice his extreme individuality and irrationality in order to be included in the team – meaning of course, the nation. Between 2001, when he first joined the national team, and up to the European Championships in 2004, this was a major issue that concerned football experts and sports journalists alike. The suburb was the place for Ibrahimovic's departure, it was Rosengård, defined as a place not entirely Swedish, that hosted narratives about the Other. In these narratives Ibrahimovic becomes synonymous with his suburban background. His doings can be put into an overall understanding of the concept of a journey. In the same year that he made his debut in the national team, he signed a contract with Ajax, a team in the Dutch league. At the beginning of 2004 he signed for the Italian club, Juventus. Each move has resulted in articles about how Ibrahimovic succeeded in escaping from an otherwise determined future of crime and unemployment. To emphasize the otherness and visualize the journey he undertakes the stories about Ibrahimovic also bring his parents (born in Bosnia/Croatia) into the narratives. This highlights the fact that, even though he was born in Malmö, the journey he has undertaken is not just a geographical journey, but is also to be understood as a cultural one.

Described as a fairy story, the young boy with nothing but problems could, with the help of his outstanding talent, irrationality and trainers, be guided to a successful career. Athletic heroes and heroines are often narrated in terms of their geographical surroundings. The landscape becomes the scene for the hero's or heroine's upbringing and rise to stardom. This mainly concerns country-raised athletes, as big city athletes are seldom connected to their landscape (Schoug 1997:43ff). This makes Ibrahimovic's constant linkage to Rosengård unusual, although the suburb is often described as being peripheral to the city. However, it is not only in Malmö where the reader finds the explanations to Zlatan's posing, gestures, statements and brilliant play, but in Rosengård, where a migrant background can be made into something reliable, and where every single one of his doings carries a vague reference to the nation. The discourses permeate the narratives of the suburb and the individual, typecast in the representation of that Otherness, also becomes a subject of the same discourses. On the one hand, the narratives praise and honour his move-away from the suburb, while on the other they indicate that he will never leave it. His mass mediated character is compared to that of his suburban background. His individual skills, techniques and aggressiveness on the football field are associated with his suburban background and to an appreciation of the stereotyped immigrant who has managed to break away from his background. But the pseudo-events portrayed and described by the journalists mean that he faces the constant risk of being knocked from his pedestal (Boorstin 1992).

*Maturity vs Immaturity*
One of the recurring media topics is whether Zlatan is mature or immature. The dichotomy cuts through most of the interviews and makes it possible for the media to discuss whether he should have a place in the national team or not. In the Swedish context, the idea of team spirit is very important. The notion of fitting into the team becomes synonymous with maturity. It is said that he has to hold himself back in order to perform for the team. The premise

applies to everything he does. One dribble too many (individualistic and immature) or a pass to the other forward (a mature working for the team) is to be understood against the background of maturity. At the same time, it is his irrationality and unexpected moves on the football field that attract the fans. As actors, suburban representatives often have these demands placed upon them in that they have to perform Otherness at the same time as they are criticised for doing just that.

Ibrahimovic has used different kinds of strategies in relation to the mass media. At one time he said that he didn't need the media. It was the media that needed him, he said. He was trying to avoid the questions because he did not think that the articles written about him were fair and representative. This attempt to avoid the mass media was then portrayed as a naïve and immature act. There was no escape, and there were no loopholes. The journalists' answer to Ibrahimovic's avoidance was to flash a patronising smile, while at the same time flirting with the audience and reassuring them that this was the Zlatan they were used to. According to Mauss' theories about gifts, the avoidance technique of Ibrahimovic is rather like a declaration of war. If you are unwilling to deliver the expected gift to the journalists, being cocky, arrogant and inviting them to a spectacle are attempts to withdraw from the mass mediated focus. The gift that journalists offer Ibrahimovic is attention (see Mauss 1997). Seen from the journalistic point of view, receipt of attention seems worthy of a return gift. When discovering that there is no actual loophole, Ibrahimovic gives the trademark *Zlatan* to the mass media, gift-wrapped.

For a while, Ibrahimovic invited the reader to think of Zlatan as a sign or an image. He often talked about himself in the third person during interviews, referring to: "Zlatan is Zlatan". Perhaps he believed that the statement – miming the sign of himself – would function as a loophole. Giving the sign of Zlatan to the mass media would keep the journalists away. Think of it as an agreement where both parties know what the other party wants. Even if the journalists have dispersed this strategy or agreement, they can still use it to describe and discuss his actions in relation to Zlatan as a sign. The newspaper, *Aftonbladet*, published an account of Ibrahimovic in June 2004. One of the headlines tells the reader that "Zlatan should be Zlatan, but..." and then the journalist goes on to talk about what we (the media and the audience) are willing to accept, and that his arrogant attitude in relation to the media has nothing to do with professionalism. The journalist wants him to show *respect* (*Aftonbladet* 02/06/2004). On the following day, another newspaper, *Expressen*, tells the reader that: "Zlatan has to be Zlatan. We must allow him to be Zlatan" (*Expressen* 03/06/2004). The emptiness of the stereotyped sign is evident when trying to analyse these kinds of articles. Could he be anyone other than Zlatan? "No", is the first answer that comes to mind, but when instead saying "Yes", even though it seems impossible, it also becomes evident that the discussion is a pseudo-event that draws attention away from the footballer Ibrahimovic, to the media character. The Zlatan *media-graphy* embodies that haunting feeling of someone uncontrollable and unpredictable.

"Q: Do you feel that the media image is incorrect?

A: I have nothing to say. Many journalists write whatever they want about me anyway, every day. It's neither the truth nor fact. I can only be me. The media goes with football.

Q: When you played for Malmö FF, you said that the reason for your arrogant attitude was 'Otherwise they put others down'

A: That was then, when I felt different. Now I have matured a lot and everything is different. Cockiness was a label that many newspapers put on me" (*Aftonbladet* 21/03/2004).

When reading the articles about Ibrahimovic, the mature vs immature dichotomy recurs and it becomes obvious that he uses it as a strategy to put the focus on the interviewer rather than on himself. The reader then sees the obvious blind spots. He "sympathetically" speaks about maturity and, without being asked, often explains his actions in terms of the dichotomy. In reporting his success in the European Championships in 2004, the journalists said that he had matured. That could have been the end of the matter. When reading articles written about Ibrahimovic during the spring and summer of 2004, however, it has to be said that journalists hovered between their demand for the arrogant Zlatan, and criticized the same behaviour as being immature. In the media discourse, the stories make him into a floating signifier, embodying the notion of a character that can display society's values and norms.

*The Mimetic Response*
Instead of abandoning the topic, Ibrahimovic does a re-run of the statements and even propose them to the journalists. The reason for that could be that Ibrahimovic knows what to expect if he keeps the conversation connected to already known subjects. Reproducing the fantasy-frame will not surprise him with anything new. Instead, he seems to take charge of the stereotyped space invented for him and thus reveals the blind spot to the reader, making the reader re-memorize.

Such articulations can also be looked at in terms of mime. Lacan describes the notions of mime as a camouflage and a mask. In Bhabhas' use of the mimetic, even though inspired by Lacan, he emphasises the ironic elements. Mime then becomes a strategy of resistance rather than a passive repetition, or attempt to hide. The mime instead becomes a double articulation. The superior's gaze follows the miming Other that it is trying to imitate. In the same mime, the subordinate can challenge and question the play or the act s/he has to perform by showing the extension of the stereotype (Bhabha 1994:85). On reading the articles about Zlatan, it is evident that the stereotyped media character of Zlatan is empty – a mimetic repetition of a media image. Article after article repeats the same theme and contains nothing new. The questions are always the same and so are the answers. After a while, the reading experience becomes comparable to listening to the so-called broken record, stuck in a characteristic loop. The reading also becomes a haunting experience. By reflecting the emptiness of the questions back to the journalists, Ibrahimovic offers resistance in a mimetic and ironic way. The mime, or the mimetic, becomes a method that the subject can use to make blind spots visible. By performing as the Other, the mime reflects the emptiness back on those who invent the scene and create the fantasy-frames. One of the characteristic features of the mime is that it is silent. In the case of resistance, however, it speaks to the observer. Ibrahimovic's mime shouts the conditions for the attention bestowed on him out aloud. The mass media haunts him with the mass mediated image of himself.

# Conclusion

In this article, I have tried to unwrap different aspects of the imaginary of the mass mediated representations of both Suburb and Immigrant. Using the notion of Žižek's fantasy-frame, and the haunting experience of blind spots as described by Gordon, I have illustrated how these images become real and have to be dealt with by those who are exposed to them. The experience of the imagery is lived out in everyday practice.

First of all there is Maya, who lives with her daughter in the suburb of Gottsunda, and shows how the blind spot of that area is produced around a specific place called Stenhammar Park. When looking out of Maya's window facing that particular area, she and I were sharing a view that was not ours but something ready-made. The emptiness of that view makes her want to leave the neighbourhood.

Following that sequence, the next scene is about how blind/white spots are produced and reproduced in mapping practices and conversations about suburbs. These images and maps create an imagined metaphoric space, and turn the migrant into the Other. The suburb becomes a place where Otherness is located and looked at. The press creates the stigmatised Other by attaching the migrant to a specific geographical space and making them collectively perform Otherness in the context of the surrounding society. The suburb becomes a scene for Otherness; a fantasy window that can be instantaneously evoked. Just a glimpse of a high building, satellite dishes on balconies, or tones of a Hip Hop beat, can set the suburban scene. They are situations created to portray the suburb and the migrant as Other.

In the final part of the article, I follow the media-graphy of the footballer, Zlatan Ibrahimovic. The mass mediated character of Ibrahimovic is stereotyped and associated with his suburban background. With that, it follows that he becomes a carrier of the differences invented for him. Instead of being able to act and communicate, Ibrahimovic has little more to do than act within the predetermined space ascribed to him. In that context, I have read the articles about him and his statements in a search for resistance, discovering that he acts out the stereotypes of the viewer, and even exaggerates them, so that the blind spot of the viewer then becomes visible. The observer's gaze turns around and instead meets the observer (audience) with her/his own perception.

## References

Anderson, Benedict 1991: *Imagined Communities: Reflections on the Origin and Spread of Nationalism*. London: Verso.
Barthes, Roland 1981: *Camera Lucida: Reflections on Photography*. New York: Hill and Wang.
Bhabha, Homi K. 1994: *The Location of Culture*. London: Routledge.
Boorstin, Daniel. J. 1992 [1961]: *The Image: A Guide to Pseudo-Events in America*. New York: First Vintage Books.
Dahlstedt, Magnus 2004: 'Betongen slår tillbaka' Hip-hop-profeter och röster från Förorten, To be published in *Häften för kritiska studier*. Stockholm: Föreningen Häften för kritiska studier.
Ericsson, Urban 2001: Mångkultur som estetik och pedagogik. In: *Nätverket. Kulturforskning i Uppsala* (htpp://publications.uu.se/journals/1651-0593/naturverket.htm). Uppsala: Etnologiska avdelningen, pp. 29–37.
Ericsson, Urban 2003: Erkännandets villkor. Om media och iscensättningen av det autentiska. In: *Kulturella perspektiv. Svensk etnologisk tidskrift*. Umeå: Föreningen Kulturella perspektiv, pp. 32–39.
Gordon, Avery F. 1997: *Ghostly Matters: Haunting and the Sociological Imagination*. London: Univ. of Minnesota Press.
Huggan, Graham 2001: *The Postcolonial Exotic: Marketing the Margins*. London: Routledge.
Marshall, David P. 1997: *Celebrity and Power: Fame in Contemporary Culture*. Minneapolis: Univ. of Minnesota Press.
Mauss, Marcel 1997 [1925]: *Gåvan*. Lund: Argos.
Molina, Irene 1997: *Stadens rasifiering. Etnisk boendesegregation i folkhemmet*. Uppsala Univ.: Dept. of Social and Economic Geography.
Morrison, Toni 1987: *Beloved. A Novel*. New York: Knopf.
Pascalidou, Alexandra 2003: *Frontkick. Samlade texter*. Stockholm: Atlas.
Ristilammi, Per-Markku 1997: Betongförorten som tecken. In: Arnstberg, Karl-Olov & Ramberg, Ingrid (eds) *I stadens utkant. Perspektiv på förorter*. Tumba: Mångkulturellt centrum, pp. 75–85.
Schoug, Fredrik 1997: *Intima samhällsvisioner. Sporten mellan minimalism och gigantism*. Stockholm/Stehag: Symposion.
Stallybrass, Peter & White, Allon 1986: *The Politics and Poetics of Transgression*. London: Methuen.
Žižek, Slavoj 1989: *The Sublime Object of Ideology*. London: Verso.

*Newspapers*
*Aftonbladet* 21/03/2004, 02/06/2004
*Dagens Nyheter* 18/06/2004
*Expressen* 29/05/2002, 03/06/2004, 22/06/2004
*Sydsvenska Dagbladet* 05/09/2002, 14/06/2004

# Afterthoughts on Modernist Necropoles

*Per-Markku Ristilammi*

*The morning flight veers towards Copenhagen. From the window I see the coastline on the other side of the Sound, and can identify Malmö, situated to the south of the nuclear plant, Barsebäck. The bridge looks like a serpent in the water below. A sandy beach and its piers are also visible. Everything looks so small from the air. Memories of my childhood flood my mind. The blue wool blanket, the wet sand, seaweed, my blue lips, the heavy breathing of children running from the sea. The sun is strong and everything seems to have been bleached white. The barrier to the subconscious is also broken, and we can access our oceanic selves. This region of beaches lends itself to the mutual possibility of liberating and formulating identity via the sea. Remembering, I twist my body and break the surface of the water.*

The Öresund region can be looked upon as a utopian white-framed evocation of a belief in the future. The artificial beach of Ribersborg, in Malmö, is part of a modernist vision of light, air and clarity. In the 1920s, the former stony beach was transformed into one of smooth sand, and framed by Malmö's first modernist high rise buildings, created by the Swedish architect, Eric Sigfrid Persson.

On the Danish side of the Sound, Bellevue Beach, created by the famous architect Arne Jacobsen in 1932, was part of the same vision. In Eric Sigfrid Persson's and Arne Jacobsen's Mediterranean-inspired ideal of modernity, the beach is bathed in white light and enhanced by a clear blue sky. The seascape horizon always forms part of the view from the large panoramic windows that were an integral part of the functional building style of the Scandinavian modernists.

The beaches, the sky and the horizon now form a double exposure, where seventy years of history is compressed into an image of never changing utopia and converted into a saleable brand. Strong brands depend on the creation of an aura that goes beyond the practical and reaches towards a realm of utopian desires. When place identity is transformed into a static brand that can be sold on the global market, the representation of place becomes one dimensional.

A question arises. Is it possible to take a critical look at this one dimensionality at the same time as being involved in a region building process? Perhaps a solution would be to drive the project of modernity to the bitter end, to the stillness of death, and see whether this leads to a reformulation of identity linked to place? One way of doing this would be to examine the connection with the sandy beach and the dynamic aspect of the modernity project.

## Spectral Modernity

The bridge building process can be linked to a notion of modernity as a form of spectral haunting; something that has lost its initial power but still lingers on. But it is also evident that such haunting is not a return in more concrete terms to an economy built on a modernist mode of production. The bridge itself may have been a triumph for modern industrial techniques, but the future management of the bridge is caught in the trappings of the new economy. Exhaustive media attention to the number of vehicles crossing the bridge creates the kind of monitoring that is usually reserved for companies on the stock market. On the one hand, the building of the bridge was a return to the large scale investment in infrastructure characteristic of industrial modernity. On the other hand, this very return created a framing for all the different branding techniques prevalent in the new economy. The industrial monumentality of the bridge formed a perfect backdrop to the different inaugural events connected to the opening of the bridge. The new economy's insistence on constant change, coupled to the need for brand stability, was perfectly merged into the image of a stable bridge with a constant stream of people moving across it.

With regard to the metropolitan region of Malmö-Copenhagen, one problem is that the bridge links two cities located in two different nation-states. It doesn't really belong to either of the cities, although Malmö has tried to replace the earlier symbol of the city – the redundant crane from closed-down Kockums' shipyard – with that of the bridge. Bridges are, of course, often used to promote visual images of cities. Tower Bridge, The Golden Gate and The Brooklyn Bridge are only a few of the famous bridges used as visual markers of the city itself. Tower Bridge is a prime example of how the interplay between selling the city and selling the bridge unfolds. A brochure on the "bridge experience" describes the bridge as the "world's most famous attraction". While the Öresund Bridge has not yet reached such a status of fame as a bridge experience, it is a powerful symbol for the Öresund-region. That it does not belong to any particular city makes it somewhat problematic.

It is a recognised fact that the concept of "region" has become increasingly important when it comes to gaining access to the EU's structural funds. It is, of course, also a fact that the national states, at least in rhetoric, are losing more and more of their former power. Attempts to create a branded regional identity for the Öresund region are therefore of crucial importance (cf. Ristilammi 2000). Having said this, one must also remember that the concepts of regions and nation states are not the only ones at stake. The bridge is also a connection between two cities: Copenhagen, the capital of Denmark, and Malmö, the third largest city in Sweden. For both these cities – but especially for Malmö – the concepts of a "new era" and a "new future", as expressed in the rhetoric of the Öresund Committee, are important indicators of a strong desire to disconnect from a recent past marked by economic recession and a growing number of social problems. These terms are also a symptom of a strongly held belief that the only way out of economic stagnation is to connect to the new economy. It is this connection to the new economy, with its claim on strong identities, that makes the connection to the sandy beaches of Öresund so alluring.

## The Power of Sand

The seductive power of a sandy beach is closely connected to modern notions of bodily movement that emphasise natural movement and freedom from constraint. Within this notion, movements and emotions flow from the solar plexus to the limbs in natural wave-like movement. The false pose or the rehearsed expression is not as important as the power that flows from the centre of the body. When it comes in contact with the warm sand, the modern body reaches its potential for movement and pleasure. At the birth of Scandinavian modernism in the 1920s and 1930s, the body was evoked through a paradoxical fascination with the oceanically organic. One of the founders of modern dance, Isadora Duncan, claimed that one of her greatest inspirations was her childhood memories of the ocean and watching the waves moving. Body and nature were one, and authentic body movement was something to be celebrated. At the same time, however, Sigmund Freud saw as his task as protecting the individual from the threat of disappearing into the oceanic. (Ristilammi 1998, 2003).

Here we have a paradoxical formulation of modern identity whose rationale is *the expression* of a non-reflexive core built purely on bodily desire. The foundation is laid for a specifically modern form of structured liberation that continuously moves between two poles; one about being imprisoned in a controlling structure and the other about being liberated from that same structure. Paradoxically, when the regional project in Öresund focuses on the freedom of a global place, the structure that connects identity to place and body is activated. In this process, those who don't fit into the modernist vision risk being outdefined. We then have a choice. Should we use globalised regionalisation processes to tie identities (and bodies) to place, or should we use them to liberate the potential movement of all the region's inhabitants? (See Ristilammi 2000, 2002.)

## Necropolis

The sea and the waves have further potential. The beach is not only a place for recreation and frolicking, but is also a spatiality that is uncontrollable, dangerous and treacherous. The sea threatens to devour the shore line. Drift wood is exposed to the forces of nature. Debris left on the beach gets blasted by waves and sand. The sun blinds and burns. When the sounds of the wind and waves disappear, and all is still, all that remains is the white noise of death.

Paul Virilio has written a dystopic account of the modern city where everything is bathed in a monochrome, almost obscene, light so that the dynamic scenic nature of the city disappears. This state comes close to the stillness of death; where everything is still, without contrast and meaningless (Virilio 1986). Just like the overexposed city, the beach is a realm of death and life. The modernist beach vision is also a necropolis where purity reflects the purity of death.[1] Divine order rules in the necropolis. Everything is in its rightful place and accords with its rightful function. The longing to return to the white order of modernism that has been latent within the vision of the Öresund region risks being stranded on the beach like driftwood. Perhaps the future does not lie in modernist purity? Perhaps what we experience in the necropolis is only phantom pain.

## The Beach as Rebirth

In the necropolis, divine order makes the order visible. What is not visible, however, are the hidden processes of putrefaction; the life that exists after death. In reality, the humanly created necropoles have never been about death, but always about life. The necropoles functioned as matrices of the perfect society (see Foucault 1986). The philosopher, Christine Battersby, has suggested the metaphor of birth as an analytical tool with which to understand processes that are still in their emergent state (1998). The metaphor of the matrix (womb) gives us an opportunity to understand how change takes place in a society where so much weight has been placed on the tension between structure and movement. If we could create a metaphor that can explain structure and change within the same conceptual framework, we might find ways to include every inhabitant in this identity project, and not only those identified by the monocultural vision of modernity.

That is why we have to be careful in our nostalgic modernist tendencies. The pure white beauty of the necropolis is seductive. But the re-birth envisaged by the region's building project encapsulates a future that is no longer one-dimensional or monocultural. It is the multicultural that shows us a holographic future, where we can see the whole in every part. That is why it is so important to create symbolic spaces where the inhabitants of the region can be part of a project of mutuality.

## Afterthoughts – Phantom Pain

The French ethnologist, Michel de Certeau, has stated that people can only live in haunted places (de Certeau 1984). That is why it is so important to evoke the hidden ghosts and learn to live with them rather than trying to suppress them. One example is the Russian painter, Kandinsky, viewed as one of the founding figures of abstract modernism. In his youth, Kandinsky was a member of several ethnographic expeditions to nomadic people in the innermost areas of Russia. Using this knowledge, an ethnographer and art historian has analysed his paintings and discovered that the shaman's drum and feathers are concealed in very the heart of these modernist abstractions.The modern is thus haunted, and by the same token, we must allow our history to haunt us.

The death of modernity has been a clarion call for several decades now. We are said to be living in a postmodern age, where our identities are as interchangeable as our clothing. Alterity becomes a product viable for consumption. Tourism, "ethnic food", exotic clothing and "world-music" are among the phenomena said to represent multiplicity.

They could, however, also be examples of what might be called cultural anaesthesia; a longing to block yourself from the pain of the other. In the consumption of the other, there is a longing to avoid being confronted with the classical modern identity question: Who am I? In other words, you don't have to think, reflect, feel, experience or have "kicks" in order to pretend.

I belong to a generation that, in its earliest years, still belonged to the paradigm of modernity. Maybe that is why my generation is so obsessed with cultural expressions of modernity. In our childhood, the future still existed. The break with modernity came when we became teenagers. Perhaps it is only now that we can see that this was a cultural trauma; the trauma of finding the adult within. Trauma is about that which is inexpressible: the silence, the loss and the wound. In one sense we are refugees in our own time. We carry traumas that can only be indirectly expressed

Perhaps this explains our compulsive search for authenticity? Many of us became fascinated with surface phenomena after having been half-hearted radicals. For us identity became a way of shutting out or harnessing, and acquiring armour of safety and security. The surface has proved to be something else – not only a visual mirror but perhaps also a membrane. Membranes such as these can be seen as semipermeable in that they allow the light and fluids to flow through.

Modernity now fulfils the function of Otherness. That which is not modern threatens to break through, like a pulse in the membrane. This is where we are now. The tactile, the haptic and the longing for closeness, paradoxically hangs onto the compulsiveness of the clean, logical, scientific modern spaceship likes a phantom limb. And perhaps it is this phantom-feeling that makes us fascinated by bridges, high-rise buildings and all that belongs to the modernist spaceship, even though we know, deep inside, that the future as it existed in the 1960s will never return.

If we are to continue with the embrace of modernity, perhaps we can paraphrase the postcolonial feminist, Gayatri Spivak's, "strategic essentialism", a concept that stresses the need for the weaker party in a conflict to hold on to a single and strong vision. Modernity played an important utopian role in the fight against poverty and inequality in 20th century Sweden. It was when the fight had been won that modernist thought began to have negative consequences. That is why we perhaps need to talk about something we might call strategic modernism; a modernism of the present where we reflect on the function and place of utopian dreams in our time.

When we break the surface of the water again and draw breath, we have a choice: We can choose to go into the perfect necropolis. We can also choose to turn away from the monument of death, go past it, and continue with life.

## Notes

1. "Necropolis (singular), plural Necropolises, Necropoles, Necropoleis, or Necropoli (from Greek nekropolis, 'city of the dead'), in archaeology, an extensive and elaborate burial place of an ancient city. In the Mediterranean world, they were customarily outside the city proper and often consisted of a number of cemeteries used at different times over a period of several centuries. The locations of these cemeteries were varied. In Egypt many such as western Thebes, were situated across the Nile River opposite the cities, but in Greece and Rome a necropolis often lined the roads leading out of town. One of the most famous necropolises was discovered in the 1940s under the central nave of St. Peter's Basilica in Rome."
Source: *Encyclopedia Britannica*.

## References

Battersby, Christine 1998: *The Phenomenal Woman: Feminist Metaphysics and the Patterns of Identity*. London: Routledge.

Certeau, Michel de 1984: *The Practice of Everyday Life*. Berkeley/Los Angeles: University of California Press.

Foucault, Michel 1986: Of Other Spaces. In: *Diacritics*, vol. 16.

Ristilammi, Per-Markku: 1998: Den kinetiska staden. In: *Aura. Filmvetenskaplig tidskrift,* vol. 4, no. 2–3.

Ristilammi, Per-Markku 2000: Cultural Bridges, Events, and the New Region. In: Berg, Per-Olof, Linde-Laursen, Anders & Löfgren, Orvar (eds) *Invoking a Transnational Metropolis. The Making of the Øresund Region*. Lund: Studentlitteratur.

Ristilammi, Per-Markku 2002: Ballonger och metaforer. Om modernistiska fantomkänslor. In: Berg, Per-Olof, Linde-Laursen, Anders & Löfgren, Orvar (eds) *Öresundsbron på uppmärksamhetens marknad. Regionbyggare i evenemangsbranschen*. Lund: Studentlitteratur.

Ristilammi, Per-Markku 2003: *Mim och verklighet. En studie av stadens gränser*. Stockholm/Stehag: Symposion.

Virilio, Paul 1986: The Overexposed City. In: Feher, Michel & Kwinter, Sanford (eds) *Zone 1/2: The Contemporary City*. New York: Urzone Inc.

# Shopping Malls and Shishas
## Urban Space and Material Culture as Approaches to Transformation in Berlin and Moscow

*Alexa Färber and Cordula Gdaniec*

Berlin and Moscow are two cities that have undergone profound changes in their urban and social structures during the past ten to fifteen years. Representing both East and West, global processes are converging on these cities and shaping their specific profiles. The shopping mall and the shisha (the Arabic pipe with water and charcoal) – two relatively new trends in these cities – are themselves emblems of East and West, the Orient and the Occident. The form in which they appear – or rather how they are being used – in these places is a representation of the local manifestation of the global.[1]

The understanding of urban culture used in this context emanates not only from the anthropological concept of cultural practices (culture in the sense of cultural and everyday practices) but also from "the cultures of cities", as promulgated by Sharon Zukin (1993, 1995), denoting special urban forms of culture linked with architecture and buildings as well as ideas of "cosmopolitanism" (Hannerz 1993; Vertovec 2000) that refer to the cultural capital that a city's visitors and immigrants bring. The city is the space in which culture(s) develop very quickly and have great impact. This is especially true for societies in transition, where major cities can be considered to be "laboratories" of the new political, economic and social orders.

In contemporary cities, consumer cultures are as central and effective as they are transitory. "The post-industrial city is the location where globalization is distilled into its local froms in the most intensive and wide-reaching way" (Clammer 2003:100). Global and local meanings are appropriated via consumer products and (re)produced in urban space. In the main it is products with ethnic connotations that symbolise the interdependence of the local and the global (e.g. in the shape of the knowledge that consumer cultures require and produce) and the attributes of a world city. In Berlin, consumer products with an ethnic reference, such as the Döner Kebab, form part of the everyday life of the city. In Moscow, such products have increasingly started to appear in the last few years. While in Berlin it is the "Turkish" cultural products – which on close inspection are actually Berlin products – that dominate, in Moscow it is the products from the Caucasus and Central Asia that dominate the street scene, reflecting the culture of the variety of the former Soviet republics. Recently Asian – and especially Japanese – food has become very prominent in the urban picture. Sushi is offered in the most unlikely places, thus indicating an infatuation with Far Eastern culture/food and its adoption into local food practices.

Nowadays, consumption cultures contribute to both the uniqueness as well as the uniformity of large cities (see King 1995). This is particularly manifest in shopping malls that highlight the tension between public and private space, global uniformity and local practices of appropriation. At the same time, urban spaces are being turned into emblems of globalised consumable cultures. In this (everyday) context, culture with ethnic connotations (e.g. in the form of restaurants, markets, music scenes etc.) promises a variety of different cultural commodities and experiences (Welz 1996). "Ethnic culture" needs to be incorporated into profitable contexts in the shape of consumable resources/products if it is to contribute to the city's image.

The relationship between the global and the local can be traced elsewhere too: Both cities have witnessed an increase in the number of shopping centres over the past few years. This type of consumer space represents globally recognisable shopping and entertainment worlds and symbols of the globalised economy. At the same time, shopping malls create new public spaces for leisure cultures which do not necessarily follow the commercial logic of consumer behaviour. In this way, the malls embody the ambivalence of local consumption practices and globalised consumer cultures. The case studies which are presented in this article focus on local and global aspects of consumer cultures in the urban topography as they are represented by specific products, spaces and forms of sociability connected with the consumption of goods. The different groups of social actors in the city – we examine Berlin and Moscow within the framework of an anthropological understanding of the world city (Hannerz 1993) – have different sorts of access to these spaces or practices. According to the model advanced by Ulf Hannerz, there are four categories of actors who, through their cultural, economic and everyday practices, as well as their transnational connections, turn a city into a world city: tourists, business people, artists and migrants (Hannerz 1993).[2] A topography of the different forms of space and access that is available or denied to the different actors highlights the opportunities and the constraints of public culture; who gains access and who is denied it.

Cultural and social spaces in or of the city are thus not only created by representation, but also – and especially – by cultural and social practices. Spaces of consumption, as well as cultures of consumption, are particularly interesting in the examination of urban developments. Although global cultural flows (Hannerz 1993) and the resulting "landscapes" (Appadurai 1996) make the world a smaller and more homogenised place, the cities, and particularly world cities, remain heterogeneous. In his study of London as a global city, Jörg Dürrschmidt talks about "the presence of the world in one city, and the world-mindedness of those cities" (Dürrschmidt 2000:13), thereby emphasizing the differences in and between big cities. While the present case studies – the shisha in Berlin and two shopping malls in Moscow – are representations of the globalised economy and finance and globalised consumer cultures, they also represent their city's uniqueness through local forms of appropriation of these flows and representations. By comparing the two cities, we can thus highlight certain phenomena of the globalisation process in transitional (world) cities. Looking at spaces in one city and practices in the other opens up a more critical and fruitful perspective on each city, and allows us to see cultural objects, everyday practices and urban spaces from an angle that would otherwise have been closed to us.[3]

The Berlin case study examines the Orient as consumable. It also examines its symbolic appropriation of urban space. One ethnographic object, the shisha, is tracked in different places in Berlin and Moscow. The popularity of this oriental accessory reflects the impact of material culture within urban space situated at the intersection of global cultural flows and local appropriation.

The Moscow case study compares a shopping centre/park in the historic city centre (Manezhnaya Ploshchad) with one of the many shopping malls that are now mushrooming at the city's periphery (Zolotoi Vavilon). Both places represent the transition to the market economy and Russia's growing inclusion in the globalised economy. However, the political/aesthetic connotations of the central space, as well as local everyday practices in both examples suggest a specific post-Soviet form of the construction and appropriation of these consumer spaces.

## Consuming Shisha: Following the Orient within the Symbolic Geography of Berlin

In analysing transformations of urban culture in both Berlin and Moscow, the perspective on consumer culture offers a wide range of approaches and field sites – a spatial approach

Shishas on display, ethnic restaurant in Mitte, Berlin 2004. Photo: A.Färber.

would focus on the different consumer spaces within a neighbourhood or on certain shops throughout the city space, whereas a group specific approach would focus on the consumer culture of a certain milieu or generation, and a material approach would build several analytical perspectives around one consumer object and follow the object through the city. I chose to analyse recent transformations within the city's landscape of consumer culture through the material approach perspective, i.e. through the object of the shisha.[4] Through this object – the oriental *nargile* or shisha – the specific tension or fusion of global and local aspects within consumer culture can be traced in urban space with respect to social contexts and cultural practices. It is the "scenography of selling and consuming" (Raulin 2000:18) exemplified with one ethnographic object that offers insights into its inscription in different urban contexts. Within this scenography, the interference of social and institutional conditions that make an ethnic consumer object a visible part of urban culture can be analysed. Thus, the "social life of things" (Appadurai 1986) may be internally linked with a "topography of things".

*The Social Topography of the Shisha in Berlin*
Everyday observations in the northern part of the district of Neukölln, in Berlin, have led to the conclusion that the shisha serves as a particularly good example for the analysis of urban transformation and consumer culture. The inner city district of Neukölln is – within the symbolic geography of Berlin – one of the neighbourhoods most often described as "the dark side of the city". Its high rate of unemployment[5] and the high proportion of immigrants among the population[6] are usually mentioned as indicators of this bad image. Approximately since the year 2000, the northern part of this district witnessed a marked change in the na-

ture of consumer goods on offer locally. As many Turkish groceries and cafés had closed down, it was a visible testimony to the district's unfavourable economic and difficult social situation and further added to the bad image of the neighbourhood. Many of these vacant shop premises were taken over by Arab entrepreneurs, which led to a different range of goods and services. Besides sophisticated nut roasters, the most prominent new item they introduced into the neighbourhood was the shisha, which today is available in grocery shops or smoke-in cafés. In these cafés, Turkish men of the first generation of economic migrants (so-called "Gastarbeiter" of the 1960s) have been drinking tea and playing cards for the last two decades – after they had realised they would be staying in Berlin indefinitely. Nowadays you see both younger and older Arab men in these cafés drinking tea and coffee, playing cards and also smoking shishas. Many of these cafés have highly symbolic names, such as "Qahwa Umm Kulthum" which refers to the prominent Arab singer Umm Kulthum, or "Qahwa al-Qahira", that indicates Cairo as the capital of Arab culture. Whether displayed in the window or represented in the logo alongside Arabic and German lettering, the shisha helps to identify these cafés as spaces of oriental sociability.

My own everyday observations of this neighbourhood (I have been a local resident myself for the past ten years) show that these places are more or less exclusively for men of Arab origin. Only a small number of non-Arab customers actually frequent these cafés. Meanwhile, snack bars and restaurants in the area have started to offer shishas in special "family compartments", or on "family days". Just like in the cities of the Arab world, restaurants now explicitly make those mixed spaces and opening hours available for men and women to smoke shishas and spend their leisure time outside the private realm. Following the introduction of the shisha into the neighbourhood, grocery stores started to sell shishas and all the necessary equipment. Apart from the café managers who sometimes buy tobacco or shishas for their cafés, both Arabs and non-Arab – i.e. German – customers buy shishas and the special tobacco for private use. An altogether new landscape of Arab shops, cafés and restaurants has thus been built on a very similar – formerly Turkish – infrastructure.

At first sight it seems as though the public and semi-public space of the streets of northern Neukölln has undergone a re-coding, in the sense that this part of Neukölln is steeped in an Arab-oriental imaginary. Consuming shisha relates to this oriental imaginary in its proper ambivalence. In addition to its exoticism, it is associated with an irritating abundance of time and with a public display of male sociability that highlights female invisibility and removal to private space.[7]

The evocation of this ambivalent imaginary was made possible by the new enterprises and the new shop owners of Arab origin. It was further made possible by the appearance of a certain product – the shisha – generating a cultural practice that is familiar to parts of the population of the area. Furthermore, it invited other local customers to take part in consuming the shisha, albeit most often in private space. This transformation, which may be seen as a sort of Arab-oriental refuge built into the city's landscape, is inscribed into the logic of the specific urban condition of marginalised neighbourhoods in Berlin.

It is important to note that this rapid and visible expansion of the shisha culture in the neighbourhood materialised at a time when Arab, oriental and Islamic cultural features easily translated into anti-Arab or anti-Islamic stereotypes – particularly after 11th September 2001, but also due to local frictions concerning Islamic teaching in public schools and the wearing of the headscarf by Muslim women in public institutions. Despite the polarising public debate about the question of "integration" that attracted a lot of media attention, a consumption and consumer culture that relied on an Oriental imaginary symbolised in the shisha proved to be extremely successful in the city's everyday culture. And this was true, as I found out by systematically following the object through the city; not only in places where Arab locals counted as the most important customers,[8] but almost all over the city.

However, I was surprised to come across shishas in neighbourhoods that are known for their stylish consumer culture, such as Mitte – a central part of Berlin which is famous for post-unification processes of gentrification.[9] Shishas are to be found in lifestyle shops and high-profile ethnic restaurants mainly frequented by tourists, people who work in the offices and cultural institutions that are located in the area, artists and also students from the nearby university departments. Here, the shisha serves, on the one hand, as an exotic consumer object within a wide range of ethnic lifestyle items from, e.g. North Africa or India. It even lends its name to a furniture and accessories shop, the "Shisha Styler". On the other hand, the shisha serves as an eye catcher in stylish ethnic restaurants offering Persian, Central Asian or North African food. The shisha is rarely smoked in these restaurants. When it is smoked, however, this never happens during the daytime, as in Neukölln or Wedding, but in the evening, thus producing a moment of leisure that is not part of everyday life. Whether on display in the window or as part of the logo, the shisha symbolises cultural difference; referring to the exotic and promising an experience of the extraordinary as a contrast to daily life. In the highly competitive landscape of stylish shops, restaurants etc., where rents are high and business is tough, the shisha is inscribed into the logic of a globalised culture of consuming cultural difference "as such" and in the form of cultural products or objects. In other words, the shisha offered in the shops and restaurants of this central district of Mitte is another visible part of the city's consumer culture. Although most of these businesses in Mitte are also run by immigrants, unlike those in Neukölln or Wedding, these cafés do not re-/create a kind of everyday life or a homely atmosphere. The shisha here forms part of the commercial logic of experiencing cultural diversity. Aided by cultural difference, this "consumption of culture" promises individual symbolic distinction – "sur mesure" or "à la carte" (Raulin 2000:14). It is a logic that is represented by one exotic product that competes with a range of others offering distinction and helping the consumer to escape from the daily routine.

Apart from these clearly polarised social and symbolic spaces, following the ethnographic object of the shisha through Berlin leads to more differentiated urban, social and symbolic contexts. For example, in the case of Kreuzberg, an inner-city district with different forms of the above-mentioned social problems and gentrification, social and symbolic associations with the shisha are more ubiquitous.[10]

Kreuzberg can be counted as the most emblematic neighbourhood, with respect to an ambivalent symbolic association with Turkish immigrant culture on the one hand and alternative political culture on the other. Since unification, Kreuzberg has undergone gentrification processes similar to those of Mitte. However, until the mid-1990s, the district had mainly been symbolically upgraded, as Barbara Lang has shown in her ethnography of Kreuzberg (Lang 1998). Today it is said to be going through a "renaissance" due to its persistent alternative culture and, as I would argue, due to a landscape of differentiated and exotic consumer culture. The high proportion of several generations of inhabitants with a Turkish background (according to the statistics, 23% of the inhabitants do not have German citizenship and almost 10% of them have a Turkish background) means that a wide variety of ethnic enterprises (see Pécoud 2001) – grocery shops, other shops, restaurants, cafés and lounges selling multicultural items – are run by locals and attract customers from all parts of the city.

In Kreuzberg, however, the shisha is not part of the urban landscape to the same extent as it is in Neukölln, although those café managers who offer shishas inscribe it into the ambivalent Turkish-oriental imaginary of the neighbourhood by re-coding it into an area that offers "the authentic atmosphere" for consuming the shisha. This kind of lounge and bar is run by the so-called "third generation", who sell oriental consumer goods and practices as part of their cultural repertoire to considerable advantage. This commodification of difference is legitimised by the transformation of the cultural knowledge ascribed to them into the display of specialised knowledge. In a conversation with the manager of a trendy lounge serving shishas, he emphasised the importance of choosing the tobacco (that he buys in grocery shops in Neukölln), that would set his venue apart from the others in the neighbourhood. He also knows that such a specialised offer resonates particularly well with the district's imaginary. This knowledge is part of turning his enterprise into a distinguished location. At the same time it is a highly localised form of knowledge, since it depends on the specific business idea and the environment that one wishes to be distinguished from (see Halter 2000:104). It is precisely this professionalisation and localisation of the consumer object that expresses the principles of a global culture of capitalism. Although global and local aspects converge on the shisha, in these places they follow the rules of differentiation of consumption.

The specific symbolic potential of the ethnographic object shisha, performed in its topography as sketched above, can be summarised as follows: Firstly, the symbolic content has to be taken into consideration. The shisha is deeply inscribed in an oriental imaginary – including its positive and negative associations. Negative aspects of this imaginary that resonate with actual global political and local social problems and fears are not always, or everywhere, brought forward. In places like Mitte, the spread of shishas even suggests complete detachment from political backgrounds in order to turn the shisha into a new oriental fashion and consumer product.

Secondly, the symbolic potential of place has to be taken into consideration. The oriental imaginary acquires very different connotations depending on the social constitution of the urban space or neighbourhood the object is found in. In order to highlight the existing social differences, the focus here is on the neighbourhoods of Neukölln and Mitte, which are at opposite ends of the Berlin social spectrum. In a socially highly stigmatised neighbourhood with very little cultural capital, such as Neukölln, the shisha becomes another symbol of an everyday practice that refers to the image of an enclosed community. As such it helps to create an exclusive feeling of being at home in a place where your presence is highly contested. Through the reconstruction of an ethnic culture, it facilitates identification with urban space. In a neighbourhood with high cultural capital, such as Mitte, the shisha is only one of the many objects that contribute to the consumption of cultural difference.

*Social Frameworks of the Topography of Things*

The shisha serves as an indicator of actual modes of transformation within urban culture that, at the same time, allows you to delve into the history of its local population and economic practice. It could even count as a symbol or the focal point of that transformation. To further contextualise the fieldwork account, the ethnographic perspective on material culture has to relate the symbolic content of the object and the symbolic potential of place to more global aspects of the character of urban space and urban culture. With regard to the concept of the culture of world cities, one can easily detect the three stages – or spaces in this case – of the market form that Ulf Hannerz has determined for ethnic cultural products: within "some subcultural community", in "its array of private settings" as non-commodified objects, where one might expect the shisha to have been used before it was introduced in cafés and grocery shops. The wide acceptance of it in the cafés points to an already present cultural knowledge and practice. This can be observed within an internally more differentiated community, "where it is profitable enough to commoditise subculturally distinctive items for consumption by community members", such as Neukölln, where the shisha is mostly smoked and offered for sale to Arab customers. And finally, the space where the product is detached from those former backgrounds, "having become more public ... in the wider cultural market-place", as we have seen in places like Mitte, where the shisha has become one consumer object amongst many that offers distinction via ethnic cultural difference (Hannerz 1993:78ff).

It is important to note that economic initiative in this specific realm of ethnic consumer culture is often a product of migrants' restricted professional possibilities. This is especially true for the transformation that has taken place in Berlin after unification and major de-industrialisation. Low-skilled immigrant workers have been hardest hit by de-industrialisation. Ethnic businesses which, in domains other than the shisha business, often rely on family-based work sharing, seem to offer a suitable space in which to make a living. At the same time, these businesses allow participation in urban culture and visibility in the public space. I would like to add another aspect to the evaluation of the ethnic consumer object in the market form. The institutional framework also comes into play and helps to differentiate and evaluate the modes of identification that urban society allocates to consumers and entrepreneurs.

The first shisha café to be opened in Neukölln six years ago, is managed by a 50-year-old Lebanese who has lived in Berlin for 30 years. A pharmacy had previously occupied the premises until the business folded. In our conversation, the manager insisted that his café was the first one to serve shishas in an original Arab atmosphere in Berlin. He kept telling me that opening the café was very much welcomed by the local political representatives. The local administration, as well as the local business community, considered the closure of an increasing number of shops along one of the main streets of Neukölln to be a real problem. The street started to look depressing with all the vacant shops; a visible manifestation of the sad social statistics and the bad reputation that was being reproduced in the local and national media, he narrated. He was only too happy to have been able to contribute to the neighbourhood's social atmosphere, so that it could once again be considered a place worth living in.

This self-representation of the café manager as being concerned about the image of the neighbourhood and the local social conditions is, in my view, a key to understanding the different layers that contribute to consuming the shisha in Berlin, in this particular space. On the one hand, he stresses the relevance of his contribution to the local culture or social environment, in a situation where an Arab-oriental culture that is almost exclusively accessible to (Arab) immigrants but not to tourists or the general public, is considered to be a threat to the public space. On the other hand, he points to the specific contribution that his café has made to the harmony of his local environment, thus entering a logic where – within urban governance – the local becomes the medium of harmonisation (see Welz 1994:224). It leads to another aspect of a specific Berlin urban practice and culture. What is described here as an individual, civil engagement to contribute to a locally based integrative culture – something that is almost more important than an economic interest in one's own business – is encouraged and structured by a variety of administrative forms of urban governance.

It is particularly in the marginalised areas where social and socio-cultural initiatives play a key role in regenerating the socio-spatial or cultural situation of these districts. The businessman seems to follow this logic. These new modes of urban governance have been implemented to prevent deeper social polarization in actually supporting creative urban culture. Formats such as that of "neighbourhood management" are meant to mediate between the local population and the district's representatives.[11] The key term is "empowerment" and a new mode of "quality policies" (Häußermann & Kapphan 2004:231), rather than routine policies, tries to respond to the social and cultural complexity of the urban condition. Thus, "quality policy" is meant to take social, cultural, economic and physical factors into consideration within an integrative development of problematic neighbourhoods: "The central aim of urban policies should be to return trust to the population in their own competence to play a role within society that is meaningful and accepted" (Häußermann & Kapphan 2004:230, author's translation). An empowered urban citizen should at least have the feeling of taking part in the development and implementation of local politics.

These modes of dialogue and this "new culture and institutions of non-hierarchical bargaining systems, forums and round tables" (Mayer 1998:72) are based on a construction of the civil subject that relies on a capacity of self-

Danilovskii Market, Moscow 2003. Photo: C. Gdaniec.

help and initiative. My argument is that this capacity of self-help and initiative is neither a mental disposition nor a cultural predisposition. It is a product of late modern, de-regulated urban governance that can be traced back to Peter Hall's concept of the "enterprise city" (1988) that is internationally oriented, and where the state retires from political forms of urban policies to instead mediate between different groups of interest. This de-formalised and de-regulated urban policy aims at setting free economic dynamics on the basis of individual initiative (see Heeg:2004). In this sense, urban institutions *prescribe* and *produce* subjects that take initiatives and civil responsibility. It is this logic of late-modern urban governance that the statement of the café house manager is based on.

In all the cases mentioned above – from the Neukölln-based shisha café manager to the trendy Kreuzberg-based third generation of young Turkish entrepreneurs – the importance of taking the initiative was not put forward in the same way: In some cases, economic aims and motivation were stressed, whereas others, as in Neukölln, highlighted social responsibility for a neighbourhood.

Consumable cultural difference and integrative locality are two codes within which objects taken as ethnic culture seem to be working "successfully" in Berlin. As a condition for this representational structure, urban policy, institutional representation and daily practices have to resonate and interact. This is certainly the case in the "shisha business", where ethnic diversity is increasingly understood as a resource not only for the city's image, but also for its local economy and social harmony, where economic initiatives on behalf of migrants melt into formats and programmes that try to project the potentials of ethnic diversity against economic crisis and unemployment (start-up businesses), and where these initiatives meet a local demand for consuming and spending leisure time. A further resource includes the trendy wave of consuming lifestyle offered by the second and third generations of migrants to young Berlin customers and tourists alike.

## Markets and Malls: Changing Consumption Cultures in Post-Soviet Moscow

"Russia [has been] ranked the number-one retail target", according to a recent *Moscow Times* article (Maternovsky 2004). The rate at which shopping malls are springing up all over the city, and especially along the city's periphery, certainly supports such an assertion. Such development has been accelerating since the year 2000, and is an indication of the increase of disposable income of a broad section of the population. Just as incomes are becoming less polarised, the city's spaces are being filled with more and more shops, restaurants, cafés and other consumer spaces that do not only cater for the rich. On the one hand, this is manifestation of Moscow's transformation from "the communist model city" into a city which is part of the globalised economy. On the other hand, it is a manifestation of the processes of economic and cultural globalisation. Post-Soviet transformation processes are coinciding temporally and spatially with an increasing dominance of global economic structures.

In the Moscow part of the research project, consumer cultures are observed from a spatial perspective; not analogous to Berlin from the material culture approach. This choice was not only informed by the nature of the research object itself, but also by the decision to demonstrate two different ethnographic approaches. Spaces of consumption are a prism through which transformations in the economic, cultural and social spheres can be examined. This is why I have chosen markets and malls as places within the urban structure in which one can observe everyday practices of consumption and leisure, official representation strategies and manifestations of the post-Soviet migration phenomenon. Moscow's food markets – the former Kolkhoz markets[12] – have become symbols of the city's multi-ethnic composition and of post-Soviet immigration processes. The markets, together with their managers and traders, evoke strong "ethnic" connotations in the minds of many Muscovites, and are often associated with the "migration problem" (Vendina 1999; Malkova 1998). The markets represent everyday life and routine shopping practices. Although the food and the atmosphere contain "ethnic" references, they do not add any symbolic value to the actual goods or practices, as is the case with the "Turkish Market" in Berlin, for instance. Judging by the offer and use of more exotic products such as the shisha, the commodification of "ethnic" cultural products plays a different role, produces less obvious symbolic capital in Moscow than in Berlin, and is therefore not included in this article. Instead I will concentrate on everyday practices and official representation strategies, both of which are played out in the chosen shopping malls.

*Consumer Culture and Public Space: Transformation of Urban Space*
The shopping mall is perhaps *the* epitome of urban consumer culture in the late modern city. The market can be regarded as the original form

of consumer space. Arcades followed some centuries later as a more sophisticated form, and in the 1970s, the pedestrian zone or the shopping street emerged in Western Europe as the latest trend in modern shopping practices. The US-American shopping mall was first developed in the 1950s, although its world-wide impact came much later. While malls have started to fade out in the USA, their management companies have found a lucrative new market in Eastern Europe. It is therefore no wonder that the shopping mall is becoming *the* new form of consumer space in Russia. In December 2003 there were 48 "quality" shopping malls in Moscow, and 35 more were expected to be completed by the beginning of 2005 (Maternovsky 2003). These are only the big, western-style shopping malls, however. The number of so-called trade centres (*torgovye tsentry*) – ranging from specialised markets to spaces similar to malls – has risen enormously and can only be estimated. According to observers, shopping in malls has become so popular in Moscow that a decline in market shopping can be detected. A real estate expert was quoted as saying that: "Western-style shopping centres offer better service and are overall far more comfortable, while their prices do not differ from those in traditional markets" (Maternovsky 2003).

While the shopping mall is an emblem, a symbol and a myth, in terms of urban culture and consumer culture it is also the antithesis to the city. It can be utopia to some and dystopia to others. "In the mall urban life is reduced to a puppet dance of the consumers. The lost city returns as a stage set, beneath the roof of glass, steel and fantastically stretchable polyethylene and behind the fully air-conditioned entrances, safe from the wind, rain, snow and the lives of its inhabitants" (Zohlen 1999). Since 1991, Moscow's urban culture and public space have gradually been rediscovered; an urbanity characteristic of a metropolis is being redeveloped. Elements of this include anonymity, freedom, the public, a heterogeneous population, cultural and ethnic diversity, niches and risk. The emergence of the shopping malls creates another form of urbanity; or rather it takes its customers out of the city into some form of parallel universe. Functionality seems to prevail in the malls around the periphery of Moscow, providing a space not envisaged by Soviet city planners.

Some of the largest malls in Moscow, such as "Megamall" on the Outer Ring Road in the south-east, however, try to emulate a city – if not a different world – within and beyond the city. Their advertisements try to persuade you that "Megamall" can supply everything you need or wish for, and that you and your family can happily spend days there. This sort of mall is the type that seems to represent US-American suburbia and the globalised consumption culture. While these malls are indeed very similar all over the globe, they do have their local specificities. The existing anthropological and sociological literature on consumption and shopping malls tends to either focus on the architectural and town planning aspects of the malls (e.g. Zohlen 1999), or the practices and strategies of the mall visitors, which might involve strategies of resistance (e.g. Bareis 2003) or a certain self-reflexivity modus of identification (e.g. Falk & Campbell 1997). Some studies do concentrate on both aspects: the nature of the "shoppingscape" as well as its uses, which range from the pragmatic to the leisurely (Lehtonen & Mäenpää 1997:137). In the current research, both trajectories play a role as a prism for the transformation of urban culture in Moscow. Practices of consumption and leisure in these new semi-public spaces of the malls, and their appropriation by the city's inhabitants and visitors, are as important as the architectural/planning issues. Both aspects demonstrate manifestations of the global in the local, or vice versa.

It can be argued that the current transformation in Moscow is as much a result of globalisation processes as of post-Soviet restructuring, and certain aspects pertain more to one rather than the other (e.g. Lentz 2003). In the Russian capital, we can witness the formation of public space in a way that did not exist during Soviet times, as well as the privatisation of public space. Places of trade and consumption are particularly good examples of this. There was little private space in Soviet Moscow, even within the home, and much of the public space served for representational rather than individual or private use. Flats were small and families of at least three, but often around five people, had to share a one- to three-room apartment. As a result, individuals – and especially the young – had to resort to using public spaces, such as the street and parks for their private affairs. This could be termed an unofficial, private use of public space which ran parallel to an official use of public space for representational purposes or collective activities. This dichotomy of public-private space persists, although is of a different quality (see also Lentz & Lindner 2003). The new public spaces that are being used for socialising and consuming are in fact private properties – cafés, restaurants and shopping centres – and therefore a symptom of economic globalisation. More private space is being created for the better-off in terms of elite or more affordable housing, so that members of a family can live separately and own a car – again a result of the globalised economy and neo-liberal economic policies. Some traditional Soviet cultural practices persist alongside these developments, however, which are often borne out in public spaces due to a lack of private space at home and lack of disposable income. The metro stations are still focal points for shopping and socialising, especially after work. Although more and more cafés and restaurants are appearing in both the city centre and on the periphery, the number of people who appropriate public space for their private lives does not appear to be diminishing. This is a paradox very much in evidence in contemporary Moscow, and is typical of globalising and transitional cities.

The Moscow case indicates a specific – perhaps a very Russian – way of appropriating global flows. A number of researchers in the social and cultural fields have argued this particular point (Pilkington 2002a; Rozanova 2003; O'Connor 2005). For instance, Melissa Caldwell, in her ethnographic study of local food practices in Moscow and the appropriation of McDonald's, writes that "Russians blur the boundaries between the personal and the public, the local and the foreign" (Caldwell 2004:7). Her observations are that Muscovites of all ages view McDonald's food as part of the Russian cuisine. On its part, the fast food giant capitalises on the Russian notion of "our" (nash) food and culture, and uses it in advertising, service and production practices. These findings are particularly telling in this context as McDonald's is, of course, emblematic of so-called "glocalization" processes (Robertson 1995; Ritzer 1998; Talbott 1996).

Two case studies help to elaborate how Moscow's public and privatised space is being used for representational purposes on the part of the city authorities, how it is transformed by neo-liberal, globalised economic practices, and how it is being appropriated through the cultural practices of visitors and inhabitants.

*Two Case Studies*
The first case study concerns the *Manezhnaya Ploshchad* complex, which consists of an underground shopping centre called *Okhotnyi Ryad* and an above ground landscaped square. The building site of Manezhnaya Ploshchad was described by real estate specialists in 1996 as a "hole in the ground – hole in the budget".[13] It was one of Mayor Yurii Luzhkov's "grands projets" which had to be finished in a hurry for the 850-year celebrations held in Moscow in 1997. The construction required far more capital investment than was anticipated by the developers, which meant heavier cash injections by Moscow city who were only supposed to own half the project (one of the typical 51%–49% deals between city and developers). Retailers were reluctant to lease space and prices had to be lowered. The available shops were eventually occupied by businesses, but there has since been a high turnover of retailers.

During Soviet times, the square next to the Manezh exhibition hall and opposite the Moskva Hotel was used as an assembly point for the military May Day parades in the adjacent Red Square. This large asphalted space was a "dead" space right in the heart of the city: open, public, generally uninviting, and only used for official events. After the collapse of the Soviet Union, this function was no longer necessary and it was important to consider how this central place could be developed. The city centre needed livening up in order to provide spaces for social and cultural interaction, as well as for trade and business. City centre space is now a focus for events or constructions which represent the city in the image it tries to create and that attracts visitors. Manezhnaya Ploshchad is important for both. There was an acute shortage of retail space when the Soviet system collapsed, and this sparked off a building frenzy. The city authorities were also keen to model a new, post-Soviet image of the Russian capital that represented Moscow as Russian and global. The resulting shopping centre and park is a representation of Moscow as a world city that hosts international retail and fast food chains in a globally recognisable setting, and which emphasises its own cultural heritage and uniqueness. This phenomenon is typical of current globalisation processes in cities undergoing political and/or economic transformations. The shopping centre, *Okhotnyi Ryad* (a reference to the historic trading rows on Red Square), is situated underground. Classical

Okhotnyi Ryad Shopping Centre, Moscow 2003. Photo: C. Gdaniec.

fountains and sculptures rub shoulders with international postmodern building designs. The roof of the shopping mall displays sculptures of Russian fairy tales and a globe that reminds us of historic world journeys of discovery and conquest. With the addition of benches, this place has been turned into an inviting space for rest and leisure.

A survey we conducted on the Square in September 2003 suggests that Manezhnaya Ploshchad mainly functions as a tourist attraction and hardly at all as a shopping facility. Most respondents were either visiting Moscow or showing their guests from out-of-town around the capital. Contrary to the pessimistic predictions during its construction and its early days of existence, both the mall and the park are popular with the visitors. While it is considered "clean" and "beautiful", few people said they would come here if it was not located next to the most important sight of the city. The shops themselves were too expensive, they said, and they were only window-shopping. The main activity of visitors seems to be strolling around or going for a walk. Young people used the Russian term "gulyat", which actually has more connotations than the English translation – including socialising and drinking (see Pilkington 2002b). For instance, the young people we spoke to used the space for "hanging out" (*tusovatsa*) with their friends; taking advantage of the possibility of spending time in a neat and comfortable environment without spending too much money. The latter term denotes activities that partly overlap with those described by "gulyat", but more specifically refers to a group and to partying. This is, on the one hand, an indication that some social practices have not changed since the Soviet era and that public space still plays a crucial role for the realisation of cultural practices in view of a scarcity of private space at home. On the other hand, it reflects a youth cultural practice of appropriating representational or consumer space for their non consumer-oriented leisure activities.

The Manezhnaya Ploshchad development thus seems to fulfil its representational purposes more than its economic logic, considering the amount of subsidies necessary to run and maintain the shopping centre. Yet, its representational function exists mainly at an abstract level of the city's image production. The way that visitors view and use the place shows a certain disregard of the official representational aspects in favour of expressing their own cultural practices. Although the respondents seem to be engaging in unspectacular activities in this place – showing their visitors from the Russian provinces the capital's central attractions, window-shopping, going for a Sunday afternoon walk, taking pictures of each other in front of the fountains – the official prestige that Manezhnaya Ploshchad carries does add a symbolic value to their practices. Wedding couples visiting the tomb of the Unknown Soldier in the Kremlin's adjacent Alexandrovski Garden, also stroll across the Manezhnaya Ploshchad square. Tourists have their pictures taken in front of the capital's main attractions and the youth come here rather than meet in their neighbourhood.

The second case study is a shopping mall on the city's outskirts, bearing the evocative name of "Zolotoi Vavilon" (Golden Babylon). It advertises itself as the "capital of rest and shopping" (*stolitsa otdykha i pokupok*), and does indeed appear to be an oasis of light, warmth, colour and comfort within a sea of standardised high-rise blocks of flats.

The mall is situated next to a metro station, and supplements the shops and cinema dating from the Soviet era (this micro-region was built during the early 1980s), and the numerous kiosks that have sprung up along the street in post-Soviet times. The shops and other facilities here serve a large population that lives within a considerable radius. This mall is first and foremost a space for meeting consumer needs in an environment of real shortage, but also provides a semi-public space in which local inhabitants can socialise and consume culture, albeit at a limited level.

The imperative of the mall developers is of course economic, although in the setting of a Soviet housing development with barely enough social or cultural amenities, the mall acquires functions, or rather possibilities, beyond mere consumerism. Again, this is a phenomenon similarly to be found in other countries, but in the Moscow context it highlights the ongoing fundamental transformations. Not unlike on Manezhnaya Ploshchad, the shops in this mall are relatively expensive, so that visitors mainly window-shop. They do, however, buy groceries in the *Perekryostok* supermarket, take their families out to dinner in one of the restaurants, play the gambling machines or watch a film in the six-screen cinema (findings based on a survey in March 2004). Again, it is the youth who most appropriate this space in a non-consumerist way, by "hanging out" with their friends at McDonald's before or after school, often making one drink or meal last for the whole socialising period. The existence of the mall in this area and the choice of chain stores and restaurants, as well as the prevalence of US-American films, is proof of the effects of globalisation in Moscow. But this has a two-fold expression in the attitudes and practices of the population. Some feel more urbane and part of a post-Soviet Russian culture (expressed in shopping habits, socialising habits such as frequenting cafés and restaurants, dress codes and attitudes), while others feel disadvantaged and experience a continuation of the Soviet shortage culture. Their lack of disposable income almost becomes more severe as a result of the opulence on display (e.g. old age pensioners buying a few items in the supermarket). Such polarisation is an effect of economic globalisation that is becoming more and more manifest in cities around the globe, and in particular in world cities such as Moscow. It is also, however, a reflection of the post-Soviet transformation.

## Conclusion

In answering the question of how transformation has been manifested in the urban culture of Berlin and Moscow since the fall of the Berlin wall/collapse of the Soviet Union, it seemed important to analyse the relationship between global and local structures and symbolic practices. Consumer cultures easily lend themselves to research and even more so in a comparative perspective. Comparing Berlin and Moscow highlights not only the character of each city, but the competitive tension between big cities today.

Following the shisha in Moscow has thus demonstrated two ideas. As far as the object shisha (*kalyan*) is concerned, what Hannerz describes as the second phase of ethnic cultural products in the world city, namely its commodification within the realm of immigrant communities, does not visibly exist in Moscow. Instead it is sold at almost any tobacco kiosk and offered on the menu of the trendiest restaurants, bars and clubs. Here, it is a consumer object in the sense of the third phase of Hannerz' market form model. Looking towards Berlin from Moscow, it becomes obvious that shisha, as an exotic consumer object promising cultural distinction, may be taken as a more global phenomenon than expected.

In contrast, the global similarity seems to be obvious in the case of new urban consumer spaces, such as malls. The comparison of Manezhnaya Ploshchad with Potsdamer Platz in Berlin seemed therefore logical. Potsdamer Platz was also built to fill a historic void in the city centre and represent the "new" capital city of Berlin as a "world city". It represents the space of globalised (consumer) cultures but, just as Manezhnaya Ploshchad, it produces different local forms of how this space is used and appropriated by visitors and inhabitants alike.

From this comparative perspective, and with ethnographic approaches to material culture and urban space, the similarities of transformation processes in cities in late modernity may be exemplified. At the same time, the appropriation of global cultural forms in local contexts may be described without understanding the local as a product of global processes, or without mystifying the local (Welz 1994:224). Berlin and Moscow are two individual cities; two urban societies that, at first glance, indicate more differences than similarities. With the help of this methodological combination, however, we reveal some of their subtleties.

## Notes

1. This article is based on a research project at the Department of European Ethnology, Humboldt University Berlin (funded by the German Re-

search Foundation/DFG, Feb 2003–Jan 2005): Urban culture and ethnic representation – Berlin and Moscow as emerging "world cities"? We would like to thank Wolfgang Kaschuba and Peter Niedermüller for valuable discussions of our work. Our thanks also to Franka Schneider for her assistance with the research and editing.
2. Anthony King (1995) added a fifth social category of actors to the world city model: urban planners and urban researchers who are actively involved in shaping the representation and discourse of the world city.
3. There are two researchers in the project, one working on each city: Alexa Färber on Berlin and Cordula Gdaniec on Moscow.
4. In my field research in Berlin, the coffee-to-go represents a second research object that enables us to describe a symbolically and socially contrasting field of consumption.
5. At about 22% it is one of the highest rates in Berlin (OECD 2003:29ff).
6. The proportion of non-German citizens in this district is approximately 21% (OECD 2003:29ff).
7. The well known Orientalism-debate serves as a major background for the discursive structure of this case, too, I would like to refer here to the main sources as Edward Said (1978) and Aijaz Ahmad (1992) as a critical response.
8. It was not therefore astonishing to find shishas for sale in grocery shops and offered for smoking in cafés in other Berlin neighbourhoods with a comparable social structure – especially with respect to the number of inhabitants with a background of migration, such as in Wedding, where consuming the shisha meets the needs of local immigrant customers.
9. For an ethnographic analysis of those transformations at one of the most prominent places in Mitte, Hackesche Höfe, see Romelli (2002).
10. Prenzlauer Berg would be another example, where, on the one hand, consuming shisha has to relate to the symbolic capital of this East Berlin neighbourhood that mainly relies on the presence of bohemian and sub-cultural scenes from before and after 1989. On the other hand it has to compete with ethnic business that, since 1989, has been predominantly Vietnamese (Bui 2003) and is now increasingly becoming a differentiated landscape of ethnic restaurants. For a sociological analysis of processes of gentrification see Häußermann, Holm & Zunzer (2002).
11. For Neukölln see e.g. the initiatives concerning a "territorial employment treaty" that is supported by the EU and embraces entrepreneurs and civic engagement. Also, an area for "neighbourhood management" has been identified since 2002 (see OECD 2003:29ff).
12. Where produce from the collective farms used to be sold; usually in purpose-built market buildings.
13. MC Securities Ltd., Report, 30/07/1996.

# References

Ahmad, Aijaz 1992: *In Theory: Classes, Nations, Literatures*. London: Verso.

Appadurai, Arjun (ed.) 1986: *The Social Life of Things: Commodities in Cultural Perspective*. Cambridge: Cambridge Univ. Press.

Appadurai, Arjun 1996: *Modernity at large: Cultural Dimensions of Globalization*. Minneapolis, Minn.: Univ. of Minnesota Press.

Bareis, Ellen 2003: Überdachte, überwachte Straßenecken. Jugendliche im städtischen Konsumraum „Mall". In: *Mitteilungen des Instituts für Sozialforschung* 15: 63–90.

Bui, Pipo 2003: *Envisioning Vietnamese Migrants in Germany. Ethnic Stigma, Immigrant Origin Narratives and Partial Masking*. Münster: LIT.

Caldwell, Melissa 2004: Domesticating the French Fry. McDonald's and Consumerism in Moscow. In: *Journal of Consumer Culture* 4 (1): 5–26.

Clammer, John 2003: Culture and Consumption in the Post-Industrial City. In: Eckhard, Frank & Hassenpflug, Dieter (eds) *Consumption and the Post-Industrial City*. Frankfurt/Main: Peter Lang Verlag.

Dürrschmidt, Jörg 2000: *Everyday Lives in the Global City*. London: Routledge.

Falk, Pasi & Campbell, Colin 1997: Introduction. In: Falk, Pasi & Campbell, Colin (eds): *The Shopping Experience*. London: Sage, pp. 1–14.

Häußermann, Hartmut & Kapphan, Andreas 2004: Berlin: Ausgrenzungsprozesse in einer europäischen Stadt. In: Häußermann, Hartmut, Kronauer, Martin & Seibel, Walter (eds): *An den Rändern der Stadte. Armut und Ausgrenzung*. Frankfurt/Main: Suhrkamp, pp. 203–234.

Häußermann, Hartmut, Holm, Andrej & Zunzer, Daniela 2002: *Stadterneuerung in der Berliner Republik. Modernisierung in Berlin-Prenzlauer Berg*. Opladen: Leske + Budrich.

Hall, Peter 1988: *Cities of Tomorrow. An Intellectual History of Urban Planning and Design in the Twentieth Century*. Oxford: Blackwell.

Halter, Marilyn 2000: *Shopping for Identity. The Marketing of Ethnicity*. New York: Schocken Books.

Hannerz, Ulf 1993: The Cultural Role of World Cities. In: Cohen, Anthony P. & Fukui, Katsuyoshi (eds) *Humanising the City? Social Contexts of Urban Life at the Turn of the Millennium*. Edinburgh: Edinburgh University Press, pp. 67–84.

Heeg, Susanne 2004: Vom Ende der Stadt als staatlicher Veranstaltung. In: *Zeitschrift für sozialistische Politik und Wirtschaft*. http://www.spw.de/118/Heeg.htm 01/09/2004.

King, Anthony 1995: Re-presenting World Cities: Cultural Theory/Social Practice. In: Knox, Paul & Taylor, Peter (eds) *World Cities in a World System*. Cambridge: Cambridge Univ. Press, pp. 215–231.

Lang, Barbara 1998: *Mythos Kreuzberg. Ethnographie eines Stadtteils 1961–1995*. Frankfurt/Main.

Lehtonen, Turo-Kimmo & Mäenpää, Pasi 1997:

Shopping in the East Centre Mall. In: Falk, Pasi & Campbell, Colin (eds) *The Shopping Experience*. London: Sage, pp. 136–165.

Lentz, Sebastian 2003: Privatisierung des öffentlichen Raumes in Moskau. In: Eichwede, Wolfgang & Kayser, Regine (eds) *Berlin, Moskau: Metropolen im Wandel*. Berlin: jovis, pp. 81–87.

Lentz, Sebastian & Lindner, Peter 2003: Privatisierung des öffentlichen Raumes – soziale Segregation und geschlossene Wohnviertel Moskaus. In: *Geographische Rundschau* 55 (12): 50–57.

Malkova, Vera 1998: *Moskva mnogonatsional'naya: konflikt ili soglasie? II. Analiz moskovskoi pressy*. Moskva: Inst. Etnologii i Antropologii RAN.

Maternovsky, Denis 2003: Mall Space Set to double by '05. In: *The Moscow Times* 09/12/2003.

Maternovsky, Denis 2004: Russia Ranked No.1 Retail Target. In: *The Moscow Times* 23/06/2004.

Mayer, Margit 1998: The Changing Scope of Action in Urban Politics: New Opportunities for Local Initiatives and Movements. In: *INURA. Possible Urban Worlds. Urban Strategies at the End of the 20th Century*. Basel/Boston/Berlin, pp. 65–75.

O'Connor, Justin (2005): "Creative Exports": Taking 'Cultural Industries' to St. Petersburg. In: *International Journal of Cultural Policy* 11 (1):45-60.

OECD 2003: *Urban Renaissance Studien: Berlin. Wege zu einer integrativen Strategie für sozialen Zusammenhalt und wirtschaftliche Entwicklung*. Paris/Berlin.

Pécoud, Antoine 2001: 'Weltoffenheit schafft Jobs': Turkish Entrepreneurship and Multiculturalism in Berlin. In: *Working Papers for Transnational Communities* WPTC-01-19: http://www.transkomm.ox.ac.uk.

Pilkington, Hilary 2002a: The Dark Side of the Moon? Global and Local Horizons. In: Pilkington, Hilary, Omel'chenko, Elena, Flynn, Moya, Bliudina, Ul'iana, Starkova, Elena *Looking West? Cultural Globalization and Russian Youth Cultures*. University Park: Pennsylvania State University Press, pp. 133–164.

Pilkington, Hilary 2002b: Reconfiguring "the West". Style and Music in Russian Youth Cultural Practice. In: Pilkington, Hilary, Omel'chenko, Elena, Flynn, Moya, Bliudina, Ul'iana, Starkova, Elena *Looking West? Cultural Globalization and Russian Youth Cultures*. University Park: Pennsylvania State University Press, pp. 165–200.

Raulin, Anne 2000: *L'ethnique est quottidien. Diasporas, marchés et cultures métropolitaines*. Paris: L'Harmattan.

Ritzer, George 1998: *The McDonaldization Thesis. Explorations and Extensions*. Thousand Oaks: Sage.

Robertson, Roland 1995: Glocalization: Time–Space and Homogeneity–Heterogeneity. In: Featherstone, Mike, Lash, Scott & Robertson, Roland (eds) *Global Modernities*. London: Sage, pp. 25–44.

Romelli, Tiziana 2002: *Ein Spaziergang durch die Hackeschen Höfe. Erkundungen eines neuen urbanen Ortes*. Hamburg: LIT.

Rozanova, Julia 2003: Russia in the Context of Globalization. In: *Current Sociology* 51 (6): 649–669.

Said, Edward S. 1978: *Orientalism. Western Conceptions of the Orient*. London: Penguin.

Talbott, Shannon 1996: Global Localisation of the World Market: Case Study of McDonald's in Moscow. In: *Sociale Wetenschappen*, Dec.1996: 31–44.

Vendina, Olga 1999: Migranty v Moskve – rost etno-kul'turnogo raznoobraziya ili sotsial'noi napryazhonnsti? In: Zayonchkovskaya, Zh. (ed.): *Migration and Urbanization in the CIS and Baltic States of the 1990s*. Moscow: The CIS Research Center on Forced Migration, pp. 297–318.

Vertovec, Steven 2000: Fostering Cosmopolitanisms: A Conceptual Survey and a Media Experiment in Berlin. In: *Working Papers for Transnational Communities* WPTC-2k-06: http://www.transkomm.ox.ac.uk.

Welz, Gisela 1994: Der Tod des Lokalen als Ekstase des Lokalismus. In: Noller, Peter, Prigge Walter, Ronneberger, Klaus (eds) *Stadt-Welt. Über die Globalisierung städtischer Milieus*. Frankfurt/New York: Campus, pp. 218–225.

Welz, Gisela 1996: *Inszenierungen kultureller Vielfalt. Frankfurt am Main und New York City*. Berlin: Akademie Verlag.

Zohlen, Gerwin 1999: Erlebnisumgebung mit kontrollierter Temperatur. In: Bollmann, Stefan (ed.): *Kursbuch Stadt. Stadtleben und Stadtkultur an der Jahrtausendwende*. Stuttgart: DVA, pp. 115–121.

Zukin, Sharon 1993: *Landscapes of Power: From Detroit to Disney World*. Berkeley, Calif.: Univ. of California Press.

Zukin, Sharon 1995: *The Culture of Cities*. Oxford: Blackwell.

# National Narratives and Cosmopolitan Dreams
## Becoming a Capital in Late Modernity

*Beate Binder*

In the fields of social and cultural sciences, the newly awakened concern with urban space and the spatial structure of society has not only given new impulse to research on cities in general, but has also produced a growing interest in the construction of urban landscapes as landscapes of meaning and, thus, the production of locality in more general terms (cf. Appadurai 1996).[1] With regard to cities being at the same time symbols and agents of the wide-reaching transformation processes, taking place in late modernity (for an overview cf. Smart & Smart 2003; Niedermüller 1998), the investigation of how cities are produced is crucial to the understanding of contemporary social and cultural transformation processes in more general terms. Refining this argument, cities are described not merely as social frames for the actions of different social groups and the performance of different forms of lifestyles. Rather, cities are interpreted as symbolic texts which are written by political, social and cultural forces (cf. Low 1999). From this perspective, cities, their architecture and spatial order represent social imagination and political visions. They are cultural constructions, places and locations for myths, memories and nostalgia as well as contemporary balances of power and hegemony. Thus, the symbolic landscape of a city represents today's political, social and cultural power and the hegemonic ideas and concepts in history. Or to put it another way, city space functions as a symbolically coded social and historical text, and in this text, different and changing political and ideological goals, historical interpretations and cultural meanings are inscribed.

Berlin is an interesting field of study to follow up these considerations. In many respects the changes taking place in Berlin are typical for the contradictory and conflicting forces that accompany the transition from the first to a more reflexive late modernity. This argument does not primarily draw on the economic and social fabric of city and society, but points towards the negotiations that produce the political, cultural and social images of the city and its landscape. Since the fall of the Wall in 1989, German unification in 1990 and, last but not least, the decision in 1991 to move the government from Bonn to Berlin, which finally took place in 1999, the city is very much "in the making", both in material as well as symbolic terms. Since then, new narratives of Berlin have emerged, and a pervasive discourse has begun regarding the possible and desirable reconstruction and rebuilding of the entire city, the ways in which to (re-)present unification, the political and symbolic dimensions of the new capital and the symbolic economy of contemporary Berlin. In effect, social, cultural and political negotiations are not only at work "as usual" but constitute a very intense and dynamic process of reworking and redefining the city's imaginary and urban landscape. This process was and still is accompanied by a lot of conflicts and discussions about what shall happen to and how to (re-)construct certain places.

However, the narratives of the "New Berlin" speak of the future of the city in contradictory ways. Simply put, the unexpected "turn" of history, the consequent collapse of socialism and the transformation of the whole economic and social system confronted Berlin with the task of having to reinvent and define itself as the cultural and political (the "national") capital of a united Germany, as well as a cosmopolitan metropolis which could cope with the economic challenges of the 21st century (Binder & Niedermüller forthcoming). Discussions regarding the impact of globalisation on urban space have highlighted the argument that "globalization generates the greater salience of both sub-national and supra-national arenas for action at the expense of the nation state (…) Once primarily structured by their place within a nested national hierarchy, cities have become more influential in defining or defending their roles for themselves within global arenas" (Smart & Smart 2003:266). As European capitals are still seen as national representations, the two aims of becoming a capital and a metropolis, co-existing side by side, cause a lot of ambiguity and contradiction. These are visible when considering the discourse on the "New Berlin". Both aims –becoming capital and developing into a metropolis – produce different narratives. The narrative of Berlin, as the national capital, is to a large extent concerned with the "own" i.e. questions of national self-representation, origin and, hence, the nation's past and the representation of the "imagined community" (Anderson 1983) – the nation as a homogenous unit. The narrative of Berlin as a "modern" city (a city capable of coping with the challenges posed by economic restructuring to postfordist modes of production and consumption) deals with images of a vivid metropolis, of multiculturalism and tolerance, of creativity, and (cultural) heterogeneity. Whereas the national project produces primarily narratives of exclusion, the cosmopolitan dreams imagine an inclusive future – at least for those who will contribute to the cities' (economic) prosperity. An important aspect, to understand the current transformation processes going on in Berlin, is to question how the ambiguities and contradictions of the national and the cosmopolitan structure the production of locality.

In the following, I will focus on how these narratives of Berlin are mapped in the city space, how meaning is inscribed in urban space and, by coming into being, how local space is transcended into its respective national and cosmopolitan representation space. Whilst there are different ways of following up these questions, I will focus on public events. To explain this approach, I will firstly concentrate on their significance as sites of anthropological research. I will then present the arguments as to why we might focus on this when the production of locality is of interest. Secondly, I will outline some events and examine those "edges", where the national and the cosmopolitan maps of Berlin overlap and intersect. My argument is that these intersections are significant spaces where the construction of a capital in late modernity takes place.

## Public Events and the Production of Locality

Looking at public events means interpreting them as sites of cultural production and representation. For a long time, the dense symbolic structure of public events turned them into outstanding sites of ethnographic investigation. For example, Emile Durkheim, Milton Singer, Victor Turner, or Clifford Geertz argued that they are keys to the investigation of societies as they enable ethnographers to grasp the symbolic structure, collective understandings or principles which building a societal order. Or, as Don Handelman put it, "they constitute dense concentrations of symbols and their associations, that are of relevance to a particular people" (Handelman 1998:9). Today, these assumptions are being criticised. Whereas Clifford Geertz (1987) interpreted the Balinesian cock fight as a key symbol of the whole Balinesian society and Milton Singer (Singer 1972) saw cultural performances as elementary for the great tradition of the Hindu Indian culture (to mention just two classic accounts of cultural performances), these holistic interpretations are being questioned today. It does not seem to be clear anymore whether it is possible at all to "read a culture from the symbols of a cultural performance" (Bailey 1996). Don Handelman notes, pointing to the same problem, that a cultural performance or public event "among a particular people communicates only *a version* of their social order". Different versions or interpretations, Handelman adds, "overlap and conflict with one another, in the knowledge and experience, and effect they convey. If events contain keys to codes, then these unlock many doors, as much to labyrinths as to great halls and cosy kitchens" (Handelman 1998:9).

With these warnings in mind, it is not possible to draw a picture of the self-image or societal order of "the Germans" or "the Berliners", based on the symbolic structure of public events. In fact, the accounts of public events will not serve this purpose in the line of my argument. Rather I will follow the argument of Orvar Löfgren and Per Olof Berg, when I focus on public events as culturally constituted focus of information processing (Handelman 1998:28). As they have pointed out whilst observing the "birth" of the Øresund region, public events are important agents in transformation processes, which do not follow a strategic plan in the first place, but are merely "concept- and event-driven". "The persuasive power of the concepts lies not least in its name giving magic, their symbolic intensity, and their character as models for future action. (…) Conferences, networks, and events stake out a future world" (Berg & Löfgren 2000:23). And public events offer stages for a special way of experiencing. In this respect, cultural performances or public events are not only something that "happens" and engages people, but something which "has effects on the world" and "does things" (Gerholm 1988; Parkin 1996; Rabinow 1995). It is the representation *work* that is most important in public events. As Yi-Fu Tuan already highlighted, the symbolic text of a landscape can only be read by a "discerning eye". That is what he named the "eye", which is able to read and interpret the meaning of urban space and to perceive the historical heritage and utopian visions incorporated in the urban environment (Tuan 1977). Thus the writing of the city as a landscape of meaning and the establishing of "rules" on how to perceive and use urban spaces is in need not only of social actors but of "agents": cultural representations which are to produce meaning, to connect narratives and space to each other and to give way to experience these connections. Consequently, one can interpret cultural performances – commemorations, demonstrations, or, in short, all kinds of modern public "rituals" – as important agents for the production and inscription of meaning. That means, that the production of locality is not only based on discourse to do with old and new architecture, the (re-)naming of streets and places, monuments and commemoration sites etc. These strategies of producing meaning are connected in manifold ways to cultural performances. Public events give space to and render visible the more "abstract" negotiations of meaning. In the context of the Øresund research project, Per-Markku Ristilammi proposed to compare the space of public events with those spaces Foucault called heterotopias – spaces which reflect and comment on the hopes and fears of society (Ristilammi 2000). Thus, the space-time structure of public events allows people to join together, to confess to the celebrated goals and symbols and to take decisions regarding their further engagement, not least because of the resulting emotional surplus that arises from taking part. The special atmosphere of public events affects people and opens them up for agency. Public events produce agency, in so far as they connect people to the envisioned projects.

From this point of view, I will examine public events to see how they take part in producing maps of national and cosmopolitan references within the cityscape and how one deals with the contradictions and ambiguities between the two and renders them visible.

## The Production of Differing Maps: Staging the "New Berlin"

I will start with short glimpses at three public events. These are taken more or less randomly from a large number of similar occasions taking place in Berlin over the last few years. The invitation to join the celebrations on the "Day of German Unity", staged every year on 3 October, the "All Nations Festival", an open house festivity, taking place in a number of embassies, and the opening of the MEXartes Festival, will give some meaning to the ques-

Invitation card for the opening of the MEXartes Festival.

tions raised above. All three are different in scale, language and purpose, but by questioning the emerging national and cosmopolitan maps they offer, it is possible to make visible some of the principles that organize the production of locality in a late modern capital.

*The "Day of German Unity"*
The "Day of German Unity" is the most recently created German national holiday. Established in 1991, this day is meant to commemorate the official act of (re-)unifying Germany on 3 October 1990. Whilst looking at "Germany's festival", I will take the celebrations of 2002 as focal point. That year, the city hosted the nationwide central festivity because Berlin was chairman of the Bundesrat – the upper house of the German parliament – then. Whilst a state ceremony was held at the Opera house, a street party at the Pariser Platz, a "Ländermeile" (mile of the German federal states) and a "Bürgerfest" (citizens' festival) took place over nearly two days and offered an atmosphere of enjoyment and pleasure. The famous square next to the

Brandenburg Gate and the avenue, Unter den Linden, turned into a huge festival ground. Like every year, the German federal states were encouraged to present their regional or local specialties, first and foremost food and drink. The visitors were able to enjoy, for example, fish from Hamburg, Hessian apple wine, Bavarian white sausages as well as folk dances, music or other "traditions" from the German federal states. Each federal state displayed an exhibition of their regional peculiarities, future plans or aspects of their regional cultural heritage. National and international dance companies, cabaret, music, and folklore groups performed their programs on two stages, especially erected that day for this occasion. At the same time, the government, its ministries, and the European Commission provided information desks with handouts and giveaways for the visitors.

The highlight of the celebration in 2002 was the unveiling of the Brandenburg Gate that had been under reconstruction over the recent years. The famous German skier, businessman and designer, Willy Bogner, slipped off the covering and lifted it out into the air, so that the rebuilt monument could come to the fore – new and bright. Even though the renovation work had been finished some weeks ago, the unveiling took place during the national holiday, and, thus, was embedded in the national narrative of unification. The event took place in the presence of famous guests. German president, Johannes Rau, German chancellor Gerhard Schröder, president of parliament, Wolfgang Thierse, the mayor of Berlin, Klaus Wowereit, and, as guest of honour, the former president of the United States, Bill Clinton, watched the unveiling and gave speeches. Framed by a rich and colourful entertainment program, they honoured the Brandenburg Gate as a symbol of German unity or, as Bill Clinton put it: "The gate was a symbol of the dividedness of Germany. Today it is a symbol of unity and a symbol of hope, the hope of freedom for all nations" (*Tagesspiegel* 04/10/2002). With rehearsals having taken place beforehand and there having been wide coverage by the press, people were very much in a mood of great expectation. Finally, the Brandenburg Gate was given back, like a gift, to the Berliners and their visitors, a site that gave them a sense of identity and belonging – on a local as well as national scale.

The symbolic structure of this event is not very sophisticated. In terms of Don Handelman it is a public event "that presents the lived-in world" (Handelman 1998:41ff). Primarily, the day was meant to commemorate unification as an important turning point of the national as well as the worldwide history and to celebrate the national self-image of Germany as a federal country. It aimed to show the progress of the unification process and stage the joy of the Wall having fallen and the overcoming of the German division. Thus, the celebrations and the festivities primarily provided Berliners as well as city visitors with a pleasant atmosphere to consume and experience the "German-ness" of Germany and its new capital.

*The "All Nations Festival"*
Lets turn to the second example. The "All Nations Festival" has taken place during the summer months for some years now. To mark this occasion, the *Tagesspiegel* invited its readers to "travel around the world – within Berlin" (*Tagesspiegel* 04/07/2003) and that is, in fact, what the day offers its visitors. The event is mainly organised by the embassies. In 2003, 36 of the meanwhile about 130 embassies, located in Berlin, opened their doors to visitors and provided a rich cultural program.

The "All Nations Festival" is strongly connected to Berlin as a capital city. The move of the German parliament forced most of the countries to follow the German government from Bonn to Berlin. Over the last decade, old representations have been reconstructed or enlarged, new buildings erected, and the old diplomatic quarters of Berlin were restored. Since most of the nations were eager to commission famous architects and to construct a really "representative" building, a rich and fascinating architectural landscape emerged in the inner districts, namely in Tiergarten. The interesting buildings – in terms of material as well as language of design – are an attraction for Berliners and tourists. There are guided walks and bus sightseeing tours all day long and some of the embassies are no longer able to cope with the public interest in their buildings.

So the "All Nations Festival" is, in some way, a prolonged and extended daily routine. On this day, the embassies make it possible to visit the buildings and provide an additional program at the same time. The visitors are encouraged to get to know their hosts' countries. Coffee, beer and soft drinks, along with "typical" dishes and drinks, are offered. Information is given on the countries and its tourist infrastructure, music and dance performances are staged and children are given the opportunity to do handicraft. Whether it is Jamaica, whose invitation has the slogan "Come to Jamaica and feel alright", or Malta, offering Kinnie, all embassies are eager to offer some specialties and highlight the attractiveness not only of the new embassy building but of their own country as a whole. A bus shuttle enables the visitors to travel easily from station to station. And last but not least, a festival pass requests visitors to collect stamps from each country. This increases that feeling of traveling – a journey around a world of colourful, distinct and different cultures, represented by different nations.

*The Opening of the MEXartes Festival*
The opening of the MEXartes festival took place at the House of World Cultures in summer 2002 (MEXartes). The House of World Cultures describes itself as one of the leading centres for contemporary art of non-European origin. It provides a platform for projects and themes transcending borders and frontiers. This is what the opening ceremony of MEXartes aimed to do, too. It announced the beginning of a rich cultural program i.e. an art exhibition, concerts and film programs, round table discussions and symposiums, all dealing with contemporary culture of Mexico and the German-Mexican cultural exchange over the last centuries. About 1000 people came to the House of World Cultures that evening. Advertised all over the city, the event obviously had a crowd-pulling effect. It offered a stage for all those involved in culture (politics) – whether merely interested in culture or Mexico (or both). It was also intended for all those Mexicans and Latin Americans living in Berlin. Underlined in speeches by national representatives of both countries, Germany and Mexico, the festival staged the benefits of cultural hybridity, multiculturalism and exchange. Furthermore, the opening offered "good to be here" feelings in terms of networking and being in the public eye.

Whilst the House of World Cultures represents the world's cultural diversity, it also shows the openness of Berlin towards the diversity of its own citizens. As Homi Bhahba put it: "In this momentous of transition, the House of World Cultures – like Berlin itself – is becoming a meeting place for dialogues between cultures, a bridge between the past and the present, East and West, North and South" (HKW). The House of World Cultures stages cultural hybridization, shows products developed from cultural contact, and its influence especially on fine arts. It opens a space for intellectual exchange on, above all, questions of cultural globalization. The former congress hall, is the home of the House of World Cultures, was constructed in the 1950s, an American contribution to the architectural exhibit "Interbau" in 1957. The language, which its architect Hugh Stubbins created within this building, is interpreted usually as transparent and, therefore, "democratic" i.e. enabling people to come together as equals. The building stands for the long established links between the US and West Germany. Today its purpose is to give Berlin a cosmopolitan atmosphere and offers the possibility to transcend the local and the national boundaries. In this spirit, German chancellor Gerhard Schröder once characterized the House of World Cultures by stating the following: "When we say that Germany has to become more international, then the House of World Cultures is doing real pioneering work" (HKW).

## Switching Scale: Local, National and Global City Spaces

All three events – Germany's festivities on 3 October, the "All Nations Festival" and the opening of the MEXartes Festival, serve different purposes and speak different languages. They differ in range and outreach. But in terms of the production of locality, they take part in mapping meaning, both in national as well as cosmopolitan terms. All three are based on and confirm national narratives i.e. narratives of the "own", and therefore they make the "new, old" capital of Berlin a "real" capital. At the same time, all three refer to the cosmopolitan insofar as they interconnect the local, the national and the global. As Susan Ruddick pointed out, "we tend to think of public space as a local phenomenon, it is, in fact, constituted at different sets of articulated scales. Public spaces can disturb our conventional hierarchical notions about scale – for instance, they can become at once local *and* national spaces for the construction, mediation, and regulation of social identities" (Ruddick 1996:140). And, to expand on this argument further, they can refer to all three: the local, the national, and the cosmopolitan and make them intersect.

To celebrate a national holiday, means to celebrate, reaffirm and reflect on one's "own" history. Thus, it is not at all surprising that national narratives structure the festivity and are presented during the Day of German Unity. Speeches by government representatives – German as well as the "foreign" guest Bill Clinton – spoke of the nation's fate and about German unification as a turning point in their national history. Finally, the highlight of the ceremony, the unveiling of the Brandenburg Gate, localized the national within the cityscape and transformed the Pariser Platz with the very symbol of German unity, the Brandenburg Gate, into a national representational public space.

In fact, the Pariser Platz has become the central location for staging national celebrations over the past years. Already in 1991, the official opening of the reconstructed Gate was meant to highlight this national symbol once again. The farewell ceremonies for the allied troops took place at the Pariser Platz in front of the Brandenburg Gate in 1994 and the official celebrations for the 9 November (which is not

The Pariser Platz has become the central location for staging national celebrations over the past years. The fence around the construction site is illustrated with European city images. Photo: Beate Binder (October 2004).

only linked to the opening of the Wall but also the *Reichskristallnacht* and the persecution of the Jews) are staged usually at the Pariser Platz, to mention just a few festivities this location hosts.[2] Since capitals are fundamentally symbolic spaces where the national history, myth of origin and a nation's fate are made visible, actually this general view is localized only in some places. In this sense, the Pariser Platz came into being as one of the most important national representational public spaces in the last decade. Here the local history of Berlin is made national, or, to put it another way, the local is transcended and transformed into the national. Today, the history of the Brandenburg Gate and its location in the very centre of the newly-built government quarter provide the "formulaic spatiality" (Parkin 1996) which imbues the staging of national commemoration with meaning and importance.

The perception of this square as national is supported by the story of its creation, i.e. its "local" history. Both square and gate were planned and constructed as part of the urban extension in the 18th century, and as the *Tagesspiegel* suggests, "gentry, intellect, and diplomacy" felt always at home on this square (*Tagesspiegel* 02-03/10/2002). Originally one of the noble places of the inner city, the Pariser Platz then became no-man's-land during the time of the city's division. The Wall passed the Brandenburg Gate a few metres west, and the Pariser Platz (which is located east of the gate) was a restricted area that was neither passable from the east nor from the west for some decades. As most of the buildings were destroyed during World War II and the ruins removed afterwards, the reconstruction began in the 1990s. It followed the guidelines of a critical historical reconstruction which were employed in order to give Berlin an unmistakable, historically saturated appearance and to support the construction of an unmistakable city image (Burg 1994). Banking establishments, the French and the American embassies (construction work of the latter only began recently), and the Hotel Adlon, with its noble suites, turned the place into one of the "first address of Germany". In this sense, the *Tagesspiegel* recapitulates: "Besides the nearby Potsdamer Platz, the citadel of globalized urban planning (with international groups, Cinemaxx, popcorn, sushi, and shopping-mall), the Pariser Platz appears as a national forum made of stone" (*Tagesspiegel* 31/12/2000). Calling the Pariser Platz a "parlour" marks its importance for both the city and the nation. Even though the institutions, located here, are transnational in scope, importance and performance, the place became a national space in the first place. Thus, the narrative of the local history is made national by infusing the local with national meaning.

But while producing and reaffirming the national map of Berlin as capital of the unified Germany, the national is positioned within the wider frame of the global at the same time, so that the production of a national map intersects with cosmopolitan endeavours even during the national celebrations. The switching of scale takes part in both directions. It constitutes a triangle of local, national and cosmopolitan reference. On the one hand, the image of the "family of nations" builds an important backdrop of this national holiday. The event connects the nation – as unity – to the global, making claims for Germany to have a seat within the family of nations. As the discourse on the metaphor of the "Berlin Republic" ("Berliner Republik") suggests, the new capital is meant not only to represent the national with its own history but to make a strong argument for the continuing reliability of German politics and the state's orientation towards Europe. In this sense, the celebration of the Day of German Unity aims to show Germany's relationship with its "neighbours" in the European context and to other powerful nations, and, last but not least, to demonstrate that Germany will take responsibility for them – knowing its own history, which is strongly connected to fascism, the Holocaust, and the destruction caused by the two World Wars (cf. Huyssen 2003; Ladd 1997).

Thus, some elements of the festivity render visible the efforts made to present Germany as a trustworthy nation. For example, giving away old bricks from the Brandenburg Gate to city mayors all over the world is meant to support the (national) self-image of friendship, tolerance, and openness. But this gesture is strongly connected to the construction of Berlin as a metropolis as well. It stresses the importance of cities as organizing points in increasingly globalised social and economic exchanges. It strengthens the networking of cities as part of their newly structured symbolic economy (cf. Zukin 1995), and supports the outstanding position of cities as important knots within global networks. And in this sense, the celebration simultaneously produces an imagined landscape of interrelatedness of the local to the global and the national.

The "All Nations Festival" reinforces this concept even more so. First of all, this festival exposes the idea of nationhood as a universal concept of societal organization. In fact, the principle of nationhood and national representation rules the whole festival. In this context, national representation means to draw on national cultural heritage i.e. draw on a "bounded concept of culture" (Gupta & Ferguson 1997). As all participating embassies are committed to producing an interesting and attractive program for visitors, they offer an image of the nation as a distinct societal and cultural unity. In effect, on the one hand there is the representation of the universal principle of nationhood, rendering invisible the power geography and hierarchies which organise the global. On the other hand, as national histories always do, hierarchies within societies, societal differentiation along the lines of gender, race, and class are made invisible in presenting national history and cultural heritage.

Thus, seen as a whole, the "All Nations Festival" represents the world as a colourful rug of different nationally-defined cultures, and so does the architectural landscape of the embassies. The embassy buildings are talking about national characteristics by bringing "traditional" cultural designs together with modern architecture. As Anthony Giddens has pointed out, heritage and tradition needs constant negotiation and confirmation in post-traditional societies. While contributing to hold the border of the "own" and the "foreign", tradition and heritage is a site and modus of societal negotiations (Giddens 1993). In this mode of producing narratives of the "own" and the "foreign", the design language of the embassies employs the strategy of exposing national heritage and combining it with codes of "modernity". The use of certain i.e. "national" materials and referring to national emblems, symbols, and stereotyped national images is about the national "own" as a distinct culture and these elements, set in contemporary design languages, refer the visitors to the modernity of the nation which is based on its cultural heritage. To mention but a few examples, the Indian Embassy is built with "typical" Indian sandstone, imported from India. The Mexican Embassy refers to architecture of the Aztec Empire. The British Embassy stresses the importance of popular culture and post-modernity and connects this endeavour with an oak "as friendly symbol of Britain continuity and lasting nature" (Britische Botschaft Berlin 2000:10). Thus, while traveling through the "Diplomatenviertel", one can encounter not only the most interesting architecture but also different cultures.

From the Berlin perspective and its urban landscape, this strategy of national representation is interpreted as a symbolic text of cosmopolitanism and multiculturalism. This is how the city makes use of the festival and how it interprets its contribution to the re-imagining of the city. The festival presents, via the embassies, the openness of Berlin toward the world and makes a strong claim for Berlin as a late modern metropolis. In this sense, the richness of cultural i.e. national representations takes part in constituting a multicultural and cosmopolitan atmosphere within the city. With Berlin as Capital, "hosting" guests from all over the world, the embassies produce a landscape of cosmopolitanism within the city – they turn the national space of the capital into cosmopolitan space. Thus, "the World within Berlin" – as the journal *Foyer* of the Berlin "Senatsverwaltung für Bauen, Wohnen und Verkehr" titled an issue about the emerging embassy quarter in 1996 – stands for a welcomed and controlled way of cosmopolitanism (cf. Binder 2004).

The opening of the MEXartes Festival is based on the concept of nations representing a distinct cultural heritage as well. Against this backdrop, the opening ceremony stages the pride Germany and Mexico have in their rich cultural exchange and celebrates their long-lasting interconnectedness. By doing so, it emphasizes the transnational space as a space that produces cultural hybridity and enables cultural enrichment. And in this sense, the opening of the MEXartes Festival points to the cultural role of (world) cities. Whilst offering a space of encounter with strangers and strangeness, cities have been playing, for a long time, an important role in the process of cultural production (cf. Hannerz 1993). Thus, the opening goes on in drawing the cosmopolitan map of Berlin, showing the metropolis as a site of cultural production.

During both events, the "All Nations Festival" and the MEXartes opening ceremony, the visitors are asked to come into contact with the "foreign" – not only in terms of the moment and the location for the event – but in terms of the city as a whole. As the mayor of Berlin, Klaus Wowereit, suggests: "In the first place, the festival opens a possibility in a city, marked by different cultures, to come into contact with the history and traditions of those foreign fellow citizens living here" (All Nations Festival 2004). Whilst employing the concept of nationhood, both the festivals takes part in constructing a map of the cosmopolitan Berlin, a map of a colourful cultural metropolis.

## Meaningful Intersections: Becoming a Capital in Late Modernity

The preceding section focused on the production of differing maps of Berlin – mainly a national and a cosmopolitan within and by public events. On the one hand, efforts to stage Berlin as a national capital refer to the "own" national history and contribute to the production of a national map of Berlin. This map is centred around the Pariser Platz, expanding to the Reichstag building and the chancellery, as well as to the Schlossplatz and the Museumsinsel, having outreaches even on the periphery of the city, e.g. the House of the Wannsee Conference[3] belongs to this national map as well. On this map, the "foreign" functions mostly as a mirror for the "own" and gives way to experience the distinctiveness of national cultures.

On the other hand, a cosmopolitan map of Berlin has also come into existence. Efforts to stage Berlin as multicultural, as open towards the world and enjoying its diversity structure a lot of public events taking place in Berlin e.g. the Love Parade for the techno kids, the Carnival of Cultures – a parade of migrant organizations (Knecht & Niedermüller 2002) –, the Christopher Street Day for the gay and lesbian local and translocal community, or the Berlin Marathon. They all operate with arguments for cultural diversity, multiculturalism and internationalism. The combination of all these events produces a text of multicultural diversity, of openness towards the world and of a rich mixture and creativity, which Berlin is able to offer and which constitutes an important aspect of the city's image. The cosmopolitan map has its centre in the newly built commercial and entertainment centres, especially the Potsdamer Platz, and consists of, to a large extent, cultural institutions and sites of cultural production. This map reveals the joyful atmosphere which satisfies curiosity and the lust for adventurous tours through the diversity of the world. The headline of this map could be "through the world within the city".

But these maps intersect and – what is most important in the line of my argument – they are made to intersect. These intersections are supposed to offer space where the contradictions of national narratives and cosmopolitan dreams are brought in line. In this sense public events produce liminal zones. As Sharon Zukin has convincingly shown, the attempt to establish a certain perception of a landscape is one of the central strategies in current social quarrels about the appropriation of space (Zukin 1992, 1995). These politics aim at giving space a singular and essential identity and at establishing a defined use of public space at the same time (cf. as well Massey 1994). But space in postmodern (as she calls it) urban landscapes "initiates and imitates" the ambiguity of cultural appropriation which came into being with the political, cultural and social changes of globalization. Sharon Zukin has named the appearance of liminal spaces in cities, spaces which link the global market to the local, and which complicate the appropriation of these spaces for constructing unambiguous spatial identities (Zukin 1992:222).

I propose to think of liminality not only with respect to the intersection of the local and the global, and, therefore, economic transformation, but to take into account the national as well. This turn in perspective renders visible different maps of belonging that are inscribed in urban landscapes. Even in late modernity, capitals still do expose themselves as national spaces. But as far as they are concerned, (as is the case with all big cities and metropolises), to gain economic and symbolic power on a global scale, they are forced to render an image of cosmopolitanism, of multiculturalism, cultural openness and diversity. In consequence, national capitals as metropolises are in need to follow cosmopolitan aims. And that is why the national has to be constituted in-between the local and the global in specific ways. Even though the rebuilding of Berlin and the construction of a new governmental quarter is strongly connected to the aim of presenting Germany as a nation, and even though the construction of a metropolis aims to establish new business and entertainment districts, both aims need to be intersected and connected to each other. The overall aim is to handle the contradictions and give room to agency in different scales. Public events especially offer spaces to present the national and the cosmopolitan simultaneously and show how they might harmonize with each other. Thus, they are important public stages, on which the ambiguity of the contradictory forces, encountered by late modern capitals, can be handled and experienced. In this sense, as Ulf Hannerz has named it, public events are to constitute a "planned cosmopolitanism": "The opportunities for the cultivation of cosmopolitanism in cities would seem to have been, as such, unplanned. That would appear, for one thing, to make serendipity an important aspect of cosmopolitanism. (…) In some of the 'cosmopolitan dreams' of today and tomorrow, perhaps there is less serendipity, more planning; sites which are rather more stages designed for the experience of novelty and diversity" (Hannerz 2002:10). Since the narrative of cosmopolitanism bears pervasive symbolic capital for nations and their capitals in late modernity, the constitution of spaces which offer the possibility to experience the cosmopolitan in a national frame and vice versa, seems to be a powerful strategy to make a capital. By switching scale, the events allow to intersect and interweave the national and the cosmopolitan, and they make it possible to handle the tensions between national narratives and cosmopolitan dreams.

# Notes

1. Many thanks to Gösta Arvastson and Tim Butler for their helpful comments on the first draft of this paper. Also thank you to Isabel Schoppe for her editorial contribution.
2. However, Pariser Platz is under construction again. During the construction of a new underground station, a "Schaustellenprogramm" (in German a play on words for: "building site as showcase program") is being staged to compensate for the loss of "the parlour": During autumn 2004, the fence presents a picture collage of European national capitals.
3. This is where the killing of the Jews was planned and finally decided

# References

All Nations Festival 2004 – http://www.allnations-festival.de/grusswort/grusswort2003.html (April 2004).
Anderson, Benedict 1983: *Imagined Communities. Reflections on the Origin and Spread of Nationalism.* London: Verso Editions and NLB.
Appadurai, Arjun 1996: The Production of Locality. In: Appadurai, Arjun (ed.) *Modernity at Large.* Minneapolis/London: University of Minnesota Press, pp. 178–199.
Bailey, F. G. 1996: Cultural Performance, Authenticity, and Second Nature. In: Parkin, David, Caplan, Lionel & Fisher, Humphrey (eds) *The Politics of Cultural Performance.* Oxford: Berghahn, pp. 1–17.
Berg, Per Olof & Löfgren, Orvar 2000: Studying the Birth of a Transnational Region. In: Berg, Per Olof, Linde-Laursen, Anders & Löfgren, Orvar (eds) *Invoking a Transnational Metropolis. The Making of the Øresund Region.* Lund: Studentlitteratur, pp. 7–26.
Binder, Beate 2004: Strategien nationaler Selbstrepräsentation. Eine Annäherung an die Botschaft der Botschaften aus stadtethnologischer Perspektive. In: Binder, Beate & Deuber-Mankowsky,

Astrid (eds) *Die Botschaft der Botschaften*. Berliner Blätter Heft 34, 24–33.

Binder, Beate & Niedermüller, Peter (forthcoming): The "New Berlin": Reconstructing the Past and Envisioning the Future. In: Dallmann, Antje, Lenz, Günter & Ulfers, Friedrich (eds) *Toward a New Metropolitanism: Reconstituting Public Culture, Urban Citizenship, and the Multicultural Imaginary in New York City and Berlin*.

*Britische Botschaft Berlin* 2000. Die Neuen Architekturführer No. 23: Stadtwandel Verlag.

Burg, Annegret (ed.) 1994: *Neue berlinische Architektur: eine Debatte*. Berlin/Basel/Boston: Birkhäuser.

Geertz, Clifford 1987: „Deep Play": Bemerkungen zum balinesischen Hahnenkampf. In: Geertz, Clifford (ed.) *Dichte Beschreibung*. Frankfurt a. M.: Suhrkamp, pp. 202–260.

Gerholm, Tomas 1988: On Ritual: A Postmodern View. In: *Ethnos*, 3–4, 190–202.

Giddens, Anthony 1993: Tradition in der posttraditionalen Gesellschaft. In: *Soziale Welt*, 44, 445–485.

Gupta, Akhil & Ferguson, James (eds) 1997: *Culture, Power, Place. Explorations in Critical Anthropology*. Durham/London: Duke University Press.

Handelman, Don 1998: *Models and Mirrors: Toward an Anthropology of Public Events*. New York/Oxford: Berghahn Books.

Hannerz, Ulf 1993: The Cultural Role of World Cities. In: Cohen, Anthony P. & Fukui, Katsuyoshi (eds): *Humanising the City? Social Contexts of Urban Life at the Turn of the Millennium*. Edinburgh: Edinburgh University Press, pp. 67–84.

Hannerz, Ulf 2002: Two-Faced Cosmopolitans: Consumer and Citizens. Cosmopolitan Dreams: Urban Life in 21st Century. Berlin, March 22–24, unpublished paper.

HKW: "Haus der Kulturen der Welt" – "The House of World Cultures": www.hkw.de/external/en/Profil/c_index.html (November 2004).

Huyssen, Andreas 2003: The Voids of Berlin. In: Huyssen, Andreas (ed.) *Present Past. Urban Palimpsets and the Politics of Memory*. Stanford: Stanford University Press, pp. 49–71.

Knecht, Michi & Niedermüller, Peter 2002: The Politics of Cultural Heritage. An Urban Approach. In: *Ethnologia Europaea*, 32, 2, 89–104.

Ladd, Brian 1997: *The Ghosts of Berlin. Confronting German History in the Urban Landscape*. Chicago/London: University of Chicago Press.

Low, Setha M. (ed.) 1999: *Theorizing the City. The New Urban Anthropology Reader*. New Brunswick/New Jersey/London: Rutgers University Press.

Massey, Doreen 1994: *Space, Place and Gender*. Cambridge/Oxford: Polity Press.

MEXartes – http://www.mexartes-berlin.de/ (April 2005).

Niedermüller, Peter 1998: Stadt, Kultur(en), Macht. In: *Österreichische Zeitschrift für Volkskunde*, LII/101, 279–301.

Parkin, David 1996: The Power of the Bizarre. In: Parkin, David, Caplan, Lionel & Fisher, Humphrey (eds) *The Politics of Cultural Performance*. Oxford: Berghahn, XV–XL.

Rabinow, Paul 1995: Repräsentationen sind soziale Tatsachen. Moderne und Postmoderne in der Anthropologie. In: Berg, Eberhard & Fuchs, Martin (eds) *Kultur, soziale Praxis, Text. Die Krise der ethnographischen Repräsentation*. Frankfurt a. M.: Suhrkamp, pp. 158–199.

Ristilammi, Per-Markku 2000: Cultural Bridges, Events, and the New Region. In: Berg, Per Olof, Linde-Laursen, Anders & Löfgren, Orvar (eds) *Invoking a Transnational Metropolis. The Making of the Øresund Region*. Lund: Studentlitteratur, pp. 95–108.

Ruddick, Susan 1996: Constructing Differences in Public Spaces: Race, Class, and Gender as Interlocking Systems. In: *Urban Geography*, 17, 2, 132–151.

Singer, Milton 1972: *When a Great Tradition Modernizes: An Anthropological Approach to Indian Civilization*. London: Pall Mall.

Smart, Alan & Smart, Josephine 2003: Urbanization and the Global Perspective. In: *Annual Review of Anthropology*, 32, 263–285.

*Tagesspiegel* 31/12/2000: Claudia Wahjudi: Platz der Republik.

*Tagesspiegel* 02-03/10/2002: Christian von Lessen: Ein Ort, der magisch anzieht.

*Tagesspiegel* 4/10/2002: Stephan Wiehler: Die Hüllen sind gefallen.

*Tagesspiegel* 04/07/2003: Auf Weltreise durch Berlin.

Tuan, Yi-Fu 1977: *Space and Place. The Perspective of Experience*. Minneapolis: University of Minnesota Press.

Zukin, Sharon 1992: Postmodern Urban Landscapes: Mapping Culture and Power. In: Lash, Scott & Friedman, Jonathan (eds) *Modernity & Identity*. Oxford/Cambridge, Mass.: Blackwell, pp. 221–247.

Zukin, Sharon 1995: *The Cultures of Cities*. Cambridge, Mass./Oxford: Blackwell.

# Creating Spaces of Fear and Spaces of Safety
## Young Natives and Migrants in Metropolitan Neighbourhoods

*Nora Räthzel*

In public image repertoires, young people of migrant background are mostly associated with problems. In the more positive versions they are seen as *having* problems: they are caught between two cultures and between two languages, fluent in neither and longing to return home. The negative versions see them as *producing* problems: they are prone to criminality, they reduce the standards of the schools they attend, and they keep to themselves and form gangs. Such common assumptions are also largely reflected in scholarly work on migrant youth. They are a problem that needs to be solved (Heitmeyer, Müller & Schröder 1997; *13. Shell Jugendstudie 2000*).

What is significant for the common sense notion, as well as for much of the scholarly work done in Germany, is that migrant youth are seldom situated within the context in which they grow up.[1] Therefore, one of the main goals of our research project on young people's everyday lives in European cities, conducted simultaneously in London and Hamburg, was to look at the *relationship* between migrant and native youth.[2] In the German part of the project (with which this article is concerned), our questions were deliberately broad: how do boys and girls of different ethnic and class backgrounds, from different neighbourhoods and in different European cities, negotiate their daily relationships? Under what conditions do they perceive each other as ethnic, male, female, rich, poor etc., and what meaning do these ascriptions take on in their relations to each other?

In Hamburg we worked between 1996 and 1999 with 160 thirteen to fifteen-year-old boys and girls from two different neighbourhoods and from three different school types: secondary school, comprehensive school and grammar school. Most of them were born in Germany, but their parents were born in 13 different countries, including Germany.[3] We gained access to the young people through the schools, and were able to conduct the majority of our research during school hours. This was certainly the main reason why almost all the young people remained in the project for such a long period. Using a diversity of methods, mainly designed in London by Phil Cohen, Les Back and Michael Keith[4], we discovered many different kinds of relationships and ways of articulating and living ethnicity, gender, and class (see Cohen, Keith & Back 1999; Back, Räthzel & Hieronymus 1999; Räthzel 1998, 2000, 2003a, 2003b; Räthzel & Hieronymus 2000).

The political background for our investigation is the tension that exists in Germany between being a country of immigration and (until the new government was elected in 1999, after we finished our fieldwork) the official notion of Germany as a nation-state consisting of a homogeneous population of ethnic Germans.

This tension leads to conflicts and limitations and has a negative effect on the migrant populations. The societal institutions have not been changed to meet the needs of a society of immigration, thus ignoring the needs and rights of such populations to full citizenship (in the juridical sense, as well as in the sense of their political and social rights, and of being seen as legitimate sectors of the population).

But this tension also has its negative bearings on the native population in that it creates an inability to deal with and accept differences and enables them to construct internal conflicts (i.e. housing problems, unemployment) as external conflicts, that is, as conflicts brought into the society from outside by immigrants – so-called foreigners – thus preventing them from finding viable solutions to these conflicts. Against this background we asked: How is the tension that exists on a political, institutional level lived in the everyday lives of young people? More specifically: Among those young people who say that they don't know anything other than growing up with "foreigners" – or "as foreigners," do we find new ways of living with differences?

The two neighbourhoods we chose for our research consisted of one in which the migrant background population formed only a small minority of 7% (12% within our researched age group between 13 and 15) and another in which they formed around 30% of the general population (51% within the age group between 13 and 15). We called the first Inlandtown and the second Portville. (The neighbourhoods will be presented in detail during the course of the article.)

One reason for choosing neighbourhoods that differed in terms of their ethnic composition was the fact that, in Germany, the concept of the "threshold of tolerance" is quite popular, both politically and academically. It is generally assumed that conflicts between newly arrived populations and those who have lived longer in the region become prominent when the first group is "too large". The definition of what can be considered "too large" varies. In our study the aim was to examine the way in which the numerical ethnic composition of a neighbourhood related to its other characteristics, such as its built environment, its history and its political tendencies.

This article focuses on the relationship between space and perceptions of safety and danger experienced by young migrants and young natives in Inlandtown and Portville. It starts by presenting the ways in which young people define dangerous places in both neighbourhoods. In Inlandtown, ethnicised groups regarded as dangerous are seen to make places dangerous, whereas in Portville people are seen as dangerous when they belong to dangerous places. After analysing the implications of these different conceptions, I elaborate on the manner in which young natives in both neighbourhoods position themselves in relation to their migrant peers. My thesis is that in both neighbourhoods, different "local spaces of normality" exist to which native young people relate in order to legitimise their relationship to young migrants. The article attempts to explain the existence of these different local normalities using Lefebvre's trialectical definition of space as space of representation, representational space and spatial practices. I conclude with the thesis that it is not so much the numbers of migrants in a certain area, but the overdetermination of the three spatial dimensions that creates local spaces of normality that can help to explain the relationship between native and migrant youth.

## Dangerous Places and Dangerous People

I begin with some quotes from young people in Portville and Inlandtown – fictitious names to protect the identity of the participants. In addition, all the names of those interviewed or involved in the project have been changed.

*Inlandtown:*

"Susi: I don't like to be in Inlandtown, 'cause there are always these kinds of people walking around. I walked there with my sister, we wanted to go home and there were some Turks or what that was and they molested us.

Simone: There are many foreigners living in Inlandtown. I find them quite violent. My father is a police officer and he told me the Turks already run around with a shooter or a butterfly knife.

Murat: I don't like to go to the station in the evening because Turks and Russians fight each other there most of the time."

*Portville:*

"Dina: I used to hang out with some German boys and they were always afraid the boys from

Koray Adan Square would steal their clothes or beat them up. But perhaps they wouldn't do anything. I haven't ever seen a real brawl there, but I've heard about some. They never touched me.

Patricia: I always make a wide berth and I don't go there, because I know, they think it's great to have a fight. Koray Adan, I have already seen an ambulance there, likeeyes having popped out and bloody noses and things like that.

Vicky: There are two from Adan Square in our youth centre. I don't like them that much, because they think they can achieve something with violence and that bothers me. But these two are quite nice.

Idi: Adan Square, there are a lot there who are into violence and I'm not. I live there, so I pass by and sometimes I play there. But they don't do anything."

From the above comments we can see that there are a number of differences between the way in which young people talk about dangerous places in Inlandtown and in Portville: The most obvious difference is perhaps that violence is linked to ethnicity in Inlandtown, while this is not the case in Portville.

A second difference is the relationship that these youngsters have towards those of whom they speak. In Inlandtown they seem to have no other relation except knowing that these violent people are Turks or Russians and dangerous, whereas in Portville they know them either from a distance or they actually meet them at the youth centre.

In Portville, dangerous places become dangerous because they are occupied by dangerous people. An (in)famous group makes for an (in)famous place. The group becomes the signifier of the place and, in turn, the place becomes the signifier of the group. Place and people reference each other as in Zora's story:

"Zora: ... for instance, when I was hanging around Koray Adan Square, a girl from the Miles quarter didn't like that, cause she had a crush on him and he was my best friend. That's why we had a fight."

Places describe people, and for anyone familiar with the scene, the place people "come from", tells them what kind of people they are. The connection between a place and the kind of people that belong to it is so self-evident for the speaker that no further explanation is needed to make sense of a story. The power of place is strong. Just by being in a certain place, one becomes a member of the group seen as owning the place:

"Zelal: I am, well, I used to be with the Jasons, because they are Spider (a youth centre in Portville)."

Knowledge of spatialised individuals is necessary in order to navigate safely through the neighbourhood.

"Zora: Well, if I go through the streets here, I am always aware that I can be attacked at any moment. Because here in Portville it's really extreme with the different neighbourhoods and different areas and streets: they are enemies but I know my way around."

Everybody seems to carry their place of belonging with them, as well as the enmities/friendships that go with it. Nevertheless, the relationship between both is in constant change. People change groups or are even in two groups at the same time.

As opposed to Zora's experience concerning the enmity of groups from different places, opposing groups sometimes support each other against others from outside the neighbourhood. "If we don't manage on our own, then we have other friends who can help us, those from Eastvillage and partly the Eriksons", says Jamal from the Jasons in talking about fights the group sometimes have with enemy groups from outside.

Relations between places and people are different in Inlandtown. They do not reference each other in an interchangeable way. Rather, the people who are seen to live in or hang out in a place denote the place as dangerous because *they* are dangerous by definition. Turks walking around with their butterfly knives transform a place into one of danger. The ethnicisation of places leads to an inflexibility in the relationship between places and people. The ethnic group becomes a signifier and the places become the signified. The relationship cannot be reversed. If you change place you do not necessarily change group. If somebody not belonging to that particular group hangs out in a place that is characterised by the presence of a specific group, he or she will not easily become part of that group if s/he does not share the group's ethnicity. We will see this later on in one of the examples.

The quotes I have chosen are not particularly exceptional as they are representative of the young people in our sample. We chose the two neighbourhoods because they had opposing positions in the local imaginary. We were suspicious of the strong impressions and differences that resulted from our fieldwork, and thought that we might have fallen prey to that dominant local imaginary. To test this we produced some statistics, and found that of the 56 young people who talked about violence in Portville, 16 (28%) connected it with "foreigners", while 17 of the 35 who constituted the sample talking about violence in Inlandtown did so (almost 48%).

It seemed apparent that our impression was correct, but as we are dealing with a relatively small sample, figures do not prove much. The question as to whether our findings indicate significant differences in the two neighbourhoods or not, can only be answered by looking more closely at the ways in which young people in both neighbourhoods talk about violence and migrants, and by analysing the actual contexts. If we find a good explanation for the different perceptions of violent youth by relating those perceptions to the social-physical context of the young people, we can claim that growing up in different neighbourhoods does indeed influence one's perception of and behaviour towards violence.

It is therefore not sufficient to just look at strong contrasts such as the ones found in the statements above. If there are significant differences in the two neighbourhoods, we might learn more about them by looking at similar statements as well. This is how a boy from Portville and a girl from Inlandtown describe their respective neighbourhoods:

"Simone: A lot of Turks or others who are violent run around here, but violence is not that extreme. Other districts are worse.

Danny: I live in Theo Street. The street is kind of OK, but just around the corner, I couldn't take a photo of that, all these ... but not that I have anything against Turks, but they are Turks, they say things like: "hey, give me money". *Interviewer: How do you know they are Turks?* Danny: Because I know them, I have some Turkish friends and they don't like them either, that's why I know that. I don't have anything against Turks, one lived in my street and he was my best friend."

The most apparent difference between the two statements here seems to be Danny's effort to avoid any impression of "having anything against Turks". It is revealing how one of the most common arguments used to assure one's anti-racist attitude (some of my best friends are ...) never ceases to be re-invented. It indicates that an understanding of racism is deeply imbedded in our everyday thinking: it equates power relations on a societal (or worldly) scale with relations between individuals in daily life. Though they may relate to and influence each other, this is not necessarily the case. Remember the way in which those Germans who counted Jews among their best friends either took part in or supported racist practices during German Fascism.

Another difference between Danny's and Simone's way of talking about Turks is to be found in the kind of stories they tell. While Simone attributes them with violence, Danny's story is more about annoyance than open violence. Perhaps this has to do with the fact that both speak on different levels of generalisation. Simone has heard her father – a policeman – say that Turks are violent and carry knives. The identification of Turks with violence must have become self-evident, otherwise she would not present the contradiction that there is a lesser amount of violence in her immediate neighbourhood even though there are so many Turks living there. Danny reports his personal experience and distinguishes between Turks who are his friends while disapproving of the behaviour of other Turks. It seems as if he is not identifying Turks in general with violence. Unfortunately, this conclusion is premature, as illustrated by another of his comments made later during the same conversation:

"Danny: For so many Turks living in our area, it is not as bad here as in other places, for that it is really peaceful, I'd say, but so many, yes, well, how should I say that, there are many Turks in our area, but hardly anything happens as opposed to other areas."

Both Simone and Danny are surprised at experiencing relatively little violence in spite of being surrounded by a supposedly violent ethnic group. This does not make them insecure with regard to their general equation of Turks and violence, however. Does it make any difference, then, that Danny comes up with his best Turkish friend in order to avoid the impression of being a racist? According to van Dijk (1992), it would only show that he is better at denying his racism than Simone is. According to Billig (1991), he is arguing with himself about the two different beliefs he holds. I want to follow the latter a bit further and look at Simone's and Danny's answers to the question posed to all our respondents in the final feedback-interview: "Is it of any importance if the parents of young people you know or they themselves were born in a country other than Germany?"

"Simone: It doesn't really bother me that they are here, as long as they don't, like some Turks, who are thugs, then I ask myself often, well, they don't belong here, but apart from that, they are quite nice, ... in my class there are foreigners as well and they are really quite nice. It doesn't matter for me. I only think that those who are so violent, I don't know.
Danny: That doesn't matter, because they are only human beings as well. Why should one get along better with one's own nationals than with foreigners? That's daft. I'm not such a right extremist or something, don't know, somehow it doesn't matter to me because one of my best friends is Turkish."

Simone maintains her position of identifying Turks with violence. She comes close to demanding the expulsion of those who are "so violent". The breaks and incoherence of her speech indicate that she knows she is on dangerous ground here, saying something that will not be seen as correct by the interviewer. In this case, the interviewer was herself of migrant background. Danny in turn, rejects any kind of differentiation between Germans and non-Germans.

## Daily Friendships and Daily Racisms

One explanation the young people in our sample gave for such differences was that there were so many – as they called them – foreigners living in Portville that there was no point in calling somebody a foreigner. Or as Clara put it: "We are used to foreigners, we grew up with them. If they weren't here – all the different shops and restaurants, something would be missing, it would be quite empty."

The latter remark reproduces one of the most dearly held beliefs of anti-racist policies (at least in Germany): when people know each other and get used to each other, they get along and racism has no chance. This view is expressed in Danny's sentence about his best friend being a Turk. There is certainly some truth in the argument that where migrants are a strong minority, as in Portville, they are better able to fight daily racism and are thus more difficult to marginalize. But I do not think this is enough, because we do find situations in which a large minority, or even a majority, is marginalized and oppressed. For instance, there is a neighbourhood in Maincity with the same degree of ethnic diversity and a very similar social structure (working class, with around 10% people living on social welfare), which, as opposed to Portville, has a strong right-extremist electorate.

A case that undermines the view that close relationships eliminate racist views is that of

Else: She attends a secondary school, which means that in her class – in relation to other schools in Inlandtown – there are a disproportionate number of young people of migrant background. Like Clara, she is used to living with quite a number of migrant youth. In addition, she is the only native person in our sample to visit the infamous Billy's disco, seen by most others as frequented by dangerous Turks (compare quotes above). In answering the question about whether a migrant background makes any difference in Inlandtown she says:

"Else: No, I have only friends who are foreigners. Not in school, but in the disco, from the disco only. You can have much more fun with foreigners. Yes, somehow they are not that prudish, you can do anything together with them. In the disco, if something happens, it's like: 'what the fuck'."

In explaining why she has predominantly migrant friends she describes them as different – though in a way that she likes. Such a positive distinction can easily turn into something negative:

"I have nothing to do with the Kurds, though, they are disgusting, they smell like hell and they think they can fiddle around with you. If you hit them you are a slut and if you put up with it you are a slut too. You feel really stupid. My friends come from Yugoslavia, Bosnia, Germans, some Turks, everything, really, Russians, Poles, except Turks and Albanians, no thanks, aaah, I mean Kurds and Albanians. Turks are okay as well, some of them. There are such foreigners and such foreigners, such Germans and such Germans, I'll say, there are more handicapped and less handicapped ones in each race."

One cannot really call Else a convinced antiracist, despite the common wisdom she displays at the end of her statement about good and bad people in any "race" and that most of her friends are "foreigners". While she excuses the Turks, the Kurds become the bearers of the traits her peers ascribe to the former. Friendship and knowledge do not lead her to a rejection of racist images, or even to a more careful usage of them.

The need for Else to produce racist images of Kurds seems to arise from the need to legitimate her unruly behaviour. By applying these images, she tries to retain her membership of the peer-group she hides her "home" (the disco) from. Additionally, she can display her expertise concerning "foreigners" when claiming that it is not the Turks that are the problem, but the Kurds.

The structures of Else's and Danny's discourses are opposed to each other. While he starts with a negative description of ethnically marked individuals, and tries to correct the impression that this may reflect his general views about them, Else starts emphasising her good relations with migrant youth, and tries to correct the impression that this may reflect a disapproval of the commonly held views of "foreigners". What Else is doing is to co-ordinate her practices and experiences with the dominating view about foreigners held by her native classmates, and in her neighbourhood in general. Although she does not go as far as to grant them their views in every respect, (when she talks with the interviewer) she does hide her visits to a place with an exceptionally bad reputation. For Else, her dissenting behaviour implies more than not fitting into the mainstream. Being a girl, she is vulnerable to losing her respectability (being seen as a slut), whereas a boy would only be seen as a wrongdoer without having to fear the loss of his integrity as a boy. She sees herself threatened from both sides: from the Kurds who may see her as a slut if she does not behave in the "correct" way and from the Germans who may regard her as such because she is seen in a place visited by Turks.

Thus, the mere friendship between migrants and natives is not in itself a basis for anti-racist views. It seems to be rather the social context within which friendships and encounters take place that is decisive.[5] Therefore, I want to proceed by trying to describe the differences between Portville and Inlandtown on a different level than that of their more heterogeneous and more homogeneous inhabitants, respectively.

To do this I shall use Lefèbvre's trialectical definition of space; the first being the "representation of space":

"Conceptualized space, the space of scientists, planners, urbanists, technocratic sub-dividers and social engineers, as of a certain type of artist with a scientific bent. This is the dominant space in any society (or mode of production). Conceptions of space tend, with certain exceptions ... towards a system of verbal (and therefore intellectually worked out) signs" (Lefebvre 1991:33).

I would like to include politicians, the media, youth workers and teachers as producers of representations of space. Their representations show Inlandtown as a place dominated by right-wing groups, while Portville is presented as a domain of the anti-racist left. Two reports (from the same conservative newspaper) about right-extremist demonstrations, which took place recently in both areas, provide good examples of such representations:

Right Extremists in Maincity

The last march of right extremist groups for the time being took place six months ago. Accompanied by a huge number of policemen, 100 Neo-nazis went through Inlandtown. The police managed to impede a clash with the 120 leftists, who wanted to disturb the group. In July 1999 more than 600 Neo-nazis marched through Inlandtown, shouting, 'fame and honour for the Waffen-SS', demonstrating against the so-called 'Wehrmachtsausstellung' (exhibition about the atrocities of the German army during World War II, NR).

Demonstrators Impede a Neo-nazi March in Portville

Meanwhile, around 50 demonstrators had sat down in front of the police in order to protect themselves from the expected water cannons. ... The water cannon should be directed towards the other side, said a woman, they have no business to be in Portville. Some of the demonstrators compared the situation with 'bloody Sunday' on the 17th of July 1932, when the SA provoked fights with the Communists and 18 people died. While the police deployed their water cannons, about 1 000 demonstrators gathered on the street. They were not only organised anti-fascists, but also ordinary residents: elderly couples and families with children. The police had to choose whether they wanted to clear the way for the NPD against pensioners and children – or change the route. They changed the route."

In these two reports, Inlandtown is represented as a place where fascists can, although not undisturbed, succeed in having demonstrations, while in Portville even elderly people and families confront them. Note the historical link made in the second report, which evokes Portville's revolutionary past. It is not so much the fact that this link was made by a demonstrator, but the fact that it is reported in the conservative newspaper that is of interest. This links to and reinforces the image of the neighbourhood as one that has "always" had a left-wing population.

The electoral results in both neighbourhoods are another source of representation – representation in the double sense of who is elected to speak for the neighbourhood, and of the kind of images the results of these elections suggest. The table below shows the result of the local elections in both neighbourhoods in the year 1997. With regard to the main parties, the Social Democrats (SPD) and the Christian Democrats (CDU), the results do not differ that much. The former rules in both neighbourhoods (like in Maincity as a whole at that time).[6] Differences occur at the margins of the political spectra, where the Green Party has 7% more votes in Portville than in Inlandtown, while the extreme right has 3% more votes in Inlandtown than in Portville. These margin differences account for the images of Inlandtown as the area of the extreme right and Portville as that of the alternative left, even though the percentage of people voting for the Green Party in Inlandtown is only 0.3% lower than in Maincity as a whole.

These spaces of representation, that is the im-

*Number of votes 1997:*

|  | Portville |  | Inlandtown |  |
|---|---|---|---|---|
| Entitled | 174 181 | % | 81 703 | % |
| Turn Out | 118 275 | 67.9 | 56 129 | 68.7 |
| Invalid votes | 2 877 | 2.4 | 1 426 | 2.5 |
| Valid votes | 115 398 |  | 54 703 |  |
| SPD | 35 773 | 31 | 19 668 | 36 |
| CDU | 37 720 | 32.7 | 18 184 | 33.2 |
| GRÜNE/GAL | 23 978 | 20.8 | 7 255 | 13.3 |
| STATT Partei | 5 156 | 4.5 | 2 299 | 4.2 |
| F.D.P. | 4 921 | 4.3 | 1 572 | 2.9 |
| REP | 2 023 | 1.8 | 1 877 | 3.4 |
| DVU | 4 686 | 4.1 | 2 974 | 5.4 |
| NPD | 254 | 0.2 | 59 | 0.1 |
| Right extrem. total |  | 6.1 |  | 8.9 |

age of Inlandtown as a centre of right extremism and the image of Portville as home to the anti-racist left, inform what I would like to call (using Lefebvre's second definition of space) young people's *lived spaces*:

"Space as directly lived through its associated images and symbols, and hence the space of 'inhabitants' and 'users', but also of some artists and perhaps of those, such as a few writers and philosophers, who describe and aspire to do no more than describe. This is the dominated – and hence passively experienced – space which the imagination seeks to change and appropriate. It overlays physical space, making symbolic use of its objects. Thus representational spaces may be said, though again with certain exceptions, to tend towards more or less coherent systems of non-verbal symbols and signs (Lefebvre 1991:245)."

Such symbols of representational spaces are nowadays used in the websites through which neighbourhoods represent themselves. As examples, I have copied the homepages of Inlandtown and one of the neighbourhoods in Portville, in which a great number of our young people lived (see next page). It can be argued that such homepages belong to the space of representation, as opposed to representational space, because they are produced by those with resources. Yet, the ones I have copied are not created by local officials but by private initiatives of people in the neighbourhoods. In this sense they represent the ways in which these initiatives live their neighbourhoods. They are like local newspapers made by committed local inhabitants.

The differences in the two homepages are striking. When visiting *www.Inlandtown.de* one is immediately confronted with advertisement from different businesses in the area – obviously the sponsors of the website. Before getting to the site itself, the first information one gets in Portville.de concerns the principles by which the site has been produced: in order to ensure that everybody has access, even if not having the latest equipment, the site has been produced without frames.

Whilst the Inlandtown site symbolises the power of individual entrepreneurship and appeals to the consumer, the Portville site is designed to be used as a means of gaining information about the community and as a means of communication between its members. Even buying and selling becomes a horizontal form of communication between those who want to get rid of things and those who want to acquire them.

The pictures of streets in the neighbourhoods are also very different. Those of Inlandtown suggest a beautiful, orderly and conflict-free neighbourhood, whereas those of Portville stress the everyday atmosphere: a rainy street, a dis-

## 1. Self-Representation: The Inlandtown Homepage

# Welcome in Inlandtown !

Your Broker

**BEST Travel agency** | **Building co-operative**

<u>Real</u>-estate market in Inlandtown – free of charge and up-to-the-minute

Monoville: Images from above order online now!

"A Landmark to be sold." <u>The</u> Inlandtown Mill faces an uncertain future.

## 2. Self-Representation - The Portville Homepage

| Network | Press overview |
|---|---|
| What really happens in the village. Here you can search for associations, initiatives, projects, branches, and private homepages. Join the network. Do you belong to Portville? Then you should be part of the mixville.de-network. As an association, a firm or a private homepage. Free of charge. Here you will learn how it works: Network under "join". | Portville in the press – Here you find all articles in TAZ, Abendblatt, Morgenpost, Welt and MainCity.de, which include the keyword Portville. |
| Market | Echo sounder |
| If you want to rent a couch, sell a husband or fall in love with a flat, place your ad here. | Information and Stories from the depths of Portville. <u>Walk</u> through Portville III |
| <u>Calendar</u> of events | Clique |
| | More then a guestbook. Talk before others talk |
| Trinkets | Gastronomy |
| The page for interactive trinkets. Choose your favourite place in Portville. | See how others judge restaurants and judge yourself. |

The Inlandtown and the Portville Homepage.

orderly but well-used place – the Koray Adan Square about which the young people spoke so much (see quotes above). At the back of the Square we can see a camping van. It belongs to young people who choose to live this way. After the picture was taken, they have been removed from the Square but have been assigned other places in the neighbourhood. The wall filled with graffiti is the back of a stage used for amateur theatre productions organised by the youth centre, The Spider.

These photos are accompanied by texts emphasising the diversity of the neighbourhood in terms of class and ethnicity. They talk about conflicts in Portville, poverty, unemployment, homelessness and racism, and about the initiatives existing in the neighbourhood to combat these problems.[7]

No text accompanies the pictures of Inlandtown. In fact, there is no overall description of the neighbourhood except for a section on its history that ends with the year 1938 – only mentioned because that was when Inlandtown became incorporated into the larger Maincity. That is all we learn about fascism on this site. The history section of Portville is notably different, however, in that it describes the fascist period in relative detail.

While the creators of Portville.de describe themselves as an initiative of individuals, who work voluntarily and are not attached to any party or to any specific politics, we learn nothing about the makers of Inlandtown.de.

A similar difference can be found in the way in which the two youth clubs of Inlandtown and Portville represent themselves. The first one shows young people in a room that resembles a family living room. The description emphasises the different atmospheres provided for different age-groups, the possibilities to play billiards and to eat fast food. This is the youth centre organising the disco, which Else attends.

The youth club in Portville is housed in a former factory, and the image shows the café where young people meet. It is described as having a special "atmosphere" of its own. The website offers young people the opportunity of taking part in creative activities and states that the young people's own ideas and suggestions are welcome. The images and the texts create connotations of a harmonious bourgeois home on the one side, and an attempt to fuse cultural creativity with a free development of young people's capabilities on the other.

## Manoeuvring Within and Creating the Local Space of Normality

I would like to expand Lefevbre's definition by interpreting the lived space as a set of practices which young people (and adults) create by making use of the dominant spaces of representation, the signs and symbols of representational space, spatial practices (see below), and their, however limited, practices of opposition. An example of such a creation becomes tangible through Susanne's account:

"Well, actually, I don't know if I am left, right or in the middle. On the one hand I don't have anything against foreigners, (…), as long as they are not Turks, especially with girls who come from a foreign country or who are born here and have foreign born parents because, they have to suffer. My friend's father is Moslem and she had to suffer a lot because of that. And in this respect I am very strongly on the left, if somebody tries to harass my friend or something."

Although she does not really know on which political side she is, wanting to defend her friend with a Moslem father automatically positions her strongly on the left, whereby left is defined through one's relations to "foreigners". At the same time, this does not prevent her from joining her fellow peers in rejecting Turks. The subject position of a leftist is somehow occupied by Susanne against her will, simply by rejecting racist harassment. This demonstrates the strong political connotations that "mingling with foreigners" has in Inlandtown. It is true that Danny created a political link by underlining his conviction that Germans and "foreigners" were equal, by describing himself as not being a right extremist. He did not imply, though, that his position was leftist.

This quote is another good example of the antagonistic ways in which discourses are structured in both Portville and Inlandtown. In the latter, it seems to be the rule that you have to say something negative about foreigners once you have opposed racism, in order to position yourself back into the group that is "entirely normal", as Daria, a friend of Susanne's calls themselves. In the first it is the other way round: once you have said something negative about "foreigners" you have to affirm your overall approving attitude. How is this to be explained?

A right extremist presence governs the representation of Inlandtown for these young people. Its consequence is that there is a large space in which to represent the Other as a threat without transgressing the boundaries beyond which a position comes to be seen as racist. By the same token, moving too far away from the beliefs represented by this group could mean to find oneself beyond the limits constituting normality. The boundaries of what I would call the *local space of normality* are drawn by the dominating and the dominated margins. Any trespassing has to be counterbalanced by a set of legitimations, which either reproduce the normal range of representations or they have to be openly opposed. Normally, a combination of both kinds of strategies will be applied – resulting in yielding to and resisting the regulating normality at the same time (see the examples of Else and Susanne).

The space of normality is created in the same way, but with a different result in Portville. Anti-racism is seen as dominating the space of representation. As Danny makes clear, believing that the country in which one's parents were born is of any importance amounts to right-wing extremism. Or as Patrick says: "It doesn't make any difference to me (national origin, NR), but for many it does, I think, they are Nazis. Such people are stupid." At the same time nobody, except one girl who dressed as a punk and had been a member of a Marxist group, spoke about being on the left because they opposed what they saw as a right extremist position. Doing this was simply being normal. As in Inlandtown, "Nazis" serve as the opponent against which one's own view is defined. However, what counts as a nazi view occupies a much broader space of representation. Consequently, the boundaries defining normality towards people of migrant background are tighter. A good example of this was Zelal's reaction to the video we had made of young people taking us on walks through their respective neighbourhoods. As soon as the lights were switched on again, Zelal immediately burst out: "Aaah, but these people in Inlandtown, they are all Nazis." "Why?" "Because all the time they are talking about foreigners, foreigners, foreigners, nothing else but foreigners." None of the young people in the video had said anything negative about "foreigners" but indeed, when the interviewer asked them what kind of people lived in their houses and what kind of people used the youth centres, in most cases their answers had been "foreigners". One can argue that Zelal is especially sensitive because she comes from another country herself. But that only means that she is especially good at capturing the subtle differences in speech and naming that exist in the two neighbourhoods.

So far, only young people of native background have been used to analyse the different lived spaces of Inlandtown and Portville. For reasons of space I cannot include the representational space of young migrants (but see Räthzel 2003b). A short summary must therefore suffice. Young migrants in Portville told us that they did not experience any racism in their environment or by their peers. Occasionally adults told them off using racist vocabulary. Young migrants in Inlandtown disagreed with their native peers that they all got on well, and stressed that they experienced racism in school as well. Yet they never talked about it with their teachers and regretted that there was no possibility for them to address these questions. The lived spaces of young migrants thus confirmed those lived by young natives, namely that migrants constituted a legitimate part of Portville, while they were seen as intruders in Inlandtown.

It is not so much that people are more or less racist in both neighbourhoods, but that they have to relate their views and actions to the local space of normality. Even when young people say the same things about migrant youth, they set them in a different context, negotiating their positions within the given normality. What is within the range of normality in Inlandtown will be seen as "Nazi-behaviour" in Portville, and what is within the range of normality there will be seen as "very much on the left" in Inlandtown. Consequently, when migrant youth is harassed, treated negatively or talked about negatively in Portville, there will be sanctions, either by peers or by the other part of that same abusing person. In Inlandtown, however, such behaviour will largely be seen as normal or as a joke, and pass unheeded.

My point is that these differences are due to the representations of these places which enter the ways in which they are lived by young people (but not only by them of course). They give meaning to daily actions and constitute the background against which people understand and judge their own and other people's actions. It is not simply the presence of the Other (in whatever numbers), but the fact that people with different background share a common space that makes for good or bad relationships. What is decisive is the meaning these relationships have through the way in which this shared space is represented.

One could say that I am arguing in a circle: Migrants are more likely to be seen as a threat in Inlandtown because the place is represented as one where migrants are seen as a threat. A third dimension has to be introduced in order to (hopefully) get out of this circle. This is where Lefebvre's third definition of space as *perceived* comes in.

"The spatial practice of a society secretes that society's space; it propounds and presupposes it, in a dialectical interaction; it produces it slowly and surely as it masters and appropriates it. From the analytic standpoint, the spatial practice of a society is revealed through the deciphering of its space" (Lefebvre 1991:38f).

Portville and Inlandtown are products of spatial practices. They are places that were built for a specific usage, following specific conceptualisations of who should use space in which way. These political goals and meanings are built into physical space and enter its representations and the way it is lived. Erdal and Angela describe the spatial practices of their respective neighbourhoods:

"Erdal: If you look at those chains of shops, the Turk starts there, and there the Albanian ends. And where the Albanian ends, the Yugoslav starts with his shop. And I mean, living together here – if we would look at Greece or Turkey and here, where the Turkish ends, you see only Greeks and they are fully satisfied with it. I am also learning Greek.

Angela: They build residential blocks for Germans, for Russians, for Turks, and now they even want to build one for Blacks. Because you have to keep the different races apart. Because they do not get on with each other. They will fight."

Both talk about differences and how places are constructed to accommodate them. Erdal speaks about the way in which differences are shared and the way in which enmities (Greeks and Turks) lose their meaning through daily encounters engendered by physical proximity. Angela talks about the danger of differences and the need to physically separate them.

In looking at the history of the two neighbourhoods, two features are particularly striking as they relate to the statements cited above. Books describing Portville tell us that it has been a neighbourhood of immigration from the beginning. Founded by Sephardim Jews fleeing from the Spanish Netherlands and situated by the sea, it has been visited by people from many different countries, some of whom have stayed and settled. Until 1867, Portville belonged to the Danish state and only became incorporated into Maincity in 1938, during the fascist period.

While Portville has always been a centre of commerce, Inlandtown was a village within an agricultural area until the end of the nineteenth century, when industrialisation started to take over and big factories were built, as well as housing for the incoming workers. The history books don't mention immigration, and only describe working class populations moving to where the factories were being built. We find the following description about an area in Inlandtown:

"Kamp: The first house was built 1869 in the later working class area of Kamp. Until well into the nineties of the last century 80 households had settled. They were separated according to professions: In Kamp the factory workers, in the south of Inlandtown, the old part, the small craftsmen, and tradesmen, in the new part the skilled worker and the white collar workers."

This statement puzzled us because it resembled Angela's description of her neighbourhood in terms of the way in which she assigned residential blocks to different "races", as she called them. What does this tell us? Are we to believe that traditions of a neighbourhood are passed on from one generation to the other? One way in which this happens might be through the stories that people hand down to the subsequent generations, as quoted in the newspaper article above.

Walking through the neighbourhoods of Portville and Inlandtown, and experiencing the different surroundings, we thought that an additional explanation might be found in the built environment, because the way those neighbourhoods are populated is reflected in their different architectures:

Inlandtown is a planned construction. By and large, old housing was knocked down to make way for new buildings, built for the use of larger groups of the population that arrived with the developing industry. The built environment reflects the concepts of mass production with its similarity and repetitiveness; its homogeneity.

In Portville, we find a stratum of different kinds of buildings that reflect the different times in which they were built and the needs they were designed to fulfil. We find houses for the working classes (Portville is a traditionally left-wing working-class area), houses for the better off, new housing to replace the damage of the war, and empty places, where nothing has been replaced. We also find a lot of rundown places. In short, the structure is chaotic rather than planned.

One could thus argue that different ways of living differences are already inscribed into the physical arrangement of a place – into its *Dispositif* to use Foucault's expression – through the spatial practices that brought it into being. Foucault's thesis was that the arrangement of things (words, rules, institutions as well as physical entities) produced certain effects. One of the examples he analyses is the way bodies were arranged in schools and in the military to produce a certain kind of discipline (see for instance Foucault 1982, 1995).

A passage in Richard Sennett's book, the *Conscience of the Eye*, provides two useful concepts to think about the different dispositif of Portville and Inlandtown. Sennett describes two streets in New York as being arranged in two different ways, in a linear way and in a way where differences overlay each other (Sennett 1992:165ff).

The more diverse built environment in Portville, together with the more planned, homogeneous structure in Inlandtown and the different ways in which these neighbourhoods are populated, are accompanied by different usages. We find a considerable number of different shops, community based initiatives and cultural centres in Portville, while in Inlandtown we find mainly German-owned shops (often chains), and as far as we could see, only two alternative community centres. The pedestrian zone in Portville is mainly used by a group of punks, occasionally by street-traders, and in the warmer periods, by men and women of different ages and ethnic backgrounds representing the variety of the inhabitants. The pedestrian zone in Inlandtown is neat and tidy. Young people hanging around might disturb the picture. And indeed, some youngsters do sit there in order to do exactly that: disturb the adults and provoke angry looks.

Overlays of differences provide an opportunity to come to terms with each other, while the linear arrangement of differences makes it easier to produce, or maintain, divisions between "us" and "them".

The way in which physical space is organised seems to impact on the way in which people perceive and live differences. The "repressive homogeneity" (to use Gerald Suttles' term, 1968) which dominates in Inlandtown and the linear arrangement of differences there, seem to make it more difficult for young people to perceive ethnic differences as opportunities, or simply as a normality. By the same token, the more chaotic structure of Portville, with its overlaid differences, seems to make it easier to enjoy differences or to take them for granted, instead of feeling threatened by them.

Physical space can be seen as signifying all three dimensions of space, thus transmitting its meaning from one generation to another. It is also, of course, constantly redefined and represented, as well as lived in different ways. There is reciprocity, I believe, between the way in which space *induces* representations, the way in which it is lived, and the way in which it acquires new meanings through new representations and spatial practices. Yet a certain stability seems to prevail.

The fact that fear of the Other also exists in Portville, though in different contexts, and also the fact that space is divided up among the different youth groups, indicates that we are not talking about an ideal place of constant harmony versus a place of constant aggression. But I do not believe that harmony is something to strive for. Harmony, as the absence of arguments, confrontations or even fights, would also be the absence of development and learning – and, according to Simmel, of social groups:

"Hostilities not only prevent boundaries within the group from gradually disappearing, so that these hostilities are often consciously cultivated to guarantee existing conditions. Beyond this, they also are of direct sociological fertility: often they provide classes and individuals with reciprocal positions which they would not find, or not find in the same way, if the causes of hostility were not accompanied by the *feeling* and the expression of hostility... The disappearance of repulsive (and, considered in isolation, destructive) energies does by no means always result in a richer and fuller social life ... but in as different and unrealizable a phenomenon as if the group were deprived of the forces of cooperation, affection, mutual aid, and harmony of interest" (Simmel 1955:18).

It was not the absence of conflicts that marked the difference between Portville and Inlandtown, but rather the way in which these conflicts were articulated. Simmel's term "reciprocal" is decisive here: In Inlandtown young people of migrant background did not appear to have a chance to take part in conflicts on an equal footing with native young people, as their presence was not seen as legitimate. In Portville, confrontations took place between various kinds of opponents; mainly between people from different places, or, sadly enough, between stronger and weaker young people, where the former made use of the latter's disadvantage. Being on the receiving end one day did not exclude the possibility of being superior the next, however. In Inlandtown, confrontations took place between different groups defined as ethnic. This meant that the same group was always made inferior, which reinforced its construction as the Other in society at large.

## To Conclude

Looking at the ways in which young people talk about violence in both Portville and Inlandtown, the most striking feature was the strong link constructed between violence and "foreigners", namely Turks in Inlandtown. In trying to understand these differences, I described the two neighbourhoods as constituting different three dimensional spaces defined by Lefebvre as spatial practices, spaces of representation and lived spaces. These three dimensions produce what I call "local spaces of normality", to which everyone arguing about ethnicity has to relate. These spaces of normality are defined through the extremes seen as dominating and being dominated. Right extremists are perceived as dominating Inlandtown. They are defined by their violence against "foreigners" with the consequence that a negative description of migrant youth becomes part of normality, while having migrants as friends constitutes an extreme leftist position.

Left anti-racists are perceived as dominating Portville. Consequently, to make a difference between natives and migrants already constitutes a rightist position, while the space of normality includes relations of equality between migrant and native youth, friendships, and the taken-for-granted nature of a migrant presence.

Individuals can, of course, cross these boundaries because they are not totally determined by them. In our sample, some young people in Inlandtown talked about their friendships with young people of migrant background while some young people in Portville talked about "violent Turks". It is therefore necessary to further specify why I suggest that these neighbourhoods constitute different local spaces of normality. It is not only the occurrence of native young people living ethnic relations differently that warrants declaring these spaces as different. It is the over-determination of differences on all the dimensions of representational space, spaces of representations, and spatial practices that leads us to the conclusion of different normalities.

If this analysis makes any sense, what does it mean for the issue of daily racism in places represented as racist or as anti-racist, as in our two cases? What I would say so far is this: within a space where anti-racism (to put it rather simplistically) constitutes the local space of normality, daily racism does not disappear altogether. However, its appearance is played down and counterbalanced, thus creating lived spaces of safety for a migrant population. Natives and migrants alike play a part in reproducing this kind of normality, which means that they subordinate themselves to the dominating representation. In Portville, this normalisation empowers migrant youth and thereby makes their lives easier and allows them to develop their capacities and their self esteem. Virtually all the young people of migrant background in our sample in Portville told us that they felt safe in their neighbourhood. At the same time, they are locked into a local normality for their feeling of safety (in Räthzel 2003b I have developed this point further). Local space does not exist in a vacuum. Young people in Portville knew that they were living in an enclave. Already the behaviour of adults, and especially leaving their area, showed them that they are not seen as a legitimate part of the population elsewhere. As institutions of society at large have not opened up and changed according to the needs of a more diverse society, the contradiction between local space and societal space in general produces feelings of ambiguity. In spite of this, young migrants' possibilities of appropriating space in Portville and their experience of being accepted as legitimate citizens may equip them with more strategies to make use of the scarce opportunities that society at large holds for them. It may also equip them with some skills to fight off daily racism.

As for Inlandtown, native and migrant youth also share the local space of normality, although they occupy different positions within it. Daily racism is experienced as damaging by migrant youth, but is not discussed openly among peers or with teachers. As a result, self-normalisation has the effect of disempowering migrant youth and they instead become outsiders; some seeking redress by retreating into their respective communities. One example of a process of self-normalisation in Inlandtown is Svetlana, who arrived four years ago from Russia. During that time, her circle of friends has changed:

"Svetlana: Now, I spend more time with the German Russians, but before I spent more time with the Germans. That has changed a bit. It's not my fault. My mother doesn't like it, she says, we are in Germany now, you have to live with the Germans if you want to go on living here. I do understand her, but, if they don't have time, then I do something with my other friends."

These young people's space of normality corresponds more to the space in society at large, and provides them with less self-confidence to confront it later in life. This may sound too bleak as a perspective, and I do not want to say that migrant youth in Germany does not have any perspective. Even under unfavourable conditions there are always possibilities and people can be lucky. However, on a more general level, and especially considering economic and political developments, there is no cause for optimism – if initiatives are not taken that is.

As young natives in Inlandtown generally construct migrants as violent and avoid contact with them, they create a more dangerous environment for themselves than the young natives in Portville. According to a quantitative study (Pfeiffer *et al.* 1999), the percentage of violent acts in both neighbourhoods is more or less the same (for instance, 27% of young people in Portville and 29% of young people in Inlandtown described themselves as perpetrators of violence). However, according to the same study, young people in Portville felt safer and liked their neighbourhood much more than those in Inlandtown. The authors had difficulty explaining this difference. Perhaps our study can provide an explanation. On all three dimensions – representational space, the space of representation and spatial practices – Portville signifies diversification and the ability of people to respect and enjoy their differences. It provides diversified spaces for different kinds of people to use the way they want, and its socio-political and historical development is linked with notions of diversity as well as of empowerment. Thus, despite the existence of danger and violence, young people are able to create spaces of safety for themselves.

Finally, and to avoid misunderstandings, when I speak about different local spaces of normality I do not assume that these localities are isolated enclaves, undisturbed by what is going on in society at large or indeed at a global level. Our two localities are to be understood as a specific blend of views, ideologies and ways of living that exist in society at large, as well as at a global level, with local peculiarities. They draw on local histories that might stand in opposition to what is hegemonic at a national level and thus, through integrating and rejecting national discourses, they deal with them in their specific ways through their specific repertoires of interpretation. While they are in constant exchange with what happens in society at large and internationally, these local normalities also serve as ways to filter and interpret what happens "outside". Therefore, such exchanges do not easily change the local brand.

## Notes

1. In contrast, see the seminal work done in Britain, for example, Back 1996, Cohen 1997.
2. A note on the usage of words: (1) In talking about young people whose parents were not born in Germany, I should really use the term "of migrant background", since most of the young people are born in Germany and are not themselves migrants. For easier reading I shall nevertheless use "migrant" as shorthand. (2) In scholarly literature, young people whose parents have not migrated are usually just called Germans. I shall not do this because it implies that the young people of migrant origin are not Germans, which in my terms they are, even if some do not have German citizenship. Therefore, I call the young people who do not have a migrant background "natives".
3. The German project was funded by the Volkswagenstiftung and co-directed by Dirk Hoerder and myself. In London, a total of 120 young people participated in the study and shared their experiences with our colleagues, Phil Cohen, Les Back and Michael Keith. The project's German title was: "Transformation of Daily Life in Processes of Migration. A Study of Immigrant and Non-Immigrant/Native Youth in Two Neighbourhoods." The British project was financed by the ESRC and its title is "Finding the Way Home". The following description of methods is taken from one of their reports (Cohen, Keith & Back 1999).
4. *Fashion Parade*: Participants were presented with 40 images of youth styles (20 of young women and 20 of young men) which where also differently ethnicised, and asked to pick and comment on three images that they liked and three they disliked.
*Photoscapes:* Young people were given disposable cameras and asked to photograph places they regarded as safe or dangerous, and places and people they especially liked.
*Photo Storyboards*: Young people were shown a series of specially constructed photographs depicting young people in peer group situations, the meanings of which were ambiguous and cut across a range of ethnic and gender relations. Informants were asked to fill in captions and dialogue to explain the scene.
*Geneogramme*: Young people plotted degrees of contact and levels of intimacy with their friends and relatives on paper and represented them spatially and with the help of colour codes indicating their emotional relation towards them.
*Guided Fantasy:* Young people were given a trigger scenario and wrote a story utilising aspects of their real and imaginary landscapes.
*Audio Diaries:* Young people kept a verbal diary over the period of a week documenting whatever they thought was important during that week.
*Video Walkabouts:* Young people planned and then conducted walks through their neighbourhoods, giving a 'guided tour'-style commentary as they went. This exercise was recorded on video.
*Journeys to London and Hamburg.* With a focus group of 22 young people, we visited London and the young people who were part of the project there. A year later, a group of 7 young Londoners came to Hamburg.
*Follow-up Interviews:* These took the form of individual semi-structured interviews in which we presented the young people with a preliminary summary of what we had learned from them, asking them to comment on it.
5. In his path breaking work on new ethnicities and urban culture, Les Back (1996) has made a similar point about the different discourses around "race" dominating different areas in London.
6. What the results do not show is the difference between the politics of the Social Democrats in

the two neighbourhoods. Pushed by the Green Party, the party's politics are much more left-wing in Portville.
7. The introductory text describing Portville says: "Maincity has 104 neighbourhoods. One of them is called Portville. It is not Maincity's biggest neighbourhood, nor is it the most beautiful, and certainly not the most modern or elegant. But many think that it is Maincity's most lively neighbourhood; some say it's most tolerant, while others complain that it's full of nooks and crannies. Some talk about a town the size of a waist pocket or about the most rebellious neighbourhood in the city."

# References

Back, Les 1996: *New Ethnicities and Urban Culture. Racisms and Multiculture in Young Lives*. London: UCL Press.

Back, Les, Räthzel, Nora & Hieronymus, Andreas. 1999: Gefährliche Welten – sichere Enklaven. In: *Archiv* 2: 7–62.

Billig, Michael 1991: *Ideology and Opinions. Studies in Rhetorical Psychology*. London: Sage.

Cohen, Phil 1997: *Rethinking the Youth Question*. London: MacMillan.

Cohen, Phil, Keith, Michael & Back, Les 1999: *Finding the Way Home: Issues of Theory and Method, CNER/CUCR Working papers 3–5*. London: Centre for New Ethnicities Research & Centre for Urban and Community Research. University of East London.

van Dijk, Teun A. 1992: Discourse and the Denial of Racism. In: *Discourse and Society*, 3, 87–118.

13. *Shell Jugendstudie*. 2000. Jugend 2000. Konzeption und Koordination: Fischer, Arthur, Fritzsche, Yvonne & Fuchs-Heinritz, Werner. Opladen: Leske und Budrich.

Foucault, Michel 1982: Espace, Savoir et Pouvoir. In: *Sous la Direction de François Ewald, Dits et éctrits* IV: 270–285. Paris: Edition Gallimard.

Foucault, Michel 1995: *Discipline and Punish. The Birth of the Prison*. New York: Vintage.

Heitmeyer, Wilhelm, Müller, Joachim & Schröder, Helmut 1997: *Verlockender Fundamentalismus. Türkische Jugendliche in Deutschland*. Frankfurt am Main: Suhrkamp.

Lefebvre, Henri 1991: *The Production of Space*. London: Blackwell.

Räthzel, Nora 1998: Listenreiche Lebensweisen: Der Gebrauch von Ethnizität im Alltag von Hamburger Jugendlichen. In: *Migration und Soziale Arbeit, Zusammenleben in den Städten,* 3–4: 32–38.

Räthzel, Nora 2000: Living Differences: Ethnicity and Fearless Girls in Public Spaces. In: *Social Identities*, 6, no. 2: 119–142.

Räthzel, Nora 2003a: Antagonistic Girls, or: Why the Foreigners are the Real Germans. In: Harzig, Christiane & Juteau, Danielle (eds.) *The Social Construction of Diversity: Recasting the Master Narrative of Industrial Nations*. New York: Berghahn Publishers. pp. 40-61.

Räthzel, Nora 2003b: Youth Groups and the Politics of Time and Space. In: *Soundings,* 24, autumn: 'A Market State?' pp. 90–111.

Räthzel, Nora & Hieronymus, Andreas 2000: The Hamburg Story: The Everyday Lives of Young People in a German Metropolis. In: *Finding the Way Home*. Working paper 6. Centre for New Ethnicities Research, University of East London.

Sennett, Richard 1992: *The Conscience of the Eye. The Design and Social Life of Cities*. New York/London: W.W. Norton & Company.

Simmel, Georg 1955: *Conflict. The Web of Group-Affiliations.* New York: The Free Press.

Suttles, Gerald 1968: *The Social Order of the Slum*. Chicago and London: University of Chicago Press.

Pfeiffer, C., Wetzels, P. & Enzmann, D. 1999: *Gewalterfahrungen und Kriminalitätsfurcht von Jugendlichen in Hamburg*. Abschlussbericht. Hannover: Kriminologisches Forschungsinstitut Niedersachsen.

# List of authors

Gösta Arvastson, Prof., Department of Cultural Anthropology and Ethnology, Uppsala University.
Gosta.Arvastson@etnologi.uu.se

Beate Binder, Dr., Assistant professor, Institute for European Ethnology, Humboldt University Berlin.
Beate.Binder@rz.hu-berlin.de

Tim Butler, Prof. of Human Geography, Department of Geography, King's College London.
Tim.Butler@kcl.ac.uk

Àngel Cebollada-Frontera, Lecturer, Department of Geography, Autonomous University of Barcelona.
Angel.Cebollada@uab.es

Margaret Byron, Dr., Lecturer, Department of Geography, King's College London.
Margaret.Byron@kcl.ac.uk

John Eade, Prof., Executive Director of Centre for Research on Nationalism, Ethnicity and Multiculturalism, School of Arts, University of Surrey.
J.Eade@surrey.ac.uk

Urban Ericsson, PhD Candidate of Ethnology, Department of Cultural Anthropology and Ethnology, Uppsala University.
Urban.Ericsson@etnologi.uu.se

Graeme Evans, Prof., Cities Institute, London Metropolitan University.
G.Evans@londonmet.ac.uk

Alexa Färber, Dr., Research Fellow, Department of European Ethnology, Humboldt University Berlin.
Alexa.Faerber.1@rz.hu-berlin.de

Jo Foord, Dr., Cities Institute, London Metropolitan University.
J.Foord@londonmet.ac.uk

Cordula Gdaniec, Dr., Research Fellow, Department of European Ethnology, Humboldt University Berlin.
Gdaniecc@staff.hu-berlin.de

Elisabeth Högdahl, Dr., Lecturer, Department of Service Management, Campus Helsingborg, Lund University.
Elisabeth.Hogdahl@msm.lu.se; Elisabeth.Hogdahl@etn.lu.se

Joanna Karmowska, PhD Candidate, Centre for European Studies, Jagiellonian University, Cracow.
Uzkarmow@cyf-kr.edu.pl

Carme Miralles-Guasch, Director, Institute of Regional and Metropolitan Studies, Autonomous University of Barcelona.
Carme.Miralles@uab.es

Nora Räthzel, Prof., Department of Sociology, Umeå University.
Nora.Rathzel@soc.umu.se

Per-Markku Ristilammi, Dr., Associate professor, School of International Migration and Ethnic Relations, University College of Malmö.
Per-Markku.Ristilammi@imer.mah.se

Stephen Shaw, Director Cities Institute, London Metropolitan University.
S.Shaw@londonmet.ac.uk